SUPERIOR RENDEZVOUS-PLACE

SUPERIOR RENDEZVOUS-PLACE

Fort William in the Canadian Fur Trade

Second Edition

Jean Morrison

NATURAL HERITAGE BOOKS
A MEMBER OF THE DUNDURN GROUP
TORONTO

Published by Natural Heritage Books
A Member of The Dundurn Group
3 Church Street, Suite 500
Toronto, Ontario, M5E 1M2, Canada
www.dundurn.com

Library and Archives Canada Cataloguing in Publication

Morrison, Jean F.
    Superior rendezvous-place : Fort William in the Canadian fur trade / Jean
Morrison. – 2nd ed.

Includes bibliographical references and index.
ISBN 978-1-55002-781-5

    1. Fort William Historical Park (Ont.)–History. 2. Fur trade–Ontario–
Thunder Bay–History. 3. North West Company–History. I. Title.

FC3099.T48M67 2007   971.3'12   C2007-903449-7

1   2   3   4   5   11   10   09   08   07

Cover illustration by Neil Broadfoot, artist-in-residence, The Canadian Canoe
Museum, Peterborough, Ontario.
Back cover photograph of Fort William Historical Park as it looks today. *Courtesy
of Fort William Historical Park*.
Back cover illustration of Fort William, 1811, by Robert Irvine. *Courtesy of
Library, Fort William Historical Park*.

Cover and text design by Catherine Hamill, Norton Hamill Design
Edited by Jane Gibson
Printed and bound in Canada by Hignell Printing Limited, Winnipeg

Care has been taken to trace the ownership of copyright material used in this
book. The author and the publisher welcome any information enabling them to
rectify any references or credits in subsequent editions.

J. Kirk Howard, President

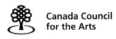

We acknowledge the support of the Canada Council for the Arts and the
Ontario Arts Council for our publishing program. We also acknowledge the
financial support of the Government of Canada through the Book Publishing
Industry Development Program and The Association for the Export of Canadian
Books and the Government of Canada through the Ontario Book Publishers Tax
Credit Program and the Ontario Media Development Corporation.

Dedicated to the memory of my mentors: Professors Elizabeth Arthur, Kenneth M. Dodd and Thomas B. Miller, History Department, Lakehead University.

Contents

vii

viii

ILLUSTRATIONS

ix

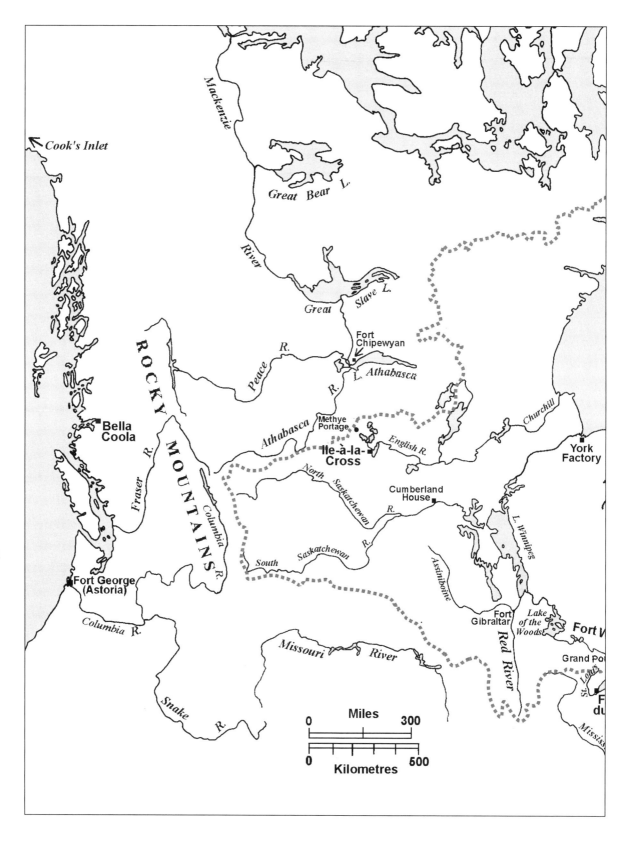

Cook's Inlet

Mackenzie River

Great Bear L.

Great Slave L.

Great Peace R.

Fort Chipewyan

L. Athabasca

R.

Athabasca

Methye Portage

Ile-à-la-Cross

English R.

Churchill

York Factory

ROCKY MOUNTAINS

Bella Coola

Fraser R.

Columbia R.

North Saskatchewan R.

Cumberland House

L. Winnipeg

Fort George (Astoria)

Columbia R.

South Saskatchewan R.

Saskatchewan

Assiniboine

Fort Gibraltar

Lake of the Woods

Red River

Fort W

Missouri River

Grand Po

Snake R.

St. Louis

F du

Mississ

x

Miles
0   300

Kilometres
0   500

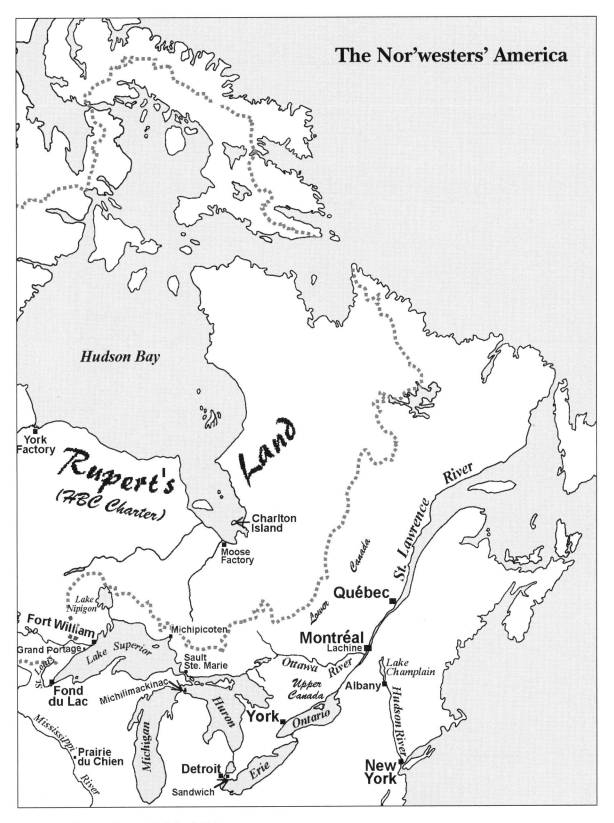

The Nor'westers' America

Hudson Bay

York
Factory

Rupert's
(HBC Charter)

Land

Charlton
Island

Moose
Factory

Lake
Nipigon

Fort William

Grand Portage

Michipicoten

Lake Superior

Sault
Ste. Marie

Fond
du Lac

Michilimackinac

Huron

Michigan

St. Louis

Mississippi

Prairie
du Chien

River

Detroit

Sandwich

Erie

York

Ottawa River

Upper Canada

Lower Canada

Québec

Montréal
Lachine

St. Lawrence River

Albany

Lake Champlain

Hudson River

Ontario

New
York

xi

Courtesy of Cathy Chapin, Lakehead University

ABBREVIATIONS

AFC   American Fur Company
ANQ-M   Archives National du Québec à Montréal
CPR   Canadian Pacific Railway
DCB   Dictionary of Canadian Biography
FWAP   Fort William Archaeological Project
FWHP   Fort William Historical Park
HBC   Hudson's Bay Company
HBCA   Hudson's Bay Company Archives
HBRS   Hudson's Bay Record Society
LAC   Library and Archives Canada
MHS   Minnesota Historical Society
MPP   Member of Provincial Parliament
NHL   National Heritage Limited
NWC   North West Company
OFW   Old Fort William
PFC   Pacific Fur Company
RRS   Red River Settlement
TBHMS   Thunder Bay Historical Museum Society
TBHS   Thunder Bay Historical Society

SUPERIOR RENDEZVOUS-PLACE

INTRODUCTION

At the juncture of McTavish and McNaughton Streets in Thunder Bay's East End, two historic monuments stand abandoned on a raised weed-strewn flower bed. Flanking them are three weather-worn poles from whose pinnacles no flags furl nor floodlights shine. Behind the granite obelisk and metal marker, a long barbed-wire fence paralleling McNaughton Street bars access to the Canadian Pacific Railway's repair yards lined with freight and grain cars. Beyond the tracks, the Kaministiquia River nears its outlet into a large bay on Lake Superior's northwestern shore known to the early Ojibwa as *Animike Wekwid* and to the French as *Baie de Tonnerre*. Both mean Thunder Bay in English.

At midday, the East End's streets are deserted. Little is left to remind passers-by that some two centuries ago this was the site of Fort William, the North West Company's inland headquarters and Lake Superior transshipment point for furs harvested in the northwest and trade goods from the east. Even the CPR's activity there today can hardly conjure up the role this site played as its transfer point for prairie grain and eastern manufactured goods for more than half a century.

The two markers at the foot of McTavish Street celebrate the location's part in the Canadian fur trade. No memorial observes its pre-World War I years of the Wheat Boom nor the contribution of its foreign-born residents to Canada's expanding economy. Nothing recalls Canada's most violent labour dispute till August 1909, when local militiamen and Winnipeg's Royal Canadian Mounted Rifles occupied this site after CPR striking freighthandlers and railway police exchanged gunfire across the place where the markers now stand.[1]

By coincidence, another military force occupied this same spot on an August 12, the same date as in 1909, when Lord Selkirk and mercenary soldiers seized the fort in 1816 in retaliation for the Seven Oaks Massacre on the Red River.[2] That such momentous events occurred twice at the Kaministiquia's entry into Lake Superior speaks to the location's significance in two different historical epochs.

A Central and Southern European cast still hangs over the East End, its homes, churches and corner stores little changed since the early 1900s. The streets still bear the names they received when the sub-division was laid out in 1892, but these have nothing to do with the immigrants who settled there. They recall instead the Highland clans of Scotland, birthplace of most fur traders associated with the site in an earlier time.[3]

Leading up to the monuments, McTavish Street recalls Simon McTavish, founder of the

3

4

The unveiling of the memorial tablet to the French and English fur trade forts on the Kaministiquia River in 1916. This was the site of Fort William, the North West Company's *rendezvous-place* from 1803 to 1821 and Hudson's Bay Company post until 1883. The Canadian Pacific Railway then acquired the property for its transshipping activities. Sir George E. Foster, holding his hat, is addressing the assembled crowd. *From a Thunder Bay Historical Society Souvenir, Jean Morrison Collection.*

North West Company, and his clansman and *protégé*, John George McTavish, the NWC's last partner in charge of Fort William. Nearby are McGillivray, McDonald, McLaughlin,[4] McPherson, McBain, McLeod and Hargrave Streets. Bordering the East End, Simpson Street, recalling HBC Governor George Simpson, cuts across other roads named for North West and Hudson's Bay Company traders.

The more prominent marker is an imposing obelisk of polished Aberdeen stone. Unveiled by the Thunder Bay Historical Society in 1916, the inscription recalls "the locality made famous by the pioneer fur traders of the great northwest." Its focus on Fort William as an HBC post is not

surprising; many donors to its erection still recalled that company's long sway at the head of the lakes. Wishing to preserve the history of the Company of Adventurers and glorify its romance, they also revelled in, and prospered from, the new steam-generated economy. The plinth could well celebrate the locale's continuity as "this gateway of commerce" to the west under the Canadian Pacific Railway.

In 1981, the Historic Sites and Monuments Board of Canada recognized the site's national historical significance by placing a simple metal marker in front of the plinth, "Here each summer from 1803 to 1821," its inscription reads, "the Montréal and wintering partners held council while trade goods were readied for the

Above: **The birchbark canoe showing partners, voyageurs and flag emblazoned "NW" is featured in the City of Thunder Bay's coat of arms today. *Courtesy of the City of Thunder Bay.***

Left: **Jean Morrison, the author, at the original site of the fur trade era's Fort William today. The obelisk dedicated by the Thunder Bay Historical Society in 1916 and the Historic Sites and Monuments Board of Canada marker erected in 1981 are seen in front of the CPR repair yards. *Photograph by Ken Morrison.***

5

Indian country and furs brought down for shipment to Montréal." Two historic markers and streets with names typically found on a clan map of the Scottish Highlands, these are the only reminders at its original site of Fort William's pivotal role in Canada's fur trade history.

Elsewhere throughout Thunder Bay, other plaques recall bits and pieces of this history. On the lawn before City Hall two markers commemorate two Europeans closely associated with the city's origins, Daniel Greysolon, Sieur Dulhut, and William McGillivray, each the founder of a Fort Kaministiquia, although 120 years apart. Also in front of City Hall are two surviving mementos of Fort William's North West Company era. These are the cannons seen in Lord Selkirk's 1816 sketch of the fort's main gate. Presented by the Hudson's Bay Company to John McIntyre, the fort's manager for over twenty years, they were donated to the City of Fort William in 1913 by his daughter Annie.[5]

Although little tangible evidence remains of Fort William in the fur trade era, one can still experience the vast complexity of the fort as the North West Company's inland headquarters. Some nine miles upriver from the original site, a striking reproduction of the original fort re-creates the ambience which research suggests prevailed at Fort William in the early 1800s. Operated by the Province of Ontario, Fort William Historical Park has been a major destination for those inquisitive about Canada's fur trade heritage since 1973.

This book begins with a brief overview of Fort William's French predecessors on the Kaministiquia River, but its emphasis is the North West Company era from 1803 to 1821. Since the Nor'westers referred to their inland headquarters on Lake Superior as their "*rendezvous-place*," the title chosen is *Superior Rendezvous-place*. The sub-title *Fort William in the Canadian Fur Trade* suggests its setting within the larger context of North American history. The book also spans the fort's Hudson's Bay Company years from 1821 to 1883, and concludes with a look at the historical attraction Fort William Historical Park and its living history programs.

Although every effort has been made to document the narrative, *Superior Rendezvous-Place* is not an academic work but is intended for a general readership. While much of this book concerns the impact of the fur trade on Native Peoples, that is not its main focus. Readers wishing to pursue this topic further may explore many excellent studies by specialists in the field. However, well-researched publications specifically on the Fort William First Nation's fur trade past have yet to appear.

During the fur trade era, American Aboriginal peoples were known as "Indians" or "Natives" and thus these terms will be used in this book. Today Native Peoples describe themselves in various ways. The *Thunder Bay Telephone Directory* for 2000/2001 lists Aboriginal Business Service Network, Anishinabek Police Service, Fort William First Nation, Fort William Indian Band, Native People of Thunder Bay Development Corp, Ojibway 1850 Treaty Council, Thunder Bay Indian Friendship Centre and Union of Ontario Indians. It seems that no one usage is "politically correct."

Weights and measures will be expressed in imperial terms to conform with practice during the period under discussion.

Jean Morrison
Thunder Bay, Ontario

6

1   HOW IT ALL BEGAN

Who was she, this Ojibwa woman whose likeness Lieutenant Robert Irvine so hauntingly captured at Fort William in 1811? The artist left no record of her name nor of the family to whom she belonged. If she had a husband of Native or French-Canadian origin, she would be known as "a woman of the fort." If married to a company officer, she would be his "little girl." If her children were among those mixed-blood offspring of fur trade marriages baptised in Montréal or elsewhere in Québec, the church register would identify her, the absent mother, as "a woman of the Indian country." Some fort records might dignify her by the title "Mrs." or "Madame" preceding her husband's name.

Perhaps we can name her *Ikwé*, the Ojibwa word for woman. The Ojibwa call themselves Anishinabek, which means human being; an Ojibwa woman is *Anishinabekwe*.[1] Like most persons throughout history, Ikwé achieved little recognition in life and complete anonymity in death. Among the many nameless Aboriginal women caught up in the North American fur trade, she almost certainly belonged to that branch of the Ojibwa tribe which arrived at the western shores of Lake Superior sometime before the mid-1750s.

One thing about Ikwé was unique. She was the only person in the North West Company era known to be illustrated at Fort William as an individual. Some drawings of the fort have people in the background, but Irvine's portrayal of this lone woman shows her as a real person going about her business within the culture of the fur trade. Her name may never be known, but this painting conveys much about its subject and the fur trade at Fort William under the North West Company.

Ikwé wears red leggings and a blue skirt covered by a white blanket as commonly worn by Native women at the time. In the tickinogan on her back, her baby is enveloped in blue cloth. Like Ikwé, a distant figure dressed in imported textiles carries a metal pail, perhaps for hauling water from the river.

The blanket and the fabric for Ikwé's clothing came from far-away England as did the metal for her pail. Transported by ship across the Atlantic Ocean and then by canoe up the Ottawa River route, textiles and metal pails of the type seen in Irvine's painting underwent a long and difficult journey before reaching Fort William. If Ikwé and other Native peoples had not wanted such imports, the fur trade may never have dominated the history of early Canada. But since the Aboriginals prized what Europeans had to offer, they had to exchange something in return, something the Europeans craved and which only Natives could supply.

7

Woman at Fort William, 1811, watercolour, by Lieutenant Robert Irvine. *Courtesy of Fort William Historical Park.*

That peculiarly shaped object above the baby's head seems to be the carcass of an animal, perhaps of a species coveted by Europeans. At great peril, traders shipped products to exchange for pelts of fur-bearing animals. To sustain the fur trade and keep the channels of commerce open, they battled competitors and their nations often went to war.

The painting shows two articles born out of the indigenous culture of the Canadian Shield. Crafted from birchbark and other forest materials, the easily portable wigwam and canoe expedited movement from one area to another. Essential to the Aboriginal's hunting and gathering way of life, the canoe also became vital to European travel on North American inland waterways. Intentionally or not, Irvine's painting symbolizes the inextricable relationship between Europeans and Native peoples in the fur trade as producers and as consumers.

The setting for Irvine's picture is the Kamin-istiquia River's exit into Thunder Bay on Lake Superior. For two periods in Canada's fur trade history, Montréal traders chose this river as their major "road" into the northwest. How did it happen that the French and later the North West Company followed this route and not some other? When did Ikwé's forebears come to live at this place? The historical processes which brought the Ojibwa and fur traders together at the Kaministiquia River are deeply interwoven, their origins stretching back to the early colonization of America.

It all began with Christopher Columbus who voyaged across the Atlantic Ocean searching for the Orient and found the Caribbean Islands instead. This monumental event in human history came at the height of the Renaissance, when intellectual fervour and ascendant merchant capitalism inspired the advances in cartography, navigation and ship building which, in turn, gave birth to the "Age of Discovery." With their goal

8

the fabled riches of the Far East, Europe's maritime states raced to reach India by ocean. In this global contest daring explorers sailed round the world, charted new routes, conquered new lands and opened up virgin territory to trade and exploitation.

First off the mark in 1486 and 1487, Bartholomew Diaz plotted a course down the African coast as far as the Cape of Good Hope for Portugal, but it would not be until 1498 that Vasco de Gama became the first European to reach the Indian sub-continent. Meanwhile Spain had commissioned Columbus to find a shorter route to the East by sailing West. The unexpected land mass in his way merely stimulated others to continue seeking a western route to the Orient. New discoveries in geography and astronomy led mariners to deduce that the Americas could be traversed around their southern or northern limits by sea.

After Spain and Portugal divided the non-Christian world between them, with the blessing of the Pope, Spain claimed the entire New World except Brazil which, along with Africa and India, went to Portugal. Thus, it was for Spain, in 1520, that Ferdinand Magellan found the Southwest Passage at the tip of South America, by sailing from the Atlantic into the South Sea (or Pacific Ocean) through the strait now bearing his name. Magellan was killed at the Philippines, yet his expedition proved that the Far East could be reached from Europe by sailing west and that circumnavigation of the globe was possible.

For the next century Spain and Portugal dominated the world's sea lanes and became fabulously wealthy from the spoils of conquest. Their grip on the New World prevented Northern European nations from establishing anything but toeholds in the West Indies and Newfoundland (which John Cabot claimed for England in 1497). But as England, France and the Netherlands established commercial and colonial bases around the world, their crusade to find an alternative to the long, hazardous and Spanish-controlled Southwest Passage became both compulsive and competitive.

Probing the St. Lawrence River as far as Hochelaga (Montréal) for France in 1535, Jacques Cartier pioneered France's future searches for the Northwest Passage via North America's inland waterway. At the same time, Martin Frobisher's voyages to Baffin Island from 1576 to 1578 presaged England's concentration on the icy waters of the Arctic Ocean as the way to the Orient.

It was while under contract from the Dutch East India Company in 1609 that the Englishman Henry Hudson sought the passage, by ascending the river which now bears his name. Hudson's mission failed, but Holland claimed the entire Hudson River basin as New Netherland. England, however, conquered the Dutch colony in 1664 and re-named it New York. By then England had founded prosperous colonies all along the Atlantic seaboard from Spanish Florida to the Maritimes (which France also claimed).

England's explorers, however, continued to seek the passage through the Arctic Ocean. Now working for England, Henry Hudson sailed deep into a northern inland sea and then south to a smaller contiguous bay. Set adrift by mutinous sailors on James Bay, Hudson perished along with his son and seven crew. Later his exploits gave England its rationale for laying claim to the entire watershed of that frigid inland sea, Hudson Bay. The future rivalry between it and the Kaministiquia River was in the making.

In the meantime, in 1608, Samuel de Champlain founded the French colony of New France at Québec. Guardian of the St. Lawrence River pointing to *La Mer de l'Ouest* and beyond to China, Champlain took his search for a route to the South Sea up the inland rivers of the St. Lawrence watershed. His successors eventually reached the headwaters of the Great Lakes and ventured beyond the height of land between the Great Lakes and Hudson Bay watersheds.

9

Often their course took them up the Kaministiquia River from one of four successive Forts near its mouth. From Champlain's wanderings to David Thompson's tracing of the Columbia River to the Pacific Ocean in 1811, this search for an inland Northwest Passage would take two hundred years.

France and Britain soon found incentives other than founding colonies and seeking the Northwest Passage to compete for control of northern North America: its abundance of fur-bearing animals. Fortunes from pelts awaited in Europe where the beaver had become virtually extinct.

What made the beaver so desirable was not its long outer hair, but the soft, downy undercoat next its skin, the best substance for making the superb brimmed hats then in vogue. Similar to a miniature fish hook, each tiny, fine hair of undercoat had barbs easily matted into felt. Although styles of brim and crown changed over time, beaver felt remained the preferred substance for fine hats until the mid-1800s.

Without North America's Aboriginal peoples, the fur trade could never have dominated the economy of early Canada. For their own survival, Indians developed skills in trapping and hunting animals and preparing their hides, skills now applied to the fur trade. Although misfortunes of war, disease and dislocation befell Native Americans from the trade's domino effect, they had one advantage over slaves in agricultural economies who could be dispensed with, one way or another. In regions where the fur trade prevailed, the slogan "The Only Good Indian is a Dead Indian" never made business sense. For the trade to prosper, Native peoples not only had to survive; they also had to pursue their traditional hunting and trapping activities but at a pace leading to the indiscriminate slaughter of animals and their own migrations to new sources of fur.

The Aboriginals willingly exchanged their furs for newfangled articles from Europe. Such imports lightened the struggle for survival. Blankets, iron pots and iron traps, guns, beads and much scorned "trinkets" provided an incentive to expand the traditional hunt to meet the demands of the overseas trade.[2] America's Natives not only insisted that their long-held present-giving rituals continue, but that before trading began certain procedures be followed around the exchange of manufactured goods and furs.

The so-called "trinkets"—an incredible variety of beads, ribbon, lace, silver ornaments, and the needles and thread with which to apply them—relieved the burden of women who fashioned intricate designs on apparel and accoutrements. Today, handicrafts created by Native women long ago are prized by museums and collectors around the world. They are also being reclaimed by descendants of those who traded pelts for "baubles."

But as beaver became scarce in the lower St. Lawrence watershed, Native hunters moved into new territory where they collided with tribes already on the ground. Well before the French reached the Kaministiquia, competition for fur unleashed havoc along the St. Lawrence and Lower Lakes as Indians allied to contending French, Dutch and English traders slaughtered one another and their foreign enemies. One horrific example, the Iroquois destruction of Huronia in 1649, led to the dispersal of Algonquian-speaking Natives towards Lake Superior and beyond.

The impact of being "discovered" on America's Native peoples can hardly be gauged. Not only did forced migrations and trade-inspired warfare take their toll, but disease carried off an estimated half the New World's Aboriginal population. As Adam Smith wrote back in 1776:

The discovery of America and that of a passage to the East Indies by the Cape of Good Hope are the two greatest and most important events recorded in the history of mankind. ... to the natives, however, both of the East and

10

Kakabeka Falls and Portage by William Armstrong. From *Canadian Illustrated News* (October 7, 1871). Known as the "Mountain Portage," this obstacle on the Kaministiquia River is just one reason why fur traders—and voyageurs—preferred the Grand Portage-Pigeon River route to the west. *Courtesy of TBHMS 976.100.1F*

the West Indies, all the commercial benefits which can have resulted from those events have been sunk and lost in the dreadful misfortunes which they have occasioned.[3]

The depletion of and disruption to Native society wrought by conquest and conflict created a dearth of Native middlemen in early New France. Something like travelling salesmen, middlemen acquired goods from Montréal merchants for trade in the interior. But with war, famine and disease reducing the Aboriginal population, the French themselves filled the void by venturing deeper into the continent to trade with Indians on their own hunting grounds. Those without the required license were the legendary *coureurs de bois*, the most famed of whom were Pierre Esprit Radisson and Médard Chouart des Groseilliers.

In 1660, Radisson and Groseilliers entered Lake Nipigon from Lake Superior where they discovered a bounty of thickly pelted beaver. Returning to New France in fur-laden canoes,

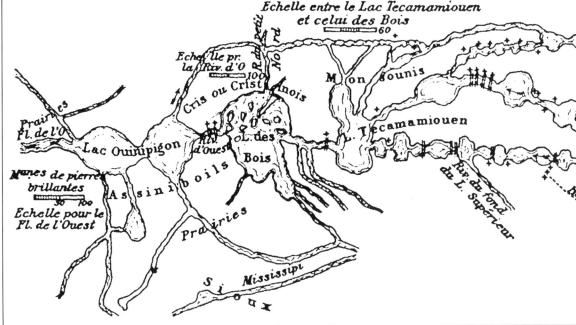

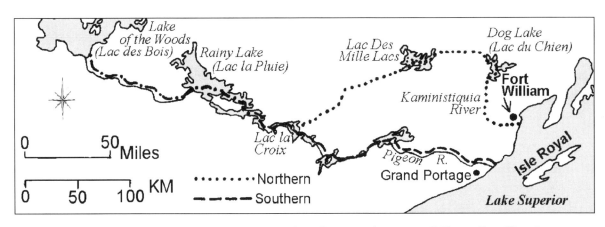

Canoe Routes Between Lake Superior and Lac la Croix

Top: **Ochagach Map, 1729. This map by Ochagach, a Cree guide, convinced La Vérendrye to use the Pigeon instead of the Kaministiquia River as his route into the west.** *Courtesy of LAC, Map Div., H2–902–1737.*

Bottom: **Canoe routes between Lake Superior and the Northwest. The Grand Portage-Pigeon River route is clearly preferable to the Kaministiquia River in terms of distance.** *Courtesy of Cathy Chapin, Lakehead University.*

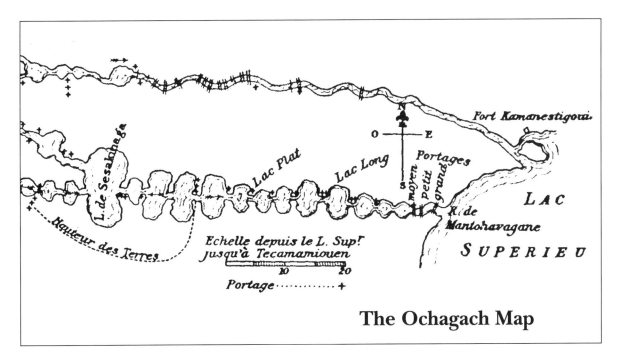

The Ochagach Map

they brought news of a great saltwater inland sea just to the north of Lake Nipigon. Instead of rewarding the *coureurs de bois* for their deeds, French officials punished them for trading illegally and for spouting nonsense about Hudson Bay's great advantage over the St. Lawrence as a shorter, cheaper outlet to the Atlantic Ocean–and France–for furs trapped north of Lake Superior.

Thus censured, Radisson and Groseilliers sailed to England where their newly acquired geographical knowledge found a receptive audience. On May 2, 1670, King Charles II granted "the Governor and Company of Adventurers of England Trading into Hudson's Bay" a Royal Charter giving the company sole possession of all "those seas, straits, bays, rivers, lakes, creeks and sounds…that lie within the entrance of… Hudson's Straits."[4] Prince Rupert, King Charles II's first cousin and the company's first governor, gave his name to this immense tract of 1.5 million square miles, but he and his fellow "adventurers" never did venture into Rupert's Land. They were called adventurers because they ventured or risked their capital in the firm.

In 1672, Radisson and Groseilliers established

Moose Factory at the bottom of James Bay, the HBC's first fort in Rupert's Land. In response to this affront to French continental ambitions, trader-explorers from New France began exploring Lake Superior's western coastline for a way into the unknown west beyond the Height of Land. Their aims were many: to discover the Northwest Passage; to claim new lands for France, to extend the fur trade and to sever Indian ties with the English now ensconced on Hudson and James bays.

Four navigable rivers enter Superior's northwestern waters. From its western tip, the St. Louis River provides an indirect way to Lake Winnipeg by the Mississippi and Red rivers. Up the coast, the Pigeon River cascades down over impenetrable falls, making it *seem* unsuited for canoe travel. From Lake Nipigon the way west is portage-ridden–and close to the English on James Bay.

This leaves the sixty-six mile long Kaministiquia River flowing into Thunder Bay from Dog Lake near the Height of Land. From the Dog River, the canoe route crosses the Savanne Portage to the Hudson Bay watershed and then passes through Lac des Milles Lacs, Lac la

13

Croix, Rainy Lake and Lake of the Woods to Lake Winnipeg and the Saskatchewan River, pointing towards the Rocky Mountains and the Athabasca country.

As it nears Superior, the Kaministiquia divides into three short outlets flowing through flat, marshy land. On its southern branch safe from the unpredictably stormy lake, Daniel Greysolon, Sieur Dulhut, built the first Fort Kaministiquia in 1679 or perhaps in 1683. This fort would be his base for western explorations, for expanding the French fur trade, and for intercepting Indians who were taking furs to the English at Hudson Bay.[5]

Kaministiquia is an Algonquian word spelt and defined many ways. Dulhut wrote it as "Caministigoya," the way he heard it pronounced by local Natives. It has been translated as "a meandering river" or "a river of three mouths," although one Ojibwa man said it means "a river with many islands covered with low bushes." Since the French apparently arrived at western Lake Superior before the Ojibwa, the word must come from the Algonquian language spoken by the Cree or Monsoni inhabiting the Kaministiquia region when Dulhut first came.

At the upper Mississippi, Dulhut encountered Siouian-speaking Dakotas at war with Ottawa middlemen who had invaded their lands in search of furs. The Algonquian-speaking Ottawa dubbed the Dakota "Nadoussioux," meaning "like the Iroquois or an adder." Although DuLhut mediated a temporary peace between the warring factions, enmity persisted between the Dakota-Sioux and other tribes west of Lake Superior for almost two hundred years.

The first French to travel beyond Lake Superior did so by permission of the Natives who demanded payment for passing through their lands and extracted generous supplies of goods, tobacco and liquor in exchange for furs. Through diplomatic skills and lavish presents, the French slowly proceeded westward in face of danger from warring tribes whom they themselves had armed.

In 1688, Jacques de Noyon voyaged up the Kaministiquia route to Lac la Pluie (Rainy Lake), the furthest west any European had yet travelled. An ominous sign of Fort Kaministiquia's future, though, was his return from Lac la Croix by the Pigeon River. The fort's fortunes also depended on international affairs. French naval and military forces captured the English posts on Hudson Bay and held them intermittently from 1682 to 1713. With English competition eliminated, the Kaministiquia's strategic location became irrelevant to French imperial and trading goals. In 1696, the first Fort Kaministiquia closed.

By the Treaty of Utrecht of 1713, Britain regained Hudson Bay, but France consolidated its presence in North America's interior with no more than a thousand French soldiers and traders combined. Securing its domain from the Gulf of Mexico to the Gulf of St. Lawrence with Indian assistance, France kept Britain's American colonies confined to the Atlantic seaboard. To ensure control over the northwest, the French founded Fort Michilimackinac on the straits between Lakes Michigan and Huron and in 1717, Zacharie de la Noue built a second Fort "Camanitigoya," this one on the river's upper branch. This fort had two purposes: to expand the French fur trade into west, and thereby keep the Indians from taking their furs to Hudson Bay, and to be the station for continuing the search for the Western Sea.

In 1730, Pierre Gaultier de Varennes de La Vérendrye made the new fort his starting point for an expedition up the Kaministiquia River, to discover the Northwest Passage and extend the fur trade. Even for the most experienced canoeist it is no easy task ascending the Kam to the Hudson Bay watershed. The lower river is well-suited to canoe travel but for a short distance only. Its shallow riverbed means that canoes be portaged at least thirteen times or lined from the rugged shoreline. Thirty miles from Superior, the almost vertical 1,426 yard-long Portage de la Montagne (Mountain Portage) bypasses the spectacular

108-foot Kakabeka Falls. Further upriver the steep 500-foot Portage du Chien (the Dog Portage) is considered the most onerous between Montréal and Lake Athabasca.[6]

In 1727, a Native guide Ochagach showed La Vérendrye a map of the Pigeon River's supposed link to the "Fl. de L'Ouest" (River of the West) and the Western Sea. From Lake Superior to Lac la Crosse via the Kam it is 230 miles but by the Pigeon only 150, a saving of one week's travel. Just one barrier stood in the way—the long series of rapids and falls tumbling down the Pigeon to Lake Superior. The only way around this obstacle was a long portage going up and down rocky and rugged terrain, a portage of almost nine miles described on Ochagach's map as a "grand portage."[7]

In 1731, the French adopted the Grand Portage-Pigeon route, but kept Fort Kaministiquia as their Lake Superior depot or *ferme*. From the Kam, the La Vérendrye family established seven forts from Rainy Lake to the Saskatchewan River despite the ever-present Dakota menace. Drawing the trade of western Indians away from Hudson Bay, they also explored the Missouri and Saskatchewan rivers searching as always for the Northwest Passage. Although they failed to find the Western Sea, their contributions to French imperial ambitions were formidable given the logistics of travel by canoe over unknown waters. Their contributions to the Natives from epidemics, slavery, dispersal, liquor and wars, however, must be placed in the category of Adam Smith's "dreadful misfortunes."

La Vérendrye took command of Fort Kaministiquia about the time the Ojibwa began arriving from Sault Ste. Marie. When the Jesuits first came to St. Mary's River, they called the Algonquian-speakers "Saulteurs" for *sault*, the French word for rapids. In the 1660s, some Saulteurs began migrating westward in two separate groups along Superior's northern and southern shorelines. A few remained at points along the way, some settled along the western Superior coast while others continued on to the prairies. Travelling westward over several decades, they ousted earlier inhabitants in their way. South and west of Lake Superior, these were the Sioux as the Dakota came to be known. Wars between the Ojibwa and the Sioux continued well into the 1800s, often at the instigation of rival fur traders.[8]

Propelled by the fur trade, the Ojibwa had started their western migrations long before they reached Sault Ste. Marie. "Where did your people come from?" I once asked an Ojibwa woman from Lake Winnipeg, Freda McDonald, supervisor of Native life at Old Fort William at that time. "My grandmother told me," she always began when asked such questions, "My grandmother told me that long ago our ancestors came to Sault Ste. Marie from the eastern sea before heading west." From generation to generation, the Ojibwa have handed down this story of their origins at "the great salt sea" to the east. The Ojibwa-European historian, William W. Warren, repeated it in his *History of the Ojibway People*, written in 1852.

The fourth chapter of this book, entitled, "Emigration of the Ojibways from the Shores of the Atlantic Ocean, to their Occupation of the Area of Lake Superior," relates how "sickness and death" drove the early Ojibwa from the "Great Salt Water," first to Montréal and then to Michilimackinac before settling along the St. Mary's River. Much later, two distinct groups left the Sault, one moving along the south and the other along the north shore of Lake Superior, eventually meeting at Grand Portage and Thunder Bay.[9]

From 1682 to 1763, France and Britain engaged in bitter conflict over the North American interior in the constant skirmishes, raids and battles known in the United States as the French and Indian Wars. In 1754, the last and most ferocious French and Indian War began as one facet in the Seven Years War, fought in Europe, India and North America over global commerce and colonial control. British supremacy in industrial might and naval power won the day.

15

In Canada, hostilities ended with Québec's capitulation in 1759 and Montréal's in 1760. By the Treaty of Paris in 1763, France ceded to Britain her possessions east of the Mississippi from the Gulf of Mexico to the Gulf of St. Lawrence. Spain acquired Louisiana, a vast vaguely defined area from the Mississippi west to the Rockies and from the Gulf of Mexico north to the Missouri River.

Diderot's famous Encyclopédie tell us:

The trade in furs was the principal object of the French in establishing themselves in this country [New France]....It cannot be denied that the fur trade, costing little in itself, was a source of wealth. The Indians bore all the expense of the hunt, and sold the finest furs for crude tools,....[10]

In pursuit of fur—and of an inland route to the Western Sea—the French had created a vast empire, an empire now vanished. In its making, the Kaministiquia River had played a pivotal role. But again, the fate of imperial powers affected not only the destiny of the establishment at the river's outlet into Lake Superior but that of the peoples within its orbit. When he learned that New France had fallen, Commandant François de La Corne abandoned Fort Kaministiquia after setting it on fire and leaving Ikwé's forebears, the Ojibwa, in sole possession of western Lake Superior.

16

2 BRITISH TRADERS AT GRAND PORTAGE

As possessors of the land, the Ojibwa governed access into the interior by the Pigeon and Kaministiquia rivers, exacting tolls in the form of gifts from anyone wishing to venture past Lake Superior.[1] During the hiatus between French rule and British exercise of power, the First Peoples held the upper hand over traders heading into the interior.

In a way the British Conquest of New France was not the end of an era for Montréal's fur trade. It merely marked a new phase in which the trade gradually resumed its former methods under new leaders. In 1763, the St. Lawrence River drainage system became British by terms of the Treaty of Paris; logically, then, Montréal's commercial rivalry with Britain's Atlantic colonies and Rupert's Land should cease. But logic and the real world of business do not always conform. Under British rule, competition continued between the St. Lawrence River and the northern and southern geographical entities named for Henry Hudson.

Even before France formally capitulated in 1763, Anglo-American colonists rushed into the interior with goods supplied from Montréal or Albany, the headquarters of New York's fur trade. Among the first to reach Lake Superior was Alexander Henry (the Elder), a New Jersey native. As Henry soon learned, one reason for

New France's dominion over North America's interior was its mastery at good relations with the Indians. In 1761, he stopped for provisions and supplies at Michilimackinac where the Ojibwa had control. There, Chief Mihnehwehna reminded him that though the British may have conquered the French:

> …you have not yet conquered us! …these lakes, these woods and mountains, were left to us by our ancestors. These are our inheritance and we will part with them to no one.[2]

Despite Mihnehwehna's warnings of revenge for Indian braves killed in war, the American frontier war hero Captain Robert Rogers and his veteran Colonial Rangers had no difficulty occupying French military posts on the Great Lakes, including Michilimackinac, and dispatching a detachment to Grand Portage where traders had gathered by 1764.

Indian resentment at military incursions into their lands was such that the British felt it necessary to secure this remote spot on Lake Superior. Independent American traders south of the Great Lakes had already alienated the Aboriginals by treating them with contempt, encroaching upon their lands and ignoring the French custom of giving presents. Canadians, as the Québec

17

French were known, and Frenchmen from Louisiana carefully cultivated Indian animosity towards their new rulers by promising to reinstate French rule in North America.

Under Chief Pontiac in 1763, the Ottawa, Ojibwa and Huron rose in rebellion, laying siege to military posts ceded by France and taking all except Detroit, Niagara and Fort Pitt (Pittsburgh). At Michilimackinac, Alexander Henry witnessed history's most famous lacrosse game when the Ojibwa lobbed a ball over the palisade to gain access to the Fort and slaughtered the British detachment. The rebellion spread from Louisiana to the Great Lakes, but thanks to the influence of a long-time trader Jean-Baptiste Cadotte Sr. at Sault Ste. Marie, the Lake Superior Ojibwa stayed out of the conflagration. Before hostilities ended in 1766, British traders were venturing as far as Lake Superior and beyond.[3]

Most traders made Grand Portage their base, but Thomas Corry set up business in 1767 at Kaministiquia where he found the old French post in ruins. His business with the local Ojibwa proved so profitable that, by 1771, he was trading goods from as far away as present-day northern Manitoba. The secret of Corry's good fortune was liberality with the Indians. He was "giving abundance of goods for nothing, and trading at a cheap rate," a Hudson's Bay Company servant grumbled.[4]

During the Seven Years War, the Hudson's Bay Company had met little interference to its trade; now it faced renewed competition from Montréal. The HBC's servants derided rough and ready independents like Corry as "pedlars from Montréal," but the pedlars easily withstood gibes from their poorly paid opponents. By conciliating Indians, paying tolls, and giving presents, they harvested fortunes in fur.[5]

South of the Lakes, American colonists on the Atlantic coast and French traders coming up the Mississippi River continued to exacerbate the general malaise in Indian affairs. In 1774, the British Parliament passed the Québec Act which virtually excluded Americans from the hunting territories and fertile lands across the Allegheny Mountains. The Act not only guaranteed the seigneurial system, French Civil Law and the rights of the Catholic Church but extended Québec's borders to the confluence of the Ohio and Mississippi rivers. American colonists, who had helped overthrow French rule in North America, felt betrayed.

The Québec Act and the ensuing American Revolution must be credited with the founding of the North West Company. For reasons both patriotic and commercial, loyalist merchants and traders fled north to Canada. The North American fur trade depended on access to British trade goods which Albany no longer enjoyed. Montréal had that access and it had the infrastructure for a prosperous trade. Before long, those nuisance pedlars plaguing the Hudson's Bay Company would be replaced by traders from Scots settlements in the British colony of New York.

The Highlanders had emigrated to British America after England defeated the clans at Culloden in 1754 and the chiefs evicted their tenants to make way for sheep. Some out-of-work estate managers (or tacksmen) and their kin settled in New York's Mohawk Valley on or near Sir William Johnson's estates. Other recipients of Johnson's patronage included Fraser's Highlanders (the 78th Regiment of Foot), veterans of Louisbourg and Québec. These Scots and their progeny provided the nucleus of the North West Company.[6]

The Superintendent for Indian Affairs in New York, Johnson became rich through the fur trade and his feudally-run estates at Johnstown. His watchword was good service, and to provide good service he needed tough subordinates who could learn languages quickly and who could command. Who better to meet these requirements than well-educated Highland tacksmen or officers and their relatives?

A good example of Scots patronage and nepotism is the case of a bright thirteen-year-old lad

18

Winter at Grand Portage. The reconstructed North West Company depot at the original site looking east across Lake Superior. No period illustration of Grand Portage before 1850 survives. *Photo courtesy of U.S. National Park Service, Grand Portage National Monument.*

from Stratherrick, Inverness-shire, whom his uncle, Lieutenant Hugh Fraser of the 78th, placed with Sir William in 1763. Well-tutored in Indian and legal affairs by age twenty, he quickly prospered in the trade. That young man was Simon McTavish, the founder of the North West Company.[7] Other Highlanders, with Johnson ties associated with the Canadian fur trade, had surnames such as Phyn, Ellice, McKay, McLeod, Macdonnell and Cameron.

The American Revolution compelled Sir John Johnson (Sir William's heir) and his tenants to escape to Canada along with other New York-based traders. Some of these Loyalists received lands up the St. Lawrence River at Glengarry or near Johnstown (renamed Cornwall in 1790), but those in the fur trade settled at Montréal to compete with Britons, Yankees and French Canadians already in the business.

By this time, the patterns of the British trade were pretty well set. Adopting practices inherited from the French, most traders west of Superior followed the Pigeon River but, unlike the French, built their headquarters at Grand

Portage rather than at Kaministiquia. Michilimackinac still supplied the southwest and provisioned west-bound canoes, but as trade routes lengthened, Grand Portage replaced it as the *rendezvous-place* for rival associations of merchants and traders. In the early years of the British trade, the Yorkshiremen Benjamin and Joseph Frobisher dominated the business.

In 1778, Peter Pond became the first European to cross from the English River (as Montréalers called the Upper Churchill) by the Methye Portage to the Athabasca watershed, beyond the limits of the Hudson's Bay Company charter. A Connecticut Yankee, Pond had the backing of Simon McTavish and other Montréal suppliers. Neither Pond nor his financiers would be disappointed. In the Athabasca, thickly pelted beaver abounded in such quantity that Pond left part of his bounty behind.[8]

In 1782, the Montréal trade benefited from two episodes beyond its control. The French navy captured and razed the HBC's Prince of Wales Fort on Hudson Bay, but more critically, a smallpox epidemic swept through Native communities

19

A re-enactor portrays a voyageur carrying two bales across the Grand Portage. *Photo courtesy of U.S. National Park Service, Grand Portage National Monument.*

from the Missouri River to the Athabasca and from Grand Portage to Hudson Bay. Wiping out some two-thirds of the Native populace, the plague debilitated its survivors and led to a dramatic shift in the balance of power from Indians to Europeans during the formative years of the North West Company.[9]

McTavish and other Montréalers had already formed a short-term partnership calling itself the North West Company when tragedy struck. In 1782, a trader in the English River district, Jean-Etienne Waddens, was killed at Lac la Ronge in a fracas with Peter Pond. Pond was never charged with murder, yet Waddens' death epitomized the ruthlessness of fur trade rivalry. The only way to end violence – and increase profits– was to eliminate competition.

In the winter of 1783–1784, the North West Company formed a more permanent partnership between merchants in Montréal and traders in the field. Known as agents, the merchants raised capital, hired voyageurs, purchased trade goods and marketed furs. The wintering partners supervised the trade in the interior. Each summer, the agents and their wintering partners held their annual meeting at Grand Portage, the company's *rendezvous-place* on Lake Superior.

The firm's name was well chosen, for McTavish now directed his energies away from the southwest trade out of Detroit and Michilimackinac northwest toward Athabasca's "Eldorado" of beaver. Affirming his choice, the Treaty of Paris of 1783, ending the American Revolution, gave the new United States of America all lands south of the Great Lakes, much more territory than its revolutionary armies had conquered. To Montréal's chagrin, British negotiators defended the interests neither of His Majesty's loyal subjects nor of his Indian allies in determining the boundary between the U.S.A. and what was left of British North America.

McTavish's faith in the northwest had been vindicated. Or so it seemed. From Cornwall, the international boundary went through the St. Lawrence River and Great Lakes but, based on John Mitchell's inaccurate map of 1755, it then crossed Lake Superior north of Isle Royale and an imagined "Isle Phelipeaux" to a nonexistent Long Lake along the Pigeon River and west to Lake of the Woods and the yet unknown source of the Mississippi River.[10]

In drawing the new border, British diplomats had but a hazy idea of Canada's east-west canoe routes. Did they realize that the entry to Pigeon River from Lake Superior was unnavigable, that it could be reached only by the Grand Portage which began six miles south of the river's mouth, well within the United States of America? Did they know that no portage was possible through the rugged terrain on the British side of the Pigeon? Since the new republic had concerns more pressing in the east than asserting sovereignty in the west, Montréal traders stayed on at Grand Portage and also at Michilimackinac and Sault Ste. Marie, all vital staging places for the western trade but now within U.S. territory.

In 1783, Simon McTavish brought his nineteen-year old nephew, William McGillivray, out from Stratherrick, Scotland as the NWC's first English-speaking clerk to serve as a trader. (In the fur trade, the term clerk applied to non-shareholding traders as well as to clerical staff.) William's brother Duncan followed him into the business in 1788, while his youngest brother Simon, born the year William left home, went into the commercial side of the business, briefly in New York and Montréal, but later in London.[11] In 1784, William McGillivray took charge at Ile-à-la-Crosse, strategically located on the upper English River near the start of the Methye Portage. Not only was the region rich in furs but from here traders could watch for competitors heading towards the Athabasca country or intercept Indians taking furs to the English on Hudson Bay.

In 1785, McGillivray had his first, but not last, taste of competition when a promising new partner in the rival firm Gregory, McLeod built a post at Ile-à-la-Crosse. McGillivray's adversary was Alexander Mackenzie, a Highlander. Like Simon McTavish, Mackenzie had emigrated to New York as a lad. The motherless Mackenzie had accompanied his father, Kenneth, who would become a lieutenant in Sir John Johnson's Royal Regiment.

Also like McTavish, Mackenzie fled to Canada during the American Revolution. In 1779, at age seventeen, Mackenzie joined Finlay, Gregory's counting house in Montréal as a clerk. In 1784, after a few months' experience in the actual trade at Detroit, where McTavish had earlier been employed, his firm, now Gregory, McLeod, made him a partner. Later, Mackenzie and McTavish would share something else in common, their enmity one for the other. Out on the English River meantime, Mackenzie enjoyed a congenial relationship with McTavish's nephew, his rival William McGillivray.

In 1787, Peter Pond again was implicated in murder, that of John Ross, a partner in Gregory, McLeod. Leaving the NWC in disgrace, Pond sold his share to McGillivray. McGillivray became a wintering partner as did Mackenzie when the NWC absorbed Gregory, McLeod. By twice capitalizing on murder, the North West Company claimed a monopoly over the north-

Simon McTavish, from the portrait by J. Hoppner. McTavish dominated the North West Company until his death in 1804. *Courtesy of Fort William Historical Park, copy of LAC 1348.*

west trade. With Simon McTavish at the helm, it would make short shrift of any upstart trying to venture west of the Grand Portage.

Any map of Canada shows that the region from Lake Superior to the Athabasca is closer to Hudson Bay than to Montréal and that Hudson Bay is closer to England than is Montréal. As the Athabasca trade expanded northward and transportation routes lengthened, the NWC's

Portrait of Sir Alexander Mackenzie by Sir Thomas Lawrence. After his explorations to the Arctic and Pacific oceans on behalf of the North West Company, Mackenzie joined the rival XY Company. When the XY Company united with the NWC in 1804, its interests were known as Sir Alexander Mackenzie & Company. *Courtesy of Fort William Historical Park, copy of LAC 1348.*

takenly named "Cook's River." Cook was killed by Sandwich Island Natives the following year, but soon his discoveries brought fortune-seekers to the Pacific coast from around the world. The sea-otter pelts which Cook's crew obtained from Nootka Indians for mere trinkets sold on the Chinese market for one hundred dollars each.

Up in the Athabasca country, Peter Pond had become obsessed by this elusive overland route to the western sea. One of his many maps shows a waterway from Great Slave Lake via Cook's supposed river. In 1787, the NWC sent its new partner, Alexander Mackenzie, to Athabasca as Pond's understudy and, on Pond's departure in 1788, placed him in charge of the district.[12]

Under Alexander Mackenzie's direction, his cousin Roderick McKenzie established Fort Chipewyan on Lake Athabasca as the district's headquarters. A clerk, Roderick had been brought into the NWC from Gregory, McLeod. Of Alexander's many kin in the fur trade, two other relatives also began their careers at Athabasca, Daniel McKenzie in 1791 and James McKenzie in 1795.[13]

Avidly devouring Pond's findings, Mackenzie himself aspired to discover the long-sought passage. In 1789, he set out from Fort Chipewyan on Lake Athabasca for "Cook's River" but, misled by Pond's maps, descended the river now bearing his name to the "Frozen Sea," the Arctic Ocean. At Grand Portage in 1790, Mackenzie evidently received no praise for a journey which failed, yet the North West Company agreement of 1792 gave him a second share over that held since 1787.[14]

The winter of 1791–1792 found Mackenzie in London honing his navigational skills with the newly improved chronometer. In 1793, he led a voyage up the Peace River, across the Rockies and partly down a turbulent river, which Mackenzie believed was the river named in 1792 by its discoverer, the American sea captain Robert Gray, for his ship the *Columbia*. Mackenzie's party retreated back up the Fraser to the West Road River where they followed its banks

22

logistical and financial problems mounted. The obvious solution was right of transit through Hudson Bay, something the HBC and the British Government adamantly refused to grant. Picking up where the French left off, the company resumed the search for an overland Northwest Passage to the Pacific Ocean for furs destined for England and China and for goods carried from the Pacific into the interior.

From its founding in 1784, the North West Company made the discovery of such a passage through the northwest a major priority. At the same time, mariners of many nations began seeking a route leading into North America from the Pacific Ocean. In 1778, Captain James Cook found a bay on the Pacific's far north coast which he misto the Bella Coola River and saltwater. With the aid of Indian guides, the indomitable Mackenzie, his clerk Alexander MacKay and six voyageurs were the first Europeans north of Mexico to cross North America to the Pacific. Yet this incredibly difficult and dangerous expedition, too, had failed. Of its 2300-mile return journey from Fort Chipewyan, only 1,720 miles were by water, hardly a practical route for commercial transportation.[15]

Depressed and anxious to quit the Athabasca, Mackenzie's prayers were answered in 1795 when he joined McTavish, Frobisher & Company, the NWC's firm of Montréal agents. Although he could now winter in Montréal and travel only as far as Grand Portage each summer, in 1799 he quit the NWC. His grand vision of one vast global trading network uniting the Hudson's Bay Company, the East India Company and the North West Company, was one not shared by the Marquis, Simon McTavish. McTavish wanted a united fur trade, but on his own terms.

Meanwhile in Montréal, the financier Alexander Ellice and his relatives John Forsyth and John Richardson had founded Forsyth, Richardson and Company to oppose McTavish, Frobisher. In 1798, Forsyth, Richardson launched a concerted opposition to the NWC as the New North West Company, better known as the XY Company.

In 1801, Alexander Mackenzie was in London for publication of his *Voyages from Montréal on the River St. Lawrence to the Frozen and Pacific Oceans, in the years 1789 and 1793*. The work gained a wide international readership including Thomas Jefferson, Napoleon Bonaparte and Thomas Douglas, the Earl of Selkirk. The next year, the book earned its author a knighthood. Mackenzie was not yet "Sir" when he joined the XY Company in 1800 but, by 1802, its firm of Montréal agents bore the name Sir Alexander Mackenzie & Company. With the prestigious explorer at its helm, the New Company's opposition to the NWC would be savage and vindictive.

Jay's Treaty of 1794 required Britain to give up its military posts in the United States by 1796. Although the British could continue trading south of the boundary, the United States had the right to levy customs duties on British goods entering its territory. In 1798, the NWC transferred its operations at Sault Ste. Marie from the south bank of St. Mary's River to the north where it built a post, canal and locks. But at Grand Portage the company stayed in place as long as possible.

In 1797, a Hudson's Bay Company astronomer defected to the NWC at Grand Portage. This was David Thompson who later had nothing but praise for "the liberal and public spirit of this North West Company of Merchants of Canada" compared to "the mean selfish policy of the Hudson's Bay Company styled Honourable." He also had nothing but contempt for British diplomats who gave "twice the area of the territory the States could justly claim." The NWC assigned Thompson the task of determining the location of NWC posts in relation to the boundary. Travelling some 4,000 miles in ten months, Thompson found, among other things, that the Grand Portage did lie in American territory.[16]

Reluctantly, the North West Company accepted the inevitable. Strangely, the old French "road" by the Kaministiquia River had been forgotten, but surely only its course, not its existence. Without guides, it would be almost impossible to travel from Dog Lake then through the maze of islands in Lac des Milles Lacs and finally to Lac la Croix where the Kaministiquia and Pigeon routes converge. In 1798, some Indians showed Nor'wester Roderick McKenzie the way to Superior via the Kaministiquia, an all-British route. What finally spurred the North West Company to move across the border, though, was price of staying put when a United States customs officer arrived at Grand Portage in 1800 to collect duties on all foreign goods crossing the great carrying-place.[17]

23

3   NEW FORT KAMINISTIQUIA

Conscious of their dependence on the goodwill of local Natives, the Nor'westers included the Ojibwa in their plans to move north. In 1798, the year Roderick McKenzie "rediscovered" the Kaministiquia route, Simon McTavish, Joseph Frobisher, John Gregory, William McGillivray and Alexander Mackenzie entered an agreement with ten "Chiefs and Old Men of the Chipeway [Ojibwa] and Kichicamingue [Lake Superior] Indians at Grand Portage." In exchange for three pounds currency, the Ojibwa yielded a tract of land five miles wide on either side of the Kaministiquia River for a distance of twelve miles from Lake Superior. In return, the agents promised the vendors the right to "peaceably quietly, have, hold, occupy, possess, and enjoy the said lands."[1]

The Indians were mystified by the need for such an agreement:

> [They] could not, or would not, understand the necessity of this movement [from Grand Portage *to* Kaministiquia], as they claimed the country as their own, and felt as though they had a right to locate their traders wherever they pleased. They could not be made to understand the right assumed by Great Britain and the United States to divide lands left to the Natives by their ancestors, and of which they held actual possession.[2]

According to the deed, the Ojibwa along Superior's northwest shore belonged to ten families or clans within a larger tribal grouping, each clan having its own base on Superior's western shoreline. On July 30, 1798, the chiefs of the clans marked the conveyance with their family symbols while the Nor'westers present signed their names. The agreement, however, had no legality. In 1799, the Administrator of Upper Canada, the Honourable Peter Russell, promised Alexander Mackenzie to "back our claim with all his Interest." (The Constitutional Act of 1791 had placed the Great Lakes watershed, including the Kaministiquia River, in the new province of Upper Canada.) Ten years later, the NWC received unwelcome news, "…the king has forbidden the sale of Indian lands to anyone but himself or their relations. The law was made for their protection." Much later, the old Nor'wester John McDonald of Garth observed, "The North West Co. were Squatters, and the H.B. Co. has no better title."[3]

The voyageurs also had to be mollified about the move north. Back in 1731, their forebears had balked at using the Grand Portage. Now the reverse was true; the notorious reputation of the Kaministiquia route had not been forgotten. In 1803, the NWC partner Alexander Henry (the Younger) noted that the "old road" deterred

24

many voyageurs from renewing their contracts; later most relented and even extolled its virtues.[4]

One of the company's priorities was to drain the low, swampy land about one mile from the lake on the Kaministiquia's upper branch. Simon McTavish chose this location for the new depot. He then ordered the work done by a readily available supply of labour, the voyageurs whose contracts obligated them to perform six days' *corvée* or mandatory labour, a convenient feudal obligation carried over from Québec's seigneurial system.

Under Québec law, employers and employees entered individual labour contracts called *engagements* before a notary. The term *engagé* applied to those hired under contract; in the fur trade it applied to engaged or contract voyageurs and other workers, most of whom marked "X" after declaring that they could not read. Once marked or signed, the *engagement* had legal status. *Engagés* failing to appear for the voyage or refusing to perform *corvée* faced the full force of the law. This remnant of the feudal system lessened the North West Company's costs for building their new fort, said to be £10,000 sterling.[5]

Unlike Grand Portage, the new Fort Kaministiquia was planned in advance. No designs have been located, yet it is apparent that William McGillivray directed the construction. In April 1802, the agents requested of the Lieutenant-Governor of Upper Canada that any survey of the Kaministiquia River:

…leave ground enough, round their possessions, so as to accommodate their Men and Indians, with sufficient Space for Places of Encampment, for Gardens, Farming, Grazing Cattle, and other suitable Conveniences.[6]

The fort's symmetrical, balanced arrangement of structures followed late 18th century architectural styles, but its model went back to mediaeval times. In North America, as elsewhere, European military posts and commercial "factories" typically featured an imposing main building facing a front gate set in high walls surrounding the complex.[7]

Fortunately for posterity, two former Astorians on their way to Montréal from the Columbia River recorded descriptions of the fort. In 1814, Gabriel Franchère recorded:

In the middle of a spacious square rises a large frame house elegantly built and painted, raised about five feet above ground level, with a verandah in front…. All of this is surrounded by a palisade of posts and occupies a considerable area.[8]

And in 1817, Ross Cox wrote:

The buildings at Fort William consist of a large house, in which the dining-hall is situated, and in which the gentleman in charge resides. The whole is surrounded by wooden fortifications, flanked by bastions, *and is sufficiently strong to withstand any attack from the Natives.*[9]

Fort Kaministiquia and similar establishments had no overt military function but served as "symbols of dominance." A description of Fort Union, an American Fur Company post at the junction of the Missouri and Yellowstone rivers, states "The dominance statement expressed through the architecture was one tool to overwhelm the local tribes. The hierarchy of a fur trade post and the isolation of its location demanded a definite line of authority and respect."[10]

This argument applies equally to Fort Kaministiquia. The few officers present at any time were prudent to flaunt their superiority over local Natives whom they had armed and supplied with liquor. They could not ignore the prospect of Americans fortifying nearby Grand Portage as a base for invading British North America. While they needed a palisade for security against vandals, thieves, wild animals, rowdy voyageurs and Natives encamped outside, they

were also aware of the continuing warfare between the Dakota and the Ojibwa just south of the Pigeon River.[11]

British authorities at Québec City had Canada's defences very much in mind when they sent the military engineer, Captain R.H. Bruyère, to survey the frontier in 1802. In his "Report on the Tradeing [sic] Establishment now forming at the entrance of the Kaministagua River Situate in Thunder Bay Lake Superior," Bruyère recommended the "Scite of the French Fort" as "the most proper situation for a Military Reserve."[12]

A military base never was built but, as Bruyère's sketch shows, its proposed location lay between the "House and Spot cleared by the New Company" and the "Picketted Fort house & ground cleared by the North West Company." The XY Company, too, was preparing for the day it would leave Grand Portage. The hostile relationship between the companies was another reason for a strong palisade around Fort Kaministiquia.

Construction was well underway in 1803 when Alexander Henry arrived for the annual meeting:

> …great improvements had been made here for the space of one Winter season, Fort, Store, Shop, &c built, but not a sufficient number of dwelling houses for all hands. There was only one range erected and that not compleat. Here was the Mess room and appartments for the Agents from Montréal with a temporary kitchen &c. adjoining. We were under the necessity of erecting our Tents for our dwelling.… Building was going forward very briskly in every corner of the Fort, and Brick kilns were also erected…[13]

Opposite: **Sketch of the Entrance of the River Kaministigua and Sketch of Thunder Bay**, 1802, by Captain R.H. Bruyère. The two Forts Kaministiquia from the French era are seen as well as the location of the planned NWC and XYC plots. *Courtesy of LAC, National Map Collection, C 85839.*

Although building continued apace, everything was not "compleat" when Henry returned in 1804. The stone structures were finished around 1810 and 1811 and the canoe sheds evidently between 1811 and 1816.[14]

The Fort would soon meet all the requirements as the NWC's "*rendezvous-place*," as the company called its inland headquarters. The NWC needed this Lake Superior depot because canoes could not make the round trip between Montréal and the northwest in one ice-free season. Lengthening fur trade routes now were such that Rainy Lake had already become the turn-around point for Athabasca canoes, while Fort Chipewyan on Lake Athabasca served as depot for Mackenzie River canoes.

The Fort not only served as the North West Company's major transshipment point for goods and furs but also as headquarters for the company's annual business meeting between wintering partners and Montréal agents. In 1803, the company held its first *rendezvous* at "Kaminitiquia." Simon McTavish did not attend this meeting. He was busy in Montréal overseeing the construction of his mansion on Mount Royal. Instead, his nephews, William and Duncan McGillivray, represented the NWC's Montréal agents, McTavish, Frobisher, which William had joined in 1793 and Duncan in 1799.

The North West Company divided its trading territory into districts, or "departments." Normally, departments were headed by one or more wintering partners or "proprietors." The few partners at the 1803 meeting came from all across the northwest: William McKay from Lake Winnipeg; Archibald Norman McLeod, Simon Fraser and James McKenzie from the Athabasca; John McDonald of Garth, Rocky Mountain House; John Sayer, Fond du Lac (Superior, Wisconsin); Duncan Cameron, Lake Nipigon; Charles Chaboillez, from the Red River; Peter Grant of Rainy Lake and Alexander Henry, Pembina on the Red River (North Dakota). Kaministiquia had no representative at the meeting. For its first five years, this department was headed by a clerk not a proprietor.

Curiously, the minutes of 1803 make no mention of the XY Company's headquarters under construction up river nor of that company's extraordinary inroads into the NWC's trade. But, in 1804, the Nor'westers had no choice but to face the impact of competition. A "system of Economy" forbade partners the use of light canoes and having more than one manservant. The only winners were the voyageurs who, benefiting from competition for their services, enjoyed a few years of higher wages.

For everyone else, rivalry between the New and Old Companies spelled disaster, especially for Indians from the volume of alcohol lavished on them by the competing firms. Until 1799, the NWC's average annual expenditure in "Spirituous liquors" was 9,600 gallons. From 1802 to 1804, it rose to 14,400 gallons annually to which must be added the XYC's output of another 5,000 gallons a year.[15]

Often liquor led to violence, but liquor did not cause all the violence. The Indian-trader relationship revolved around credit. Before the hunt, the Indians received credits in goods to be repaid in furs. But this system fell apart as rival traders waylaid Indians and seized furs owed their creditors. Brawls over pelts could have fatal results, but as a new NWC clerk, Daniel Harmon, wrote in 1800, "Here a murderer escapes the gallows as there are not human laws that can reach or have any effect on the People of this Country."[16]

Murder over fur proved too much for imperial officials in London. As Canada had no right to lay charges for crimes committed in the Indian Territory, Parliament passed the Canada Jurisdiction Act in 1803 which empowered Justices of the Peace, appointed by the government at Québec, to arrest offenders in the Indian Territory and send them to Lower Canada for trial.

The magistrates chosen then (and later) were hardly unbiased. In 1803, they were Duncan McGillivray, William McGillivray and Roderick McKenzie, agents of the North West Company and Sir Alexander Mackenzie and John Ogilvie, agents of the XY Company. This act gave the North West Company the authority to construct a "common gaol" (pronounced jail) at the Fort. It also prompted both sides to consider ending their contest.[17]

While the NWC was fighting the XYC, it also had to contend with Montréal's ancient rival, the Hudson's Bay Company. As the Nor'westers pushed deeper into the Athabasca country, they resented more and more the HBC charter to the Hudson Bay watershed. In London, the NWC's agents pleaded with government for a right of transit through Hudson and James bays but in vain. In 1803, Simon McTavish sent his kinsman, John George McTavish, by sea from Québec to occupy Charlton Island in James Bay and William McGillivray's brother-in-law, Angus Shaw, overland to build posts on the Bay's southern coast.[18]

Three years later, the NWC abandoned these efforts. Yet geography dictated that without access to the Bay, the NWC would either have to amalgamate with the Hudson's Bay Company, or try to take it over. But first, the New and Old North West Companies had to present a united front before their mutual enemy, a seemingly remote possibility.

On July 6, 1804, Simon McTavish's unexpected death in Montréal removed a major barrier to union between the rival firms. Despite their recent animosity, William McGillivray and Mackenzie ended their feud with the active assistance of Edward Ellice, the XYC's London agent and trans-Atlantic merchant, banker and landowner. On November 5, 1804, the rivals, "being desirous to put an end to said opposition and to avoid the waste of property" agreed "to coalesce and join their respective interests"

Opposite: **Engagement of Alexis Matte to McTavish, McGillivrays for three years, 1815. The third paragraph from the top shows** *six jours de corvée. Courtesy of Fort William Historical Park.*

28

PARDEVANT LES NOTAIRES de la Province du Bas-Canada à Montréal, y résidant, soussigné; fut présent

Alexis Matte de la Tonel

lequel s'est volontairement engagé et s'engage par ces présentes à Messrs. *William McGillivray, Simon McGillivray, Archibald Norman McLeod, Thomas Thain, et Henry Mackenzie,* de Montréal, Négocians et associés, sous le nom de McTAVISH, McGILLIVRAYS & Co. & PIERRE DE ROCHEBLAVE, *A. N. McLeod*

Ecuier, à ce présent et acceptant pour, à leur première réquisition, partir de Montréal en qualité de *Milieu* dans un de leurs canots, pour faire le voyage, et pour hiverner durant *trois* année *dans* les dépendances du Nord-Ouest dans le Haut-Canada,

(ne sera libre de ce présent engagement qu'à son retour à Montréal, à la fin de son hivernment) passer par Michilimakinac, s'il en est réquis, donner six jours de corvée, faire deux voyages du Fort-William au Portage de la Montagne, ou au lieu d'iceux donner six jours de tems à d'autres ouvrages à l'option des dits Sieurs, aider à porter les canots à trois dans les terres, et avoir bien et dûment soin pendant les routes, et étant rendu aux dits lieux des marchandises, vivres, pelleteries, ustensiles, et de toutes les choses nécessaires pour le voyage; servir, obéir, et exécuter fidèlement, tout ce que les dits Sieurs Bourgeois ou tous autres représentans leurs personnes, auxquels ils pourroient transporter le présent engagement, lui commanderont de licite et honnête; faire leur profit, éviter leur dommage, les en avertir s'il vient à sa connoissance; et généralement tout ce qu'un bon engagé doit et est obligé de faire sans pouvoir faire aucune traite particulière, s'absenter ni quitter le dit service, sous les peines portées par les loix et ordonnances de cette Province, et de perdre ses gages. Cet engagement ainsi fait, pour et moyennant la somme de *Septcent*

livres ou chelins, ancien cours de cette Province, qu'ils promettent et s'obligent de bailler et payer au dit engagé un mois après son retour à Montréal; et avoir pour équipement une couverte de trois points, une couverte de deux points et demie, six aunes de coton, une paire de souliers de bœuf et un collier, pour la première année et les Gages et conditions du poste où il hivernera pour les autres

reconnoît avoir reçu à compte d'avance *dix piastres lecavra Sep en partant*

s'oblige de contribuer d'un par cent sur ses gages pour le Fonds des Voyageurs. Car ainsi, &c. promettant, &c. obligeant, &c. renonçant, &c.

Fait et passé à Montreal, en l'étude du Notaire soussigné l'an mil huit cent vingt *—* le *quinze* de *Xbre —* et ont signé, à l'exception du dit engagé qui, ayant declaré ne le savoir faire, de ce enquis, a fait sa marque ordinaire après lecture faite.

Alexis X Matte
marque

A. N. McLeod

beginning with the outfit of 1805 and ending in 1822. Replacing his uncle as McTavish, Frobisher's principal director, McGillivray now headed the united North West Company and would continue to do so until the NWC's union with the Hudson's Bay Company in 1821.

In the hundred share "joint" firm, the Old NWC had a three-quarters interest with twenty-five shares allotted to McTavish, Frobisher and fifty to its wintering partners. The XYC had twenty-five shares, six for its wintering partners and nineteen for its firm of Montréal merchants known as Sir Alexander Mackenzie & Company but dominated by the partnership of John Forsyth and John Richardson, Edward Ellice's cousins.

It was an immigrant from Waldorf, Germany who revitalized the New York fur trade by associating with Alexander Henry the Elder, now an independent Montréal merchant. John Jacob Astor needed Montréal's commercial connections with London, but his long-term ambition was to rid the United States of British fur traders. Already conducting business with China from Atlantic ports, he looked to an early discovery of an overland route to the Pacific, an idea he had picked up from Henry, who in turn had heard Peter Pond propound his theories about such a passage to the sea.

In 1802, another American seized upon the urgency of finding a route to the Columbia. President Thomas Jefferson had read Sir Alexander Mackenzie's *Voyages* and found the following proposal for advancing British imperialism in North America a threat to the territorial ambitions of the United States:

Whatever course may be taken from the Atlantic, the Columbia is the line of communication from the Pacific Ocean, pointed out by nature…. By opening this intercourse between the Atlantic and Pacific Oceans…the entire command of the fur trade might be obtained.[19]

Spain's cession of Louisiana to France gave Jefferson his opportunity. In 1803, he bought Louisiana on behalf of the United States of America for $15,000,000. With the Louisiana Purchase, the U.S.A. doubled in size, its western boundary now the Rocky Mountains instead of the Mississippi River and its northern limits some vaguely defined line with western British North America.

In 1804, Jefferson commissioned the famed Lewis and Clark expedition to explore America's newly acquired territory and beyond to the Pacific Ocean. After their two-year journey, the explorers urged the United States government to forestall North West Company ambitions on the Pacific by "the establishment of a trading post at the mouth of the Columbia River, for expediting the commerce in furs to China." These proposals reinforced similar plans already forming in the mind of John Jacob Astor.[20]

When the united North West Company met in 1805, Fort Kaministiquia was still under construction. The merger made it possible to rationalize resources and cut costs. But the intransigence of the HBC and the looming menace of John Jacob Astor kept the "joint firm" focussed on its perennial quest for a navigable, overland passage to the Pacific Ocean.

30

4 WILLIAM'S FORT

"Active intelligent enterprising ambitious obstinate and vindictive." Written by an enemy, this observation still had a certain validity. As Simon McTavish's worthy successor, William McGillivray commanded North West Company operations on all fronts until 1821. From the minutest arrangement inland to the grand sweep of international affairs, he devoted abundant energy and astute attention.[1]

In Montréal, he set policy at meetings of McTavish, McGillivrays, the merchant firm which succeeded McTavish, Frobisher in 1806. With his brother Duncan, he virtually controlled this agency firm which, in turn, held four shares in McTavish, Fraser of London. Of the remaining five shares, his brother Simon and his cousin John Fraser had two each and the bookkeeper one. McTavish, Fraser controlled three-quarters of the London business. Inglis, Ellice held the other quarter on behalf of Sir Alexander Mackenzie & Company of Montréal.[2]

Most summers, William travelled to the *rendezvous* by express canoe manned by twelve voyageurs. His many business trips to Britain and the United States took four or five days in open boats or canoes between Montréal and New York, and several weeks by ship across the Atlantic. He collaborated with John Jacob Astor about the NWC's China trade from New York and Boston via Cape Horn. In Lower Canada, McGillivray had personal property to administer, including an estate of 11,550 acres granted by the government in 1802, along with similar largess to Simon McTavish and other fur magnates *cum* landed proprietors.[3] In 1808, he would represent Montréal West in the Legislative Assembly of Lower Canada.

In Montréal, McGillivray attended glittering parties and grand dinners at private homes and the famed Beaver Club, founded in 1785 for veteran traders of the *pays d'en haut*. Until his 1800 wedding in London to Magdalen, the sister of Nor'wester John McDonald of Garth, he and his then friend Alexander Mackenzie enjoyed the club's all-night drunken revelries, a privilege granted non-married members only.

Among the club's distinguished guests were John Jacob Astor and Lord Selkirk. But no intelligence these guests divulged *in vino veritas* could augur their future hostile relationship with McGillivray. Perhaps what equipped him most for tribulations yet to come were the Beaver's Club's motto, "Fortitude in Distress" and the North West Company's "Perseverance."

William was absent on legislative duties when the annual meeting in 1807 honoured this man at the head of the North West Company. As the minutes state somewhat tersely:

William McGillivray by Sir Martin Archer Shee.
Courtesy of Fort William Historical Park, copy of original at LAC C-167.

The Wintering Partners having proposed that the name of this place should be changed & that of Fort William substituted in its stead as being more simple and appropriate the Agents gave their assent and the name 'Kamanistiquia' is accordingly discontinued & abolished for ever & that of Fort William is adopted in its place.[4]

Suitably, the port from which most Highlanders sailed to the New World was Fort William at the Great Glen's outlet to the North Atlantic, but, as the clerk Daniel Harmon recorded on July 19, the Nor'westers had McGillivray in mind when they re-named their fort on the Kaministiquia's outlet to the Great Lakes:

This which formerly was called the New Fort is now named Fort William, in honor of William McGillivray, Esqr, on which occasion the Commerce made a present to their common labouring men of a considerable quantity of Spirits, and Shrub, & C, and also a similar present was made to the Natives encamped about the Fort.[5]

The enthusiasm of all partners may not have been universal, given Daniel McKenzie's later complaint that the celebration's costs were charged, without permission, to the wintering partners' accounts by order of the agents.[6]

During these heady times, Fort William on Lake Superior gained an almost mythic reputation, a reputation enhanced in its decline by Washington Irving in his stirring *Astoria*:

To behold the North West Company in all its state and grandeur, however, it is necessary to witness an annual gathering at Fort William.... On these occasions might be seen the change from the unceremonious times of the old French traders; now the aristocratical times of the Briton shone forth magnificently, or rather the feudal spirit of a Highlander. Every partner who had charge of an interior post, felt like the chieftain of a Highland clan, and was almost as important in the eyes of his dependents as of himself.[7]

Witnesses of life at other NWC posts confirm the company's cultivation of Scottish hierarchical traditions. Joining the NWC after its purchase of Astoria from the Astor's Pacific Fur Company in 1813, Alexander Ross observed a marked change on the Columbia from the egalitarian style of the Americans. The Nor'westers demanded seating at dinner according to station and three qualities of tea, tea pots and sugar for three ranks of personnel. As for the NWC's depot on Lake Superior:

This portrait of William McGillivray is owned by Simon McGillivray's great-great-grandson. The tartan is worn in Thunder Bay today by the Lake Superior Scottish Regiment and the Macgillivray Pipe Band. *Courtesy of Fort William Historical Park, copied by the kind permission of Gianni Lombardi, Rome.*

Fort William, the great *rendezvous* of their trade throughout the North, was in show and grandeur little behind their princely establishments in Montréal. Their buildings there were elegant, their style of living costly, and altogether the establishment presented a very imposing spectacle to the eye of a stranger.[8]

His impoverished childhood in Stratherrick, Inverness-shire well behind him, William now proved himself equal to the lairds of Scotland by this display of grandeur named in his honour.

The magnitude of the fort also testified to the giddying achievements of the North West Com-pany, its explorations and trade proof, in Duncan McGillivray's words, that "the spirit of commerce is fertile in expedient and unwearied in pursuit of new sources of wealth." The trade across the Rockies, which he himself had initiated, well reflected the age's rampant spirit of commerce.

Although the trans-mountain business had yet to make a profit, Duncan wrote in 1807, the company planned "a general establishment for the trade of that country on the Columbia River." In pursuit of that objective, Simon Fraser explored a river to the Pacific in 1808 which proved not to be the Columbia, as expected, but the turbulent river now bearing his name. The

Great Hall at Fort William Historical Park showing reproduction paintings of Lord Nelson and the Battle of Trafalgar by William Berczy. The original paintings are at HBC Head Office, Toronto. *Photograph by Joe Winterburn, Fort William Historical Park.*

Fraser proved impractical for traffic but Simon's explorations added the Caledonia Department across the mountains to the NWC's domain.

The NWC's shareholders (the agents and partners) and the would-be shareholders (the clerks) personified this spirit of commerce. Together they typified the rising bourgeoisie depicted in Max Weber's *The Protestant Ethic and the Spirit of Capitalism*. As summarized by R.H. Tawney's succinct foreword:

> The pioneers of the modern economic order were, he argues, *parvenus,* who elbowed their way to success…. The tonic that braced them for the conflict was a new conception of religion, which taught them to regard the pursuit of wealth as, not merely an advantage, but a duty…. Capitalism was the social counterpart of Calvinist theology.[9]

Calvinist theology, in turn, so imbued the culture of these Nor'westers that it had drawn the few Catholics, like Simon Fraser, amongst them into its powerful grasp.

At Fort William each partner no doubt "felt like the chieftain of a Highland clan," while the buildings in which they worked, caroused and slept reflected their status as gentlemen. Lieutenant Robert Irvine's almost photographic view of the fort (see back cover) depicts their dwelling, dining and business quarters as painted, but with rough exteriors on warehouses, workshops, farm buildings and quarters for the lesser folk.

Within the managerial group, the hierarchical principle extended to the sleeping quarters. Raised above all other buildings on the main square, the Great Hall had two bedrooms at each end for Montréal agents. At the square's northwest corner, the appropriately-named North West House contained twelve bedrooms for wintering partners. East of the Great Hall was the Bell House with twelve similar rooms for "superior" clerks. From its bell tower, fort personnel were summoned to work and to meals. On the square's east side, the East House housed apprentice clerks and interpreters, the latter mostly French Canadians with fluency in Indian languages.

In 1807, the mess house walls featured two new paintings donated by William McGillivray. William Berczy's full-length likeness of Admiral Lord Horatio Nelson and depiction of the Battle of Trafalgar symbolized company loyalties during the Napoleonic Wars. The Nor'westers had already contributed to the Nelson column in Montréal, erected in 1809, years before Nelson's column stood in London's Trafalgar Square. This romantic hero of triumphant sea battles and his tragic death in victory inspired patriotic fervour in all Britons. The Fort William paintings and the Nelson statue, still standing in Old Montréal, symbolized the NWC's empathy with Britain's cause—and its stake in British control of the high seas.[10]

The mess house also displayed portraits of past and present Nor'westers and a bust of Simon McTavish, the company's founder. Revelling in past triumphs and future exploits, the Nor'westers no doubt quaffed many salutations to the great personalities depicted around them, perhaps repeating the mandatory toasts proposed at Beaver Club meetings in Montréal:

The Mother of All Saints
The King

The Fur Trade in All Its Branches
Voyageurs, Wives and Children
Absent Members[11]

Such festivities furthered the *esprit de corps* of those eligible to partake. The winterers had undergone long and strenuous journeys to reach the fort and, despite such luxuries as coffee, tea and chocolate, they endured months of monotonous diet, sometimes near starvation, in remote, lonely outposts. Meals taken at Grand Portage, as described by Alexander Mackenzie, differed little from those at Fort William:

> The proprietors, clerks, guides, and interpreters mess together, to the number of sometimes an hundred, at several tables, in one large hall, the provisions consisting of bread, salt pork, beef, hams, fish, and venison, butter, peas, Indian corn, potatoes, tea, spirits, wine, etc., and plenty of milk, for which purpose several milch cows are constantly kept. The mechanics have rations of such provisions, but the canoemen, both from the North and Montréal, have no other allowance here, or in the voyage, than lyed corn and melted fat.[12]

At Fort William, the upper ranks enjoyed produce from the fort's farm and products shipped from afar—double Gloucester and American cheese, ham, raisins, brown and loaf sugar, Hyson and green tea, port, Madeira, Teneriffe wine and brandy. To run the farm, the company hired agricultural workers from Lower Canada; to manage the mess room and supervise the cooking, it brought in a butler or *maître d'hotel*, cooks and *domestiques* from Montréal. Elaborate meals and gala dances with fiddle, fife and bagpipe, attended by local Native women, provided a much needed boost to morale.

The dining and working environment at Fort William gave clerks from the Indian country the opportunity to be observed by their betters.

35

This illustration of Fort William by William Armstrong, circa 1870, shows the fort during the Hudson's Bay period.

Most clerks entered the trade at around age eighteen to serve as apprentices for five to seven years at £100 for the entire term. Those not voted into a partnership after their apprenticeship worked as "superior" clerks at £80 to £200 a year in anticipation of future promotion, but if lacking "connexions" they stayed on salary for the rest of their careers. Ross Cox well explained the incentive to undergo the long, poorly-paid process to become a NWC partner:

> ...as each individual was led to expect that the period for his election to the proprietory depended on his own exertions, every nerve was strained to attain the long-desired object of his wishes. Courage was an indispensable qualification not merely for the casual encounters with the Indians, but to intimidate any competitor in trade with whom he might happen to come in collision...provided he obtained for his outfit of merchandise what was considered a good return of furs, the partners never stopped to inquire about the means by which they were acquired.[13]

As Lord Selkirk came to understand:

> The hope of obtaining the envied station of a partner, being kept alive among all the senior clerks, excites among them an activity and zeal for the general interests of the concern, hardly inferior to that of the partners themselves.[14]

Despite, or because of their hardships, the wintering partners in the North West Company acquired a unique kind of panache which still clings to their names. The system of giving those in charge of the trade a share in the profits and a voice in company affairs gave rise to the company's spectacular successes, especially compared to the Hudson's Bay Company, whose traders on fixed salaries had no inducement to "extra exertion." Lord Selkirk looked on the NWC's system of selecting partners with admiration:

> No candidate can have much chance of success, unless he be well acquainted with the nature of the trade, the character and manners

of the Indians, and the mode of acquiring influence with them.[15]

Fort William's Counting House best revealed the relationship between agents and partners and clerks. This was the office of the company's interior headquarters where clerks from Montréal recorded and analyzed the annual returns in furs, the deployment of canoes, provisions and men, balances in employee accounts and Indian credits, and examined departmental inventories.

By the 1802 agreement, the Montréal agents brought one complete set of NWC accounts to the *rendezvous* for the wintering partners' perusal. In the fur trade, each year or "adventure" paid for its own outfit which included supplies, goods, provisions, wages, equipment, shipping costs and duties, interest on loans and other necessities. Furs harvested that year were the adventure's "returns." Every adventure could take years to wind up since expenditures for each year's outfit and receipts for each year's furs continued over time.[16]

Each partner had his portion of the outfit's costs charged to his account and its returns similarly credited. Since payments for an outfit's returns could come in some four or more years after the purchase of its outfit, new partners started out in debt to the agents. Examining the general accounts and their individual statements naturally had great interest for partners attending the *rendezvous*. For their part, the agents required that the partners bring from their own departments:

> …a true faithful and exact account and Inventory of all the goods, provisions and other effects…remaining on hand as well as of the Peltries, debts due by the Indians and canoemen …[17]

In the counting house, the Montréal firms' professional bookkeepers scrutinized, calculated, recorded and copied these accounts which affected profit estimates, the assignment of personnel and allotment of good and provisions for the coming year. In the spirit of commerce, the moneyed partners needed to know, in R.H. Tawney's words, the initial balances to calculate "an enterprise's probable profitableness, and at

Fort William is mistakenly entitled *Grand Portage on Lake Superior* in an inset on Joseph Bouchette's *A Topographical Description of Lower Canada, 1815*. Courtesy of LAC, National Map Collection, C 17761.

the end a final balance to ascertain how much profit has been made."[18]

The several currencies prevailing in British North America made the bookkeeper's tasks extremely complex. Alexander Henry the Younger's statement for the Lower Red River Outfit of 1802 shows that one account could have entries in many currencies. Costs incurred in Canada are given in Halifax (Hx.) currency whose units were the same as sterling but whose value was lower, fluctuating according to the rate of exchange. The cost of merchandise and the sale price of furs in England are given in sterling. In Lower Canada, the *livre* prevailed in transactions with French Canadians. North West (or Grand Portage) *livres* expressed men's wages and expenses in the interior. Halifax currency and the *livre* had no specie; they were merely forms of reckoning. The coinage most in circulation was the piastre or Spanish dollar.[19]

£1 Hx = 24 livres Québec = 12 livres NW = $4

The North West Company held its annual meetings in the council house. Minutes of the Fort William meetings, which have survived for the years 1803 to 1814, provide a wealth of information about the diverse issues facing the company. In 1814, partner-agent differences over accounts surfaced: "Various explanations of the Accts were asked and given by the Agents," and, "The Exchange was again objected to on which account the general accounts were not signed." Presided over by William McGillivray or his alternate, the meetings debated a diversity of topics, all ultimately concerning profit and the value of each partner's share as revealed in the accounts. At Fort William, frugality dominated the proceedings of the North West Company.[20]

38

5   THE TRANSFER OF GOODS

Along British America's fur trade transportation routes, products of distant lands and domestic origin flowed from Montréal through Fort William into the north and west. Back along the same waterways, animal pelts moved to Montréal on their way to overseas markets. Distance determined that the vessels carrying goods from the east and furs from the northwest turn around at a Lake Superior port. History determined that, from 1803 to 1821, this point be at the mouth of the Kaministiquia River.

This transfer of cargo at Fort William coincided with the need to employ different vessels on the eastern and western laps of the route, huge Montréal canoes for the Ottawa River-Lake Superior run, *batteaux* and schooners via the Great Lakes, and smaller north canoes on inland waterways. But before goods and furs left the fort, they had first to be aired, cleaned, sorted, consigned and repacked for loading into the appropriate vessels.

Moving goods through Montréal was labour-intensive and complex. After clearing customs at Québec, imports went by ox-cart or watercraft to Montréal warehouses. There, smaller goods were packed into ninety-pound *pièces*, the bales, crates and kegs designed to fit into canoes and be portaged two at a time on men's backs. Bulk materials went in large containers for shipping via the Great Lakes on schooners and *batteaux*.

From Montréal wagons carried the cargo to warehouses at Lachine above the St. Lawrence rapids where *pièces* were loaded into thirty-six foot *canots de maître*, each carrying four tons of freight along with provisions and personal baggage. The freight canoes travelled in brigades of three or more, following the Ottawa (or Grand) and Mattawa rivers, Lake Nipissing, the French River, Lake Huron's north channel and St. Mary's River. With thirty-six portages, this route could take four or more weeks to the Sault and another ten days along Lake Superior's north shore.

Each summer, several hundred voyageurs descended on Fort William from east and west. Most were French Canadians, natives of seigneuries along the St. Lawrence and Ottawa rivers. The summermen, who signed a new contract each year for the round trip from Lachine, were also known as *allants et venants* (goers and comers) or *mangeurs de lard* (pork-eaters) for the salt pork added to their daily ration of dried peas or beans. If required to go on to Lac la Pluie (Rainy Lake), the turn-around place for Athabasca canoes, they received additional pay, usually half again what they received for the Lachine to Fort William run.

The northmen or *hivernants* had three-year contracts renewable at either Fort William, at an

SUPERIOR RENDEZVOUS-PLACE

inland post or in Montréal. Over the winter, the northmen laboured at hunting, fishing, constructing or repairing buildings and canoes and trading at Indian encampments. As soon as the ice was out in spring, they brought the past year's returns in furs down to Fort William in twenty-four-foot north canoes. These *hivernants* had nothing but contempt for the summermen who had the luxury of wintering in Lower Canada.

Besides his wage, the voyageur's *engagement* specified the contents of his equipment. A summerman's normally included one pair of beef shoes, a tumpline (or portage strap), a three-point blanket and three ells (1 ell = 45 inches) of cotton while a *hivernant* had the generous allotment of an additional two-point blanket and another three ells of cotton. Once engaged, he received an advance, usually of thirty piastres (Spanish dollars), and on departure another ten piastres. Some contracts designated the *engagé's* wife or mother as recipient of the advance. Most voyageurs were obliged to perform six days *corvée* at Fort William and either make two trips from the fort to the Mountain Portage depot above Kakabeka Falls or provide an additional six days' labour.

Within both groups, a strict hierarchical structure and pay differential prevailed based on the voyageur's position in the canoe. The middlemen or *milieux* had the lowest rank, then the *gouvernail* at the stern and then the *avant* or *devant*

Opposite top: Tracking the Rapids **by Neil Broadfoot. Where possible, tracking was undertaken to avoid the onerous portaging of canoe and freight around hazardous waters.** *From* **Superior Illusions** *by Richard Pope. Courtesy of Neil Broadfoot.*

Opposite bottom: Voyageurs at Dawn, **1871, by Frances Anne Hopkins. Travelling conditions beyond the settled areas of Canada had changed little since the earliest days of the fur trade as seen by the cooking pots and pans, baskets and crates and sleeping arrangements for voyageurs. Of special interest is the Native woman going about her tasks.** *Courtesy of LAC, C-002773.*

in the bow. At the highest level were the *guides* who led brigades of three or more canoes. At Fort William, the guides had the privilege of eating in the Great Hall and sleeping in a building reserved for them within the fort. All other voyageurs slept along the river under canoes or a tarp or perhaps in a "leathern tent"; for meals they had the same rations of dried peas or lyed corn and grease as doled out to them on the voyage. To curb feuding between winterers and summermen, they stayed in separate encampments, the *hivernants'* of "the utmost cleanliness" west of the palisade and the pork-eaters' in "filthy" conditions to the east.[1]

When weather permitted, the voyageurs paddled from sunrise to sunset, taking five minute breaks each hour or so for a "pipe." They portaged heavy loads over rugged terrain, often on very slender provisions, but just how harshly the Nor'westers treated the voyageurs is subject to debate. In 1794, Duncan McGillivray put down a strike of voyageurs at Lac la Pluie by sending its ringleaders to Montréal in chains, but most traders praised the carefree voyageurs for their "principles of passive obedience and nonresistance." In his nine years as a winterer, William McGillivray declared that he "never confined or punished a Servant for ill conduct." En route, the Nor'westers had no choice but to trust the voyageurs' expertise. Alone at isolated posts far from law enforcement agencies, they dared not risk being heavy-handed.[2]

Despite its hardships, tradition and family pride led generation after generation to the life of the voyageur. Among its rewards was a salary, especially welcomed in a cash-strapped society. Those who saved their wages returned to their village with ready money, as seen at Sorel where estates of deceased voyageurs included far more coinage than those of other inhabitants. Their camaraderie born of shared sufferings and their ostentatious attire made them the envy of fellow habitants.[3]

Many voyageurs, however, came to grief

41

Canoes in a Fog, Lake Superior, 1869, **by Frances Anne Hopkins. This brigade of three canoes eases its way along Lake Superior's perilous waters. The artist has painted herself into the last canoe.** *Collection of Glenbow Museum, Calgary, Canada.*

42

through indebtedness brought upon themselves by reckless spending at Fort William and inland posts. Some ended their contracts by owing the company more than the company owed them. To pay off their debts, they had to sign up for another term. Some never did break the cycle; they remained in the north as "free" Canadians for the rest of the lives, eking out a living and marrying Native women according to "the custom of the country."[4]

For voyageurs, the *rendezvous* meant hard work readying cargo and repairing canoes, but it also allowed ample opportunity for frivolity. At the fort's canteen within the palisade, voyageurs charged liquors, tobacco and provisions to their accounts; they also bought clothing and luxuries on credit for themselves and families in the Equipment Shop. At a distance west of the fort,

one Jean-Marie Boucher ran a separate *cantine* where voyageurs could buy liquor, tobacco and provisions but, according to Boucher's agreement with the Montréal agents, for "ready money" only.[5]

Forbidden to become indebted to Boucher, the voyageurs paid him with their cash advances or the "two Buffaloe Robes or two dressed skins or one of each" they could take out of the country each year. Voyageur rowdiness centred at Boucher's House instead of in the fort itself, but this was not the main motive for the enterprise. Boucher's contract guaranteed him 2,000 livres a year; otherwise two-thirds of the profits went to the Montréal agents. And since most voyageurs spent their year's wages at Boucher's, they ended up in debt to the Montréal agents by purchasing goods on credit at the "company store."[6]

During the NWC era, the number of French-Canadian voyageurs gradually declined. In the west, it became advantageous to hire men on the spot, the mixed-blood sons of voyageurs and Native women. The company also hired Iroquois from Lac des Deux Montagnes and Caughnawagna near Montréal as canoemen and hunters, a practice continued by the Hudson's Bay Company. Like the other *engagés*, the Iroquois had written contracts which many signed, not with an "X" but in writing, a reflection perhaps of missionary work in Lower Canada.[7]

At Fort William, the Iroquois had their own encampment, quite separate from the voyageurs and the local Ojibwa. By hiring Iroquois as voyageurs and as hunters on lands inhabited by other tribes, the North West Company inflamed old animosities and created new ones. Some Iroquois served as pork-eaters as far as Lac la Pluie

Bill of Lading, 1802, for a Montreal freight canoe leaving La Chine for Grand Portage. *Courtesy of Thunder Bay Historical Museum Society, 972.2.218.*

43

THE TRANSFER OF GOODS

Fort Kaministiquia, circa 1805, artist unknown. Published in Father Aeneas McDonell Dawson's, *Our strength and their strength* (Ottawa, 1870). Note schooners, *batteaux* and canoes at the wharf, voyageur tents to the left of the palisade and Indian encampment to the right. *Courtesy of LAC, C-24733.*

but others went to the foothills of the Rockies where, as hunters, they proved more reliable and more ruthless than local Natives whose livelihood they disrupted.[8]

Despite voyageur indebtedness, the company had a heavy payroll, to which must be added such embarkation costs such as room and board at Lachine. The company also paid into the provincially regulated Voyageur Fund which provided a little insurance to infirm and aged voyageurs or their widows. As required by their *engagements*, the voyageurs contributed one percent of their wages as well. At its annual meeting in 1811, the NWC agreed to give £100 to the fund because of "the unavoidable pressure upon it from the distress among the Voyageurs the last two winters," but in 1812, with no reason given, the "Wintering Partners do not wish to contribute any sum of money for the Superannuated Fund."[9]

When the Great Lakes opened to private shipping in 1791, Montréal traders eagerly resorted to this route for transporting bulk goods. Although *batteaux* had to be dragged and poled up the St. Lawrence from Lachine to calm water at Prescott, the flat-bottomed craft could be sailed across Lake Ontario to Queenston. Freight then went across the Niagara Portage by ox-cart to Fort Erie for transfer to NWC schooners on Lakes Erie and Huron. At the Sault, the goods by-passed St. Mary's rapids by ox-cart or went by *batteau* through the canal and locks for loading into one of the company's Lake Superior schooners.[10]

The company's need for lake transportation spawned a modest ship-building industry on the Detroit River and at Point aux Pins on St. Mary's River above the rapids. For Superior, it launched the *Otter* at Point aux Pins in 1793. In 1801, the XY Company built a schooner at

Sandwich, and then dismantled it and transported it to Point aux Pins for completion as the *Perseverance*. In 1802, the NWC responded with the *Invincible*, also built at Point aux Pins, the vessel Alexander Henry (the Younger) noted at Fort Kaministiquia in 1803 along with the decrepit *Otter*. With the XYC-NWC merger, the *Perseverance* replaced the *Otter* as the NWC's second ship on Lake Superior.

After the American Revolution, an attack on the Great Lakes route from the United States seemed inevitable. In 1793, Lieutenant-Governor Simcoe chose York on Lake Ontario as the capital of Upper Canada, and as the start of a road to Lake Simcoe and the Nottawasaga River route to Georgian Bay on Lake Huron. Yonge Street would allow the North West Company to avoid risks to its shipping along the Lower Lakes. The NWC made limited use of this road until the War of 1812, at which time both the company and the military sent supplies from York to Lake Simcoe and Lake Huron by both the Nottawasaga and a new passage to Penetanguishene which the NWC had helped finance. Both routes proved invaluable to the North West Company during the war period since they ensured the safe transportation of its bulk cargo between Montréal and Fort William.[11]

6 "Emporium for the Interior"

"Fort William is the great emporium for the interior." Thus Ross Cox described Fort William's role as the North West Company's major inland transshipment point. As Cox so aptly observed, the fort had one main purpose: to ship an "extensive assortment of merchandise" inland and "the produce of the wintering posts" to England via Montréal. Nothing the former Astorian had seen on his east-bound journey from the Columbia River in 1817 could prepare him for this "metropolitan post of the interior."[1]

The assortment of merchandise which amazed Cox in 1817 amazes still. Just one cassette destined for the west in 1816 held rolls of ferreting silk and ribbons of many colours, papers of pins, playing cards, shaving boxes, common razors, beads, brass "jews-harps," sets of violin strings, fine scissors, silk hat covers, tooth brushes, Windsor soap, rolls of blacking, nutmegs, jockey hats and coloured thread.[2]

Not all these items were destined for the trade with Indians; some were intended for distribution or sale to company personnel. Of the fort's eleven buildings on the main square, seven contained merchandise and provisions. Six were "stores" while one housed three "shops" under its roof. Stores contained wholesale goods; shops were retail outlets. As described by Gabriel Franchère in 1814:

On the west side is a row of houses or sheds...[One] is used as a retail store for quality merchandise intended for the use of partners and clerks. A little farther north is another shop with effects intended for the *engagés*, where their outfits are issued to them. Adjacent to this is the warehouse where the outfits are assembled for the different posts in the interior.[3]

In a sense, the NWC's Montréal agents were wholesalers and its wintering partners retailers. The agents assembled the outfit in Montréal and accompanied it to Fort William. The dry goods went to the "General Store" where each proprietor selected his department's outfit. The person in charge of the Fort William Department (or district) divided its outfit between the Indian Shop, the local trading post and the Fort William Shop.

The Fort William Shop was one of three retail outlets in the "General Equipment Store." From here, necessaries were distributed for running the department and goods were sold to the fort's year-round staff. During the *rendezvous*, the Little Shop served partners and clerks while the Equipment Shop supplied *engagés* with equipments or sold them goods on account.

The fabrics inventoried at Fort William might well be the basis for a study of British textiles, then in the process of supplanting the output of foreign cottage industries. Most cottons with East Indian names were woven in England from raw material shipped from India. The Little Shop stocked fine, printed and furniture calico; dimity quilting waistcoats; fine calico and common cotton shirts; large, middle and small printed cotton shawls; Madras, Bangladore, Britannia, red Turkey, and red or blue barred handkerchiefs.

This also applies to silk goods stocked at Fort William. Although the finest silks came from China, English mills now used domestic silk for fine cloth, brocade, galloons (braiding), gartering, ribbons, handkerchiefs, hosiery, hat bands, hat covers, clothing and thread.

As Irvine's painting of the woman at Fort William shows, Indians wore warm but light woollen blankets as a covering, but traders, voyageurs and Indian men also wore blanket coats and *capotes*, the *Canadien* version of the parka. Of English manufacture, blankets ranged in size from one to four points, each point indicated by a black bar along the selvedge.

When the Hudson's Bay Company introduced the point system in 1779, one point had the value of one prime beaver skin, or in HBC terminology, one Made Beaver (MB). In the North West Company, one *plus* had the same value as one MB. Inflation prevailed then as now. In 1821, a one-point blanket at Fort William cost two *plus*. Hudson's Bay Striped Blankets were so popular that, despite the name, the NWC ordered them in large quantities as trade goods and as equipment or merchandise for its personnel.[4]

Among the other woollens were strouds and molton, flannel, hosiery and worsted yarn. Fine Irish linen came by the yard or in shirts while coarser linens included list cloth, ticking and strong, untwilled Russia sheeting for trousers, tents, tarps and sails.

In the fur trade, gentlemen and *engagés* alike revealed their social origins and culture by their clothing. Thanks to Fort William's extensive inventories, individuals dressed much the way they did back home if not better. The "travelling necessaries" of NWC partner James Keith in 1816 give no sign of "roughing it in the bush":

1	Dress coat black, black breaches & white vest
1	Travelling suit—immaterial as to colour
1	Hat & Travelling cap
7	fine linen shirts ruffled
2	Pairs Pantaloons
2	do Boots—4 Pairs Stockings
2	do Black Silk Hose & 1 Pair under drawers of worsted gauze
1	do Dress shoes—12 neckcloths
6	silk Pocket Handkfs; Bandanna or flags, Dickies, &c[5]

One mark of a gentleman was his hat. The purpose of the fur trade—the beaver hat—now found its way from England to the Indian territory, the source of its felt. Fort William stocked London Beaver hats for men, women and children; and London Plated hats (of inferior fur glued over with a thin layer of beaver felt) for voyageur guides and Indian chiefs who bedecked them with tinsel and ostrich feathers. Practical headgear included peaked jockey caps and fine or common wool hats.

Fur-trade fashion decreed good grooming and clean-shaven faces. According to Nor'wester Charles McKenzie, keeping up appearances impressed the Natives:

Men of dignity must deck themselves better than the common voyageur if they wish to be considered as they should be...there must be some thing in the outward appearance to attract notice and command respect.[6]

Alexander Henry (the Younger) and Charles Chaboillez criticized McKenzie for wearing "the Indian costume" in the Mandan country on the

47

North West Canoe on Lake Ontario, 1840, by Mary Millicent Chaplin. The company officers and voyageurs (as well as their status) are easily recognized by their appearance. *Courtesy of Library and Archives Canada, C-82974.*

Upper Missouri River, but according to McKenzie, the Indians despised the two traders for arriving shabbily attired:

> M. Chaboillez had on a *capot* which had once been white…and a weather-beaten hat, with a stout black beard of nine days' growth. Mr. Henry only differed in the *capot* as he had a corderoy jacket!…to say the least, their appearance was not to their credit, nor to the interest of the Company.[7]

Most Nor'westers took time to look respectable, even under difficult conditions. On their journey to the Pacific, (Sir) Alexander Mackenzie and crew cleaned up before meeting unfamiliar Indians. Toiling through terrain "the most savage that can be imagined," Simon Fraser and his men "shaved and dressed in our best apparel," again before meeting unknown Indians. After descending the Columbia River, David Thompson reached Astoria "relatively well-dressed." Such fastidiousness was made possible by the great emporium, Fort William.

The fur trade spawned a flourishing clothing industry in Lower Canada. Voyageurs almost universally wrapped Assomption or Achigan sashes around their waists, but Natives and traders also adopted these finger-woven belts. In 1820, the North West Company bought 99 belts and 20 narrow belts from "Ignace's wife," 21 fine belts and 6 NW belts from "Ignace's' wife's sister" and 82 narrow belts from Hannah. Tanneries near Montréal supplied ox and cow hides to cobblers who made sturdy "beef" or leather shoes for the trade.[8]

Seamstresses in Montréal workshops sewed most of the trade's ready-made clothing. In one order from the NWC for *capotes*, Dominique Faron provided 1693 Molton, 152 Blue List, 20 Gray list, 20 gray ratteen (a thick twilled woollen), 414 Illinois cloth. She also supplied 20 scarlet land coats, 120 blanket coats and 13 fine corduroy jacket. In another order, her workshop made 183 pair common corduroy trousers, 112 of blue list, 1310 of Russia sheeting and 81 tents in size from 20 to 10 ells. This small sampling of industries spawned in the Montréal region by the fur trade shows their significance to the Lower Canadian economy.[9]

Four warehouses for consumables stood along the south side of Fort William's main square: the Provision Store, two Corn Stores raised on stilts, and the Liquor Store. Despite their titles, the first and last named also stocked unrelated objects.

In the Provision Store, saws, window glass, ball, beaver, snipe, duck and "pidgeon" shot, bar iron, square iron, steel, plough shares; in the Liquor Store soap and candles, tobacco, iron works (axes, hoes, picks, chissels, augers, fish spears, frying pans, traps), Indian and fort flags, oil cloths and empty kegs and cases. The massive Stone Store in the main square's southwest corner kept the schooner's fall shipment of perishables safe over winter.[10]

The foods stored in these warehouses reflect the thriving market for farmers in Upper and Lower Canada in the fur trade. Through Montréal merchants, the company bought common and fine biscuit and bread; pork, bologna and sausage; butter, Indian corn, hogs lard, cheese and, in 1814, eight oxen weighing 6603 pounds. At Sandwich (Windsor, Ontario), schooners took on bags of Indian corn, oats and flour, kegs of beef, ham, pork and butter, and live cattle, sheep and swine, all bound for Fort William.

"Long experience has shewn that Boatmen & Voyageurs uniformly prefer Pork–it is almost impossible to keep Beef exposed in open Boats to a Hot Sun from spoiling." This report to Lord Selkirk explains the 6,000 pounds of salt pork in the Provision Store in 1816 compared to 154 of beef. That year, the fort stored 74,516 pounds of flour in casks, barrels and bags, 50 bags of hulled corn and 228 barrels of rough corn, dried kernels before their tough outer skins had been leached off in a lye solution.[11] If the crew of each fur trade canoe can be considered its engine and their provisions its fuel, then Indian corn propelled the canoes at least as far as Lac la Pluie where wild rice and pemmican took over. Corn was stored at Michilimackinac or St. Joseph's Island to replenish Montréal crews on their way to or from Fort William. But most was doled out to voyageurs at the fort for consuming at the *rendezvous* and on their journeys to and from the fort. For boiling with corn and frying flour, the Provision Store had hog's lard and north grease, a product of the Métis buffalo hunt. Some prairie posts were vital for their returns in grease and pounded meat, the pemmican which provisioned the western brigades.

For the trip back to the *rendezvous*, supplies of corn and grease were stashed along the way. The balance between adequate provisions for

From the mess room window, circa 1816, by Lord Selkirk. This drawing of Fort William shows the Corn Stores raised on stilts. Here "rough" and "lyed" corn was stored for distribution to voyageurs. The two cannons facing the main gate now grace either side of the entrance to Thunder Bay City Hall. *Courtesy of Fort William Historical Park, copy of Archives of Ontario, F481 MU3279.*

voyageurs and starvation was always delicate. The 1813 meeting at Fort William chastised Duncan Cameron, proprietor at Lac la Pluie, for exhausting the corn and grease set aside for the spring brigades; had he not done so, Cameron argued, his men and the Indians would have starved, given the failure of the fishery.[12]

In 1816, the fort's provision store contained 6,231 pounds of maple sugar packed in kegs or makaks (birch bark containers), most purchased from Indians on St. Joseph's Island or near the Sault, although a small amount perhaps had been made by Fort William's Indians at the sugar bush on the "mountain." Provisions shipped through Fort William not only provided income to farmers in Lower Canada and along the Ottawa River, Great Lakes and Yonge Street transportation routes but also to Indian producers of edibles such as the maple sugar and grease listed in Fort William's inventories.

The indiscriminate dispensing of liquor had such a disastrous effect on Native well-being that English reformers questioned the morality of the fur trade. In 1811, the company was sufficiently concerned about the influence of the "*Saints in Parliament*–in their mistaken notions of Philanthropy" that it agreed to reduce its annual consumption from 10,000 gallons to 5,000 "in order to prevent its total prohibition."[13]

"When a nation becomes addicted to drinking, it affords a strong presumption that they will soon become excellent hunters." Duncan McGillivray's honest rationale partly explains the vast quantities of spirits at Fort William, despite the "saints in Parliament." But company personnel as well as Indians imbibed rather heavily. For gentlemen travelling from Montréal to Fort William, for example, one canoe brigade carried "six flagons of Jamaica, Shrub & wine, besides other small Kegs of two Gallons each." When they reached the fort, plenty of port, Madeira, Teneriffe (from the Canary Islands), Jamaica spirits and brandy awaited.[14]

The partners treated voyageurs en route to drams of rum after onerous portages or on special occasions. On arrival at Fort William, they rewarded their paddlers with a *régale* of brandy, meat, bread, and butter. Otherwise, the voyageurs had to satisfy their thirst at their own expense. At the *rendezvous*, "between rum and baubles the hard-earned wages of years are often dissipated in a few weeks."[15]

The first Europeans in America were so enthusiastic for the tobacco which Indians grew for religious and medicinal purposes that, in Brazil, Portuguese colonizers cultivated fine leaf known as "Brazil" or "twist." Tobacco of lesser quality came from Virginia. In 1817, the fort's warehouses stocked 73 tobacco rolls weighing an average of 95 pounds each, 32 tierces (casks of 45 gallons) of carrot tobacco and quantities of pigtail and plug tobacco. These amounts were destined for the outlying departments and do not include local supplies available in the fort's shops for Indians, gentlemen and *engagés*.[16]

The business of acquiring, transporting and distributing immense inventories of goods and consumables had one purpose—high returns in fur. The "Northwest Returns of Outfit of 1805 receipted at Kaministiquia" in 1806 are staggering. That year, 2,332 packs of fur arrived from the outlying departments. Since each "pack" (the term for bundle of fur) weighed an average of ninety pounds, this comes to 209,880 pounds altogether. A total of 142,721 beaver skins, weighing 162,182 pounds, counted for about three-quarters of the 1805 returns, while muskrat, marten, otter, mink, fisher, bear, deer, moose, wolf, raccoon, ermine, fox and buffalo made up the rest.[17]

The Kaministiquia Department returned forty-six packs in 1805, but this figure pales before the 302 packs from Northwest Lake Superior (Lake Nipigon, Lac des Isles, Monontagua, Le Pic, Michipicoten and Batchewana Bay). South Lake Superior in the United States (Fond du Lac, Folle Avoine, La Pointe and Montréal River) topped that figure with 361 packs. Returns for 1804 from

Screw press at Old Fort William. Incoming furs are aired and cleaned, sorted by category, weighed, pressed into standard-sized packs marked NW, outfit year and pack number and then sealed prior to being transferred to east-bound Montréal canoes or schooners. *Courtesy of Fort William Historical Park.*

the Mackenzie River in the reputedly fur-abundant northwest totalled but seventy-nine packs. Comparing the time (two years), distance (some 2,500 miles) and cost for the Mackenzie River furs to reach headquarters compared to those from nearby South Lake Superior, it is easy to see why the NWC hung onto its trade south of the border as long as possible.

At Fort William, incoming furs were taken to the pack stores, a complex formed by a large warehouse on the main square and two smaller structures behind it. After long exposure to all kinds of weather, the maggot-ridden furs had to be cleaned and aired before being pressed into new packs for the eastbound journey. Under the agents' supervision, clerks marked each pack with "NW," the outfit year and a number to correspond with the invoice. One of Daniel Harmon's first tasks as a new apprentice clerk in 1800 was marking packs at Grand Portage.[18]

Packs of 90 or so pounds containing beaver and marten either went by canoe all the way to Lachine or by schooner to the Sault canal for transfer to Montréal canoes. Heavier packs of 112 to 120 pounds with bearskins, buffalo robes and less valued furs went by relays of schooners down the lakes.

Non-fur items in the annual returns included by swanskins and castoreum. In 1816, the fort receipted 2,904 swans or swanskins with 1,112 from Fort des Prairies alone. Swanskin provided down for soft powder puffs, small feathers for wispy trim on ladies' dresses, and quills for quality pens. Castoreum, the dried castors or perineal glands of the beaver, was an ingredient in antispasmodic medicines and in cure-alls for earache, epilepsy and madness. Today it is used in the manufacture of perfumes.[19]

In the fur trade, castoreum hastened the beaver's near extinction as an Indian lamented to David Thompson about this irresistible bait in the newly introduced steel traps:

> …all of them [the beaver] were infatuated with the love of their own species and more fond of it that we are of fire water. We are now killing the beaver without any labour, we are now rich, but shall soon be poor, for when the beaver are destroyed we have nothing to depend on to purchase what we want for our families.[20]

In Fort William's pack stores, the North West Company's annual northwest returns furthered the conspicuous consumption of luxuries abroad. Military bearskin hats and bear or buffalo rugs, gowns, robes, muffs and cloaks of fox, mink, martin, lynx and ermine all made statements of their owner's social class.

51

Nothing, however, symbolized the essence of the fur trade more than the thousands of beaver skins flowing through Fort William each year to London for producing that ultimate symbol of conspicuous consumption, the beaver hat. Fort William became a great emporium filled with foreign and domestic merchandise for one principal reason: to acquire the raw material for elegant hats. But the process to obtain that material led to the near extermination of the beaver with unhappy results for the hunters. As David Thompson lamented:

> …the Natives became poor, and with difficulty procured the first necessaries of life, and in this state they remain, and probably forever.

Just how poor the Indians became as a result of the fur trade is subject to much review in today's academic circles, as has the degree of Native victimization in the trading relationship. The application of revisionist thinking to the fur trade at Fort William is worthy of further investigation. Nothing discovered in the preparation of this book, however, leads the author to dispute David Thompson's observations.[21]

7 THE FORT WILLIAM DEPARTMENT: RESPONSIBILITIES AND DUTIES

As each summer came to its close, Fort William seemed deserted, its population reduced from a thousand or so at the height of the *rendezvous* to a scattering of North West Company personnel and their families. As the centre of the department of the same name, the fort had responsibility over the trade in the entire Kaministiquia River watershed but, as the NWC's inland headquarters, it also had duties preparing for the coming *rendezvous* and shipping season. Beyond these obligations, the fort's small complement of contract and casual workers by necessity devoted much of its energy merely on surviving the long, cold winter months.

In the North West Company, one or more wintering partners (the proprietors) usually headed each department or district but, until 1808, a clerk had charge of Kaministiquia/Fort William. The first was Dr. Henry Munro, the surgeon and clerk in charge at Grand Portage since 1798. When the NWC transferred its headquarters to British soil, Munro held the same positions at the new fort. He thus became the first doctor to practice medicine at Thunder Bay.

Also making the move was Kenneth MacKenzie who joined the NWC in 1800 as an apprentice clerk and Dr. Munro's assistant at Grand Portage. Kenneth's entry into the NWC may have been eased by Roderick McKenzie, now McTavish, Frobisher's agent at the *rendezvous* in place of the defecting Sir Alexander Mackenzie. Kenneth apparently showed great promise for in his first year he headed operations at Grand Portage over the winter during Dr. Munro's "rotation" or leave.[1]

When his apprenticeship ended in 1805, Kenneth replaced Munro as the principal wintering clerk at Kaministiquia. Munro's next posting was the less prestigious Pic on Superior's north shore (near present-day Marathon). In 1807, the partners voted overwhelmingly to promote MacKenzie to a share, beginning in 1808, over the claims of Robert Henry, the brother of Alexander Henry the Younger. Henry received his promotion in 1810.

In 1803, a second doctor arrived for Kaministiquia's first *rendezvous*, the eighteen-year old John McLoughlin. McLoughlin had just received his license to practice medicine after apprenticing for almost five years with Dr. James Fisher at Québec. Like many Nor'westers, McLoughlin had Fraser connections, his through his maternal grandfather, Captain Malcolm Fraser, the seigneur of Mount Murray. Unlike most Nor'westers, though, he was at least a third-generation Canadian on both sides of his family.[2]

McLoughlin entered the NWC as an apprentice clerk and surgeon through the influence of his uncle, Dr. Simon Fraser of Terrebonne; during

53

the winter of 1804–1805 he wintered with another uncle, the NWC partner Alexander Fraser. For several years, he combined trading over winter at some nearby post and practising medicine in summers during the *rendezvous*.[3]

The NWC's permanent officers at Fort William lived in separate dwellings on either side

John McLoughlin, hired as an apprentice in 1803, worked as a surgeon at Fort William each summer and as a clerk at an outlying in winters. Made a partner in 1814, he served as proprietor first at Rainy Lake, and later at Fort William in 1815. *Line drawing by John Marden for OFW, artist's impression of McLaughlin, circa 1815.*

54

of the main gate just within the palisade. MacKenzie shared the wintering house to the left with the captain of one of the NWC's two schooners on Lake Superior. John Maxwell served as captain from 1800 to 1810; in 1812 Robert McCargo assumed this position. With the status of clerk, the captain performed the duties

of "ship carpenter" as well as mariner. Aided by a crew of seven sailors, over winter he constructed and repaired schooners for Lake Superior and *batteaux* for local use and at the Sault canal.[4]

Paralleling the wintering house, the doctor's apothecary and residence was located between the gate and the Indian Shop, perhaps by design. At larger posts, physicians often did double duty as traders. The North West Company devoted much attention to health care since sick or injured personnel could be a liability. By 1816, it added a hospital to its medical facilities. Among the common hazards of the fur trade were venereal disease, hernia, broken limbs, infections and ague, a mild form of malaria emanating from mosquito-infested swamps throughout the wilderness and at the Kaministiquia's entry into Lake Superior.

Current medical practice favoured ridding the body of harmful fluids by bleeding, cupping, purges, emetics, enemas and expectorants, theories put into practice at Fort William with its well-stocked apothecary and instrument cabinet. For treatment of pain and hysteria, Dr. McLoughlin had a modern electrifying machine with two Leyden jars. To keep abreast of recent medical theory, he consulted his extensive library of medical books and corresponded with his uncle, Dr. Simon Fraser of Terrebonne.[5]

During his apprenticeship, McLoughlin chafed at his status and pay of £20 a year, arguing that his qualifications equalled those of Dr. Munro who received a "superior" clerk's salary. At his insistence, he received £200 annually when his apprenticeship ended in 1808, but still he fumed at not being promoted to a partnership. "I would much rather have gone to the West Indies as you propos'd," he wrote Dr. Fraser. "People talk of the dessert [sic] of Siberia, but this is as bad."[6]

McLoughlin has been described as a "reluctant fur trader," someone with no alternative but to leave Lower Canada for his "own want of conduct." Over his long years in the fur trade, from which he never did escape, he exhibited an "ungovernable Violent temper and turbulent disposition" on many occasions.[7]

Another permanent officer at the fort, James Taitt had his own dwelling house in the naval yard adjoining the main palisade. A native of Perth, Scotland, he had joined the XY Company in 1801 as clerk and carpenter and joiner at Grand Portage but, on the NWC-XYC merger, the company made him its clerk and foreman of the Kaministiquia work force.[8]

Taitt kept accounts, disbursed provisions and supplies to personnel and traded with the local Indians. His daily log of the fort's weather in 1806 is preserved in the National Archives of Canada. In charge of law and order, Taitt acted as "Gaoler" of "recalcitrant" voyageurs and the occasional company antagonist. With no expectation of promotion, he held a rank quite unusual for a tradesman, that of clerk and "gentleman." To superiors and inferiors alike, he was "Mister" Taitt.[9]

Winterers in the Indian Territory never described their lives as romantic. In the interior, some even ate moccasins, parchment windows or *tripe de roche* (lichen) to survive. Between *rendezvous*, the fort's food supplies had to be distributed with care, especially if the fisheries failed. William McGillivray's detailed orders to Kenneth MacKenzie about winter duties at Grand Portage in 1800 concerned food rationing rather than matters of great moment. To prevent shortages, McGillivray gave instructions about dividing potatoes evenly between fort people and sailors while keeping enough "for the Table next Summer," distributing salt fish, corn and flour and doling out "a glass of Grog now and then."

As befitting their station, Captain Maxwell and MacKenzie had more generous allowances: a keg of butter and one of wine, three bags of flour and one hundred pounds of sugar, a share of meat brought in by Indians and of a large hog being fattened, as well as the output of a "milch" cow. The distribution of food continued to be among Kenneth MacKenzie's many responsibilities at Kaministiquia.[10]

The fort's year-round labour force included *engagés* from Lower Canada, local Indians and "free" Canadians. Most, though not all, the *engagés* were French Canadians hired as voyageurs for the journey and as skilled or general workers year round. Driven by diminishing game resources to exchange their labour for goods and provisions, the local Ojibwa performed such traditional activities as fishing or canoe making as well as newly-learned tasks on the farm. "Free" Canadians, former *engagés* whose contracts had expired, remained in the northwest instead of retiring back to Lower Canada. Intermarried into the local Native community, they provided a handy pool of casual labour paid by the job rather than for the duration of a three-year contract.[11]

The Industrial Revolution was well underway by the early 1800s, but most manufactured items were still made with the same tools as in ages past. Fort William's extensive inventories of tools and materials reveal that traditional crafts flourished far from large urban centres. Its skilled craftsmen had separate workshops in the tradesmen's square. Here, Franchère observed "shops of the blacksmiths, tinsmiths, cabinetmakers and so on;" while Ross Cox noted, "a forge; various workshops, with apartments for the mechanics, a number of whom are always stationed here."

Inventories of woodworking tools at the fort shows a high level of joining taking place in the carpenter's shop. With its planes (over twenty types), drawing knives, chisels, gouges, and lathes, the fort's fine furniture could well have been made on site. In 1816, its most highly valued piece of furniture was a cherry table in the great hall worth 400 shillings. There is little reason to doubt its local manufacture. It was more cost-efficient to bring tradesmen, tools and materials to the fort than transport finished pieces over laborious routes from Montréal.

55

Fort William, 1866, by William Armstrong. Although it shows Fort William as a HBC post, as seen from across the river, this painting shows a continuity in activities from the NWC era. *Courtesy of TBHMS, 976.46.1.*

The fort's wooden structures needed constant maintenance. Labourers replaced rotting lumber with timbers squared with broad axes, planks and boards made at the pit saw, and shingles hewn with special shingling axes. In preparation for winter, masons repaired fireplaces and chimneys, blacksmiths repaired stoves, woodsmen felled trees for construction and firewood and labourers caulked year-round dwellings and workplaces.

The wooden cask, made with staves, two heads, and hoops is a remarkable invention, its ability to be rolled being especially convenient in transportation. At Fort William, coopers repaired large barrels for schooners and made smaller kegs and firkins for canoes. Casks at the fort stored such wet and dry materials as gunpowder, liquors, vinegar, pork, beef, butter, sausages, raisins, figs, prunes, cheese, sugar, tobacco, spruce gum, flour, salt, dried peas, fish and furs. In 1816, the cooperage had wood for one hundred and fifty kegs and, in 1820, for two hundred.

Most ironware at the fort was produced in Montréal from British metal, but the fort's black-smith also made axes, traps, fish spears, canoe awls, nails and bolts. Since the company traded guns and kept an armoury at the fort, it also hired a trained armourer for their maintenance and repair. Tinsmiths supplemented Montréal-made tinware with bedroom candlesticks, quart and pint pots, tureens, oval dishes, canoe pans and tea and kitchen kettles, some in nests of eighteen ranging from ten gallons down.[12]

Skilled and unskilled *engagés* alike also performed tasks outside their specialties. Pierre LeBlanc's versatility led to a successful fur trade career. He joined the XY Company in 1803 as a writer to copy accounts and correspondence; his contract stipulated that he serve as a middleman on the voyage to Grand Portage but exempted him "from Nipigon and from wood-cutting in winter." On the XYC-NWC merger, the NWC hired him as a carpenter and painter at Kaministiquia.

On the HBC-NWC merger in 1821, the HBC hired LeBlanc to supervise improvements at York Factory. He then superintended construction at Upper Fort Garry at the junction of the Red and Assiniboine rivers and later down

56

the Red at Lower Fort Garry. George Simpson described him as, "A very active useful man as a Tradesman, conductor of Work [,] Indian Trader or in any capacity in which he might be employed."[13]

The French and British colonizers of North America adapted the Indian birchbark canoe for their own purposes by developing huge Montréal canoes for large bodies of water and relatively smaller north canoes for inland lakes and rivers. For travel between Montréal and Fort William, the agents had sleek express canoes manned by twelve select voyageurs and unencumbered by cargo other than personal baggage and no other passengers besides their manservants. The NWC established a large canoe making and repair facility at Fort William for these large craft, as well as for smaller "bastard," fishing and Cree canoes.

Although the company had other canoe building operations at Trois-Rivières, Griffintown (a Montréal suburb), Lachine, St. Joseph's Island and Lac la Pluie, the winterers also had canoes built at inland posts or purchased them from Indians along the route. Fort William's facilities included two enormous canoe sheds within a spacious enclosed yard. In 1816, an inventory taken at the fort shows eighty-three new north canoes and thirty-nine old canoes of various sizes.

The NWC hired experienced canoe makers for Fort William from Lower Canada, among them Joseph Longeuil dit Renard of Cedres as a summerman in 1808; Joseph Hamel of Fauxbourg des Recollets as a winterer in 1817 "to make canoes, to raise bark and wood, to do any other work concerning canoes, to work as a cooper when required;" Louis Durant of L'Achigan to "go to Fort William as a guide and make and repair canoes until his return;" and, in 1820, Hamel for three years at Fort William or Lac la Pluie as a canoe and barrel maker. Another canoe maker and a freeman born in the Lake Superior region, Antoine Collin worked under contracts entered into at the fort.[14]

The process of canoe building was usually divided along gender lines. *Engagés* and Indian men went into the forest to cut long sheets of birchbark for the outer shell and cedar for thwarts, dowelling, ribs and gunwales, which they assembled back at the fort. Women from the local Indian encampment sewed the bark onto the frame with *watape*, long spruce roots which they had first cut from the forest floor, soaked to remove the outer bark and spliced into sinews. They then waterproofed the seams with spruce gum gathered in the forest.

Old Fort William interpreter Cheryl Kylander is seen preparing cedar ribs as part of the process of building a birchbark canoe. In the background are canoes built at Old Fort William. *Courtesy of Fort William Historical Park.*

Each night en route, the voyageurs repaired their fragile craft with supplies from the *agret*, which Sir Alexander Mackenzie's *Voyages* describes as "two oil-cloths to cover the goods, a sail, &c. an axe, a towing-line, a kettle, and a sponge to bail out the water, with a quantity of gum, bark, and

57

watape." At Fort William, *engagés*, free Canadians and Natives assembled stores of gum, bark, and watape for agrets while tradesmen produced the axes, tinware and oilcloths.[15]

Engagés, free Canadians and Natives also worked together in the fall fishery which provided protein for winter consumption. Before fishing began, James Taitt issued thread to male and female net makers, pig lead to the blacksmith for making sinkers and hooks; nets, cod line and sturgeon twine to fishermen who set up camps and spread nets at the Kaministiquia rapids and at Welcome, Sheep and Pye islands or at Thunder Cape in Lake Superior. Men did the fishing while women cooked and helped salt the trout and whitefish in fort-made barrels, toted back to the fort by *batteaux* for storage.

Its layout based on British agricultural practice, the fort's farm had two barns for crops,

three stables for cattle, sheep and horses, a dairy for preparing milk, butter and cream, and an ice house. Its extensive acreage included fields for oats, peas, buckwheat, Indian corn and barley and a large kitchen garden. The farm provided fresh meat and dairy products to the mess house and sustained the work horses and oxen needed for carting year round.

In the fall, the farm harvested great quantities of potatoes. Potatoes with salt fish made up the staple fare over winter. Each spring, *engagés* manured and ploughed the fields while Native women cut up and planted old potatoes; in summer, *engagés*, freemen and Natives hoed the ground; in autumn, "all hands" joined in harvesting. The fort had seventy-two "souls" to support over the winter of 1827–1828, for example, which required 104 pounds of salt fish and 27 gallons of potatoes daily.[16]

Detail from an engraving by C. Graham showing two men harvesting fish from a canoe. *Courtesy of TBHMS, 976.100.1KK.*

58

The fort's teamster since at least 1805, Pierre Masta of Terrebonne and Montréal ploughed fields, carted fish barrels, ice and firewood and perhaps hauled *pièces* to the Mountain Portage for transfer to west-bound canoes. Before joining the NWC, he may well have been a teamster at the Terrebonne seigneury north of Montréal, owned by Simon McTavish and then Roderick McKenzie.

A former XY Company employee at Grand Portage, Vincent Dauphin gardened, looked after the *cavreau* (root cellar), slaughtered farm animals, salted beef and fish and cleaned fish barrels. He and Masta were typical of the *engagés* who farmed, fished, cut wood and maintained the fort. Along with local Natives and freemen, they performed the mundane but necessary tasks which kept Fort William functioning from *rendezvous* to *rendezvous*.

Enemies of the NWC accused it of opposing any kind of agriculture at its own establishments, but this was not the case at Fort William or at inland posts. The NWC encouraged farming and gardening but only to support its own operations. It adamantly opposed independent farming outside its jurisdiction. This became clear when Lord Selkirk founded his Red River Settlement in 1811. Such settlements destroyed the habitat of wild animals, offered an alternate way of life for Indians and provided a resource base to rival traders.

The North West Company employed Indians on its Fort William farm but obstructed agriculture by Natives on their own behalf. To stay in business, the company required Native dependence on the goods and provisions it exchanged for raw materials and labour or presented as rewards for past and future services.[17]

8 FUR TRADE FAMILIES

According to a "Report of North West Population 1805," the number of Indians at Kaministiquia, Lac des Miles Lacs and Lac des Chiens totalled 70 men, 84 women and 178 children.

Another population survey of the same period estimates that some 150 local "Algonquins" (or Ojibwa) lived in this area. These low figures may explained by declining wildlife resources and the devastating smallpox epidemic of 1782, but they also may be found in the boreal forest's inability to sustain large populations at any time.[1]

In the North West Company's Fort William Department, which covered the entire Kaministiquia watershed, some Ojibwa attached themselves to the fort while others lived further afield. Most of the latter visited the fort during their seasonal round to receive advances in goods and pay their debts in fur. Perhaps theirs was the encampment seen east of the fort in the 1805 "Fort Kaministiquia" drawing and perhaps the local Natives had the wigwams seen across the river in other illustrations. While these assumptions cannot be confirmed, it is known that traders also travelled into the district to collect furs and that Indians, integrated into the fort's labour force, also went on hunting expeditions in return for credits.

At some posts, Indians approached the trading shop by a palisaded passageway and made their transactions through a small wicket. Fort William's Indian Shop not only lacked such a pathway but apparently gave its patrons full view of the goods. Its merchandise generally had practical use, fire steels, steel traps, shot and muskets, for example, or molten capotes, ivory awls and tin kettles. Some items had decorative or symbolic value, white, enamelled and seed beads from Venice or Canton, crimson sash ribbon, trade silver crafted by Montréal silversmiths, wampum beads of Atlantic seashell or its imitation, and Indian Flags (the Red Ensign). Impractical adult and children's beaver hats from London made a status statement, and the quantity of tobacco suggests its consumption for pleasure as well as for religious purposes.

The trader recorded each transaction in the "Indian debts" account book, a debt being the price of the goods supplied in advance of the hunt. On delivery of the furs, their value was entered in the credit column but not in monetary figures. Furs and goods were priced in terms of one prime beaver skin referred to by the NWC as one *plus* (pronounced "plew"); in the Hudson's Bay Company, "Made Beaver" or "MB" meant the same thing. For a four-point blanket, a hunter might trade the following:

Debit	1 four-point blanket [= 8 prime beaver]	8 plus
Credit	1 brown bear skin	3 plus
	1 lb. Castoreum	1
	2 beaver cubs	1
	2 prime martin	1
	3 mink	1
	1 red fox	1

Labour and other services were paid for on the spot. In a typical exchange, Madame (Antoine) Collin received six yards of Bath coating and one gallon of rum (!) for knitting snowshoes, and in another, five quarts of corn, four quarts of flour and two pounds of sugar for cutting moose hide and dressing the skins.[2]

In 1816 and 1817, Lord Selkirk's occupation at Fort William left invaluable information about the area's ordinary inhabitants. The Red River Settlement Day Book kept at the fort, for example, gives the names of local Indians and the activities for which they were paid out of NWC stock. Those working at road-building included Cawicappo, Cutuon & Son, Kitshimagus, Lesmehago, Massidision's Son, Mikkeockeishuk, Nachobe, Nanachushick "an Indian from Grand Portage," Oprikwaikustiquan—"fish for his mother," Pisiquakustiquan, Skandiga, Visignan's Son and Billau. In return they received guns, knives, powder, shot, rum, tobacco, tobacco pipes, scissors, needles, corn, grease, potatoes, earrings, beads, thread, earrings and belts. A noteworthy reverse of past trading practice is suggested by entries for moccasins, soles and hides sold to Natives.

Just as traders and voyageurs insisted on distinguishing attire, so did the Indians. At Fort William they typically dressed in imported cloth, not in furs or skins. Since the North West Company was in the business of importing British fabric to exchange for fur, it needed the produce of the hunt for itself. Neither did Indians wear clothing of homespun. Spinning and weaving would deter Native women from occupations essential to the trade such as preparing and tanning the skins upon which company revenues depended.

Native women readily adapted their traditional dress to imported textiles. Eastman Johnson's paintings of women at Grand Portage in 1857 conform quite remarkably to Peter Grant's observations of 1804:

> The women wear petticoats of blue cloth, which come down to the ankle, and cover their bodies upwards to the pit of the shoulder with the same stuff. Their sleeves, made of red or blue molton, come down near the wrist and open along the inside of the arm.... A narrow slip of cloth is fixed across the breast, from the end of which two other slips are suspended carefully ornamented with white beads and various other trinkets.... They wear silver bracelets on their wrists, rings on their fingers, beads about the neck and a profusion of silver crosses and other ornaments...[3]

When Native women entered into a marital liaison with an NWC officer or servant, they changed to styles current in their husbands' culture. Traders' wives might wear the high-waisted empire line while *engagés'* wives dressed in a shirt, short gown and petticoat in "Canadian" fashion. No matter the style, they invariably wore molton leggings and covered themselves with a blanket.

Indian men also wore leggings often topped by a long calico shirt. Traders "made chiefs" of favoured males by giving them military "chief's" coats, beaver hats and trade silver, often in formal exchanges. On the HBC-NWC merger in 1821, two chiefs preceded by an English flag (the Union Jack), and accompanied by "all the Tribe," presented twenty fine beaver skins to "their great Father" William McGillivray. After this:

Ojibwe Women at Grand Portage, 1857, by Eastman Johnson. The clothing in the painting conforms exactly to Peter Grant's description of Indian women's attire written fifty years later. The original is the property of the St. Louis County Historical Society, Duluth. *Courtesy of Fort William Historical Park.*

…Mr. McGillivray's Presents were brought in which consisted in two red Coats faced with blue and gold Braid, a round Hat and a Shirt….Then Rum and Tobacco in considerable Quantity was divided amongst them. After this they gave Mr. McGillivray the Pipe to Smoke and then they departed…

One of the chiefs proudly wore his new coat the next day:

The Indians at Fort William represented today their War Dance. The Chief dressed in a red Coat faced with blue and laced with Gold Tinsel entered the Fort followed by the whole Band of Indians amongst about 30 Dancers all men.[4]

Indian women changed their racial identity as well as their attire on marriage to a European. The Report of North West Population 1805 give the number of "whites" in the Kaministiquia district as: 62 men, 16 women and 36 children[5]

Some men classed as white perhaps were construction workers on the new fort for many fewer normally wintered in the area. But what of the sixteen "white" women and thirty-six "white" children?

Men associated with the North West Company typically had one of three origins—Indian, French Canadian or Anglo-Scot. All the women, however, were Aboriginal or of mixed blood; European women simply did not belong in the fur trade. Women classed as white were Native or mixed-bloods who had married, *à la façon du pays,* white men, officers or servants of the NWC; since the children had white fathers, they, too, were designated as "white."

Most men joining the North West Company did so when young and single. In the Indian country, many entered into marital relations with "little girls," often aged twelve or thirteen, but without benefit of clergy. Clergy were unwelcome in the Indian country. Indeed, one incentive for entering the trade was its freedom from religious constraint. In 1806, the NWC balked at supporting an increasing body of Native families. Resolving to "reduce by degrees the number of women maintained by the Company," it forbade:

…either Partner, Clerk or Engage…[to take] any woman or maid from any of the tribes of Indians…to live with him after the fashion of the North West, that is to say, to live with him within the Company's Houses or Forts & be maintained at the expense of the Concern.[6]

The Red Lake Chief with some of his Followers arriving at the Red River and Visiting the Governor by Peter Rindisbacher. The subjects in this 1820s scene appear much like Natives and NWC personnel around 1815. Note the blue and red leggings of British wool; a "chief's outfit" and a painted buffalo robe. All wear clothing typical of fur trade social groups. (The party is from Red Lake, Minnesota.) *From a postcard issued by the Toronto Reference Library.*

63

The company still allowed marriages but to daughters of white men only, though perhaps for devious reasons. For a woman like Ikwé, marriage to a trader or *engagé* had many attractions. She had regular rations as well as access to awls, pots and pans, ribbons, lace, beads, cloth and needles by charging them to her husband's account. Alexander Fraser, a blacksmith at Fort William in 1816, resisted such a marriage:

…[he] was frequently advised and desired, from the time he was first in the service of the North-West Company, and even by several of the partners, to take a Squaw as a wife; but as he conceived this was wished for, for the purpose of getting him to run in debt to the North-West Company, he had never been prevailed upon to do so.[7]

For the average *engagé*, taking an Native wife had many advantages. Besides being "bed fellows," women relieved the harshness of wilderness life by making moccasins, snowshoes and clothing, gathering edible forest products and hunting small game. They also eased the company's trading relationships with their relatives and smoothed the way into Native society for spouses remaining in the northwest instead of returning to Canada.

Scattered references to Fort William's fur trade families allow for little more than conjecture about their lives. The *engagés* apparently stayed in farm cottages, the tradesmen's house, huts outside the palisade and perhaps lofts over trades shops, but information about the distribution and preparation of their rations of fish and potatoes or corn and grease is skimpy. Dr. John McLoughlin's daughter has provided some clues about daily routines in her recollections of Fort Vancouver on the Columbia River where McLoughlin introduced practices followed at Fort William:

They [the labourers] got up at five o'clock in the morning at the ringing of the bell, and would go to work until eight o'clock, and then it rung for breakfast. At twelve o'clock they would ring for dinner, and at one o'clock it would ring to go out. Then, at six o'clock again for quitting work. That finished up the days work.[8]

Native women married to traders spent the day quite apart from their husbands:

The ladies who were there lived separately in their own Mess room. When my father had company distinguished visitors or others, he entertained them in the general Mess room, and not in the family mess room. The families lived seperate [sic] and private entirely. Gentlemen who came trading to the Fort never saw the family.[9]

Just as details of daily life at Fort William are not easily uncovered, the same is true for personal details of its year-round inhabitants. No regular birth, marriage and death records of the local Indians, for example, were kept until the Jesuits arrived in 1849. With few exceptions, the identity of women married to *engagés* and other fort personnel is almost impossible to discover. Family histories, thus, must be pieced together from scattered references in accounts, contracts and journals.[10]

Recent research has revealed something of the genealogy of Antoine Collin, a canoe maker at Grand Portage and Fort William born about 1780 in the Lake Superior area. *Engagés* named Collin had worked along the Upper Lakes during the French regime; records show an Antoine Colin hired for Sault Ste. Marie in 1743 and Michilimackinac in 1752, and a Claude Colin for Kaministiquia in 1752. Although the Fort William canoe maker's parentage is unknown, his Lake Superior origins imply Ojibwa matrilineal descent. The birth of his son Michel at Kaministiquia (or perhaps Grand Portage) in 1799 suggests that Antoine, too, had an Ojibwa wife.[11]

64

The Collins belonged to Fort William's population of "free" Canadians, those former *engagés* who stayed in the Indian country, for one reason or another, on the expiry of their contracts. This term apparently applied to their descendants as well. But although "free" meant without contract, it did not mean freedom from company control. Neither the NWC nor the HBC tolerated independent entrepreneurship within their domains. As Chief Factor John Haldane bluntly explained to Lieutenant Bayfield at Fort William in 1823:

> …although these freemen were not in the Company's permanent Employ; they derived the whole of their Support from the Company; and that in every Estimate made for the Supply of the Indians, the necessaries required by these people were always included in consequence of which, they were to be considered as on the same footing with the Indians; and any Clandestine Trade carried on with them, as an infringement of the Company's rights.[12]

At Fort William, the mixed-blood families of "free Canadians" did not seem to evolve into a distinct society as did the Métis on the Red River. Through marriage into Native society over generations, most of their progeny became absorbed into the Fort William Band. The many Collins living on the Fort William First Nation Reserve today, for example, are descended from Antoine Collin and his son Michel.

The "white" family of Fort William's teamster, the *engagé* Pierre Masta, had a somewhat different future. Pierre's contracts with the NWC identify him as a carter at Fort William, while HBC documents show him at Fort William well into the 1820s, his name often associated with Vincent Dauphin. Other records refer to a Jean-Baptiste Masta. The HBC's journals of "transactions and occurrences" in the 1820s record Pierre often working alongside with Vincent Dauphin. This entry for February 23, 1824, reveals that he had a wife: "On July 25, 1826, Masta and Dauphin left Fort William for Michipicoten in a *batteau* loaded with canoe bark." Their names never appear again in Fort William's HBC's records.

Genealogical records possessed by their descendants show Jean-Baptiste Masta as the son of Pierre Masta and Marie Dauphin, apparently Vincent's daughter, and the Mastas and Dauphin families moving to Sault Ste. Marie in Canada and then to Michigan. Today, the Mastaw family abounds along the St. Mary's River on both sides of the U.S.–Canada border.[13]

The gentlemen in charge at Fort William also had wives of Native origin. All that is known of Kenneth MacKenzie's wife comes from his will of 1816. Its terms stipulate that Louisa MacKenzie, the mother of his natural daughter, Margaret, receive twenty pounds Halifax currency annually as long as she had charge of the child or was otherwise unprovided for. Louisa's tribal origin and parentage, however, remain a mystery, as does her fate and that of Margaret, following MacKenzie's untimely death in 1816.[14]

In 1815, James Taitt received a letter from Qu'Appelle on the Assiniboine River that his "little Girl" was well. This chance reference to Taitt's "little girl," the term traders used for Indian wife, shows that Taitt not only had married *à la façon du pays,* but that his wife may have had a tribal origin other than Ojibwa. Genealogical records held by Taitt's descendants show her as Susan McKenzie, but how she came by that name is unknown.[15]

The best documented wintering family associated with Fort William is Dr. John McLoughlin's. In 1812, McLoughlin married Marguerite Waddens MacKay, the former wife of Alexander MacKay and daughter of the slain Jean-Etienne Waddens and an unknown Cree woman. MacKay left Marguerite and the North West Company in 1808, taking their son

Thomas to Glengarry for education by Alexander Ross before joining Astor's Pacific Fur Company in 1811. When John and Marguerite took up year-round residence at Fort William in 1814, they brought with them John's son Joseph, born in 1809 to an Indian woman who died in childbirth, Marguerite's daughters Mary and Nancy McKay, and their children in common, John, age 2, and Marie Elizabeth, an infant. During the McLoughlins' stay at Fort William, two more children would be born, Eloisa in 1817 and David in 1821.

Sometime before 1816, Nancy McKay married Captain McCargo who lived next door in the Wintering House. After the North West and Hudson's Bay Companies merged in 1821, the McCargo and Taitt families moved to Chatham in eastern Lower Canada. There, two sons of the McKay-McCargo marriage would marry two daughters born to James Taitt and his "little girl" from the Assiniboine.[16]

In the past few decades, studies of fur trade families have given fascinating insights into a hitherto neglected or often denied aspect of Canada's social make-up, its strong Aboriginal component. In succeeding generations, the offspring of these families took many paths as they assimilated into either Native or white society or identified themselves as Métis. Although light continues to be shed on fur trade families associated with Fort William, the topic deserves much more investigation as a means to understanding our past and the complexity of today's society.[17]

66

9 THREATS FROM ALL DIRECTIONS

In 1806, the Nor'wester Alexander MacKay had a most unusual assignment. He was to be the proprietor, not of a geographical district, but of "to Watch DeLorme." An independent trader, DeLorme attempted to take two canoes into the northwest by the Grand Portage on behalf of his Montréal supplier, Dominique Rousseau. MacKay did more than watch DeLorme. He and his pugnacious *engagés*, known as *batailleurs*, cut trees all along the portage, blocking traffic in either direction. Unable to advance or retreat, DeLorme sold his goods to the North West Company at Montréal prices and left empty-handed. The portage would be impassable for years, forcing all traffic into the northwest to pass by Fort William or Fond du Lac. Thanks to MacKay, no trader or Indian could travel from Lake Superior into the interior without the NWC's knowledge or consent.[1]

Compared to more menacing threats, independent traders from Montréal proved a mere nuisance easily disposed of by the NWC's *batailleurs*. From its origins in the era of New France, however, the Montréal fur trade and its inland base on the Kaministiquia River never escaped perennial threats from the Atlantic seaboard to the south and Hudson Bay to the north. But before the outbreak of war between the United States and Great Britain in 1812, new

threats would emerge from the mid-west on the Red River and from the far west on the Pacific coast.

In stopping DeLorme, the North West Company had more in mind than barring Grand Portage to petty traders. Over the winter of 1805-6, Lieutenant Zebulon Pike of the United States Infantry led an expedition towards the source of the Mississippi River to assert U.S. sovereignty over the region in which the NWC's Fond du Lac department operated. Pike found the NWC's "commerce and establishments extending beyond our most exaggerated ideas" with major posts at Fond du Lac, Red Lake, Sandy Lake and Leech Lake, all in present-day Minnesota.[2]

Jay's Treaty of 1794 had allowed British traders to do business in the United States as long as they paid U.S. duties on goods and supplies. Pike found that British merchandise traded in Fond du Lac had not gone through U.S. customs at Michilimackinac as required, but had been distributed directly from Kaministiquia.

To Pike's dismay, the North West Company flaunted U.S. sovereignty in more symbolic ways. The British flag flew over NWC establishments and several Indian villages in the United States. Moreover, Indian chiefs and elders displayed King George III medals, presents from the NWC. The Indians willingly

Chief Mike Flatte (Michael Nah-Bah-Ga-Do-Way) of the Grand Portage Band of Minnesota Chippewa, with his wife. Flatte is wearing epaulettes, gorget, armbands, and three peace medals (two of Great Britain's King George III and one of the United States of America). Photograph dates to the 1920s. The King George III medal has belonged to the Maymushkowaush family of Grand Portage for many generations. (The Minnesota Chippewa or Ojibwa obviously did not hand over all their British flags and medals to to U.S. authorities.) *Photo courtesy of U.S. National Park Service, Grand Portage National Monument.*

68

exchanged their British flags and medals for American flags and medals, but at Leech Lake, headquarters of the NWC's Fond du Lac Department, Pike ordered the Union Jack shot down from the flag staff.

Reciting NWC misdemeanours on U.S. soil, Pike formally requested Hugh McGillis, the department's proprietor, to "make representations to your agents, at your headquarters on Lake Superior" that future shipments of goods for Fond du Lac be shipped through U.S. customs at Michilimackinac. McGillis responded in tones most conciliatory, his errors caused by ignorance, not intention, he insisted. Despite his promise that the NWC would henceforth pay the required duties, Pike recommended that a U.S post be established near the mouth of the St. Louis River at the western end of Lake Superior, to intercept smuggling.[3]

The Pike expedition was just one omen of coming threats to North West Company operations south of the border in an area menacingly close to Kaministiquia. To counter American inroads both east and west of Lake Michigan, McTavish, McGillivrays formed the Michilimackinac Company in 1806. The anticipated threat to the southwest trade (east and west of Lake Michigan) came in the person of John Jacob Astor of New York City, fast becoming the wealthiest man in the United States through his multitudinous enterprises. Astor had by-passed his country's restrictions on trade with Britain by acquiring trade goods and furs through merchants in Montréal, but he also determined to break Montréal's hold over the Michilimackinac trade and block any NWC establishment at the Columbia River.

In 1808, Astor founded the American Fur Company (AFC). By 1811, the American Fur Company's strength was such that it forced the Michilimackinac Company to join in a coalition called the South West Company. Despite their reservations, the NWC's wintering partners accepted one-third of the Montréal agents' interest and the international boundary as the border between the South West and North West Companies. Soon, however, the boundary question would be fought out, not in New York boardrooms or Fort William's Council House, but by force of arms along the Great Lakes in the War of 1812.

Astor founded the Pacific Fur Company (PFC), in 1810, as a subsidiary of the AFC. The PFC's aim was to establish a post named Astoria at the Columbia's outlet into the Pacific Ocean. Again, Astor offered the North West Company a share. The Nor'westers had not made up their minds about Astor's overture when the PFC sent a sea expedition from New York via Cape Horn to found Fort Astoria at the Columbia. Among the PFC's partners on board the *Tonquin* were former Nor'westers Duncan McDougall, Alexander MacKay and David and Robert Stuart. (Other passengers included Thomas McKay, the son of Alexander MacKay and Marguerite Wadden, and his teacher, Alexander Ross of Glengarry.)

Hudson's Bay Company flag dating to 1842, in possession of Chief Mike Flatte (Michael Nah-Bah-Ga-Do-Way) of the Grand Portage Band of Minnesota Chippewa. This flag is similar to the Union Jacks presented to Indians in Minnesota by the North West Company. *Photo courtesy of U.S. National Park Service, Grand Portage National Monument.*

Although the North West Company's wintering partners seemed tempted to have some kind of partnership with Astor's Pacific venture, Simon McGillivray's persuasiveness changed their minds:

> If you do not oppose the Americans *beyond* the Mountains they will bye and bye meet you on this side; and even if you should ultimately be inclined to make an amicable arrangement with them, the only way to do so upon an independent footing, or to obtain good terms, is to have rival establishments previously formed in the Country on the same footing as theirs.[4]

To obtain the same footing as the Pacific Fur Company's, the 1811 meeting at Fort William resolved that "Mr David Thompson should be left to prosecute his plans of discovery on the west side of the Rocky Mountains towards the Pacific." Thompson now began his great exploratory voyage from the Athabasca Pass down the Columbia River to the sea.[5]

The NWC also resolved to enter "into adventure and a Trade from England, and China to the North West Coast of America–provided a suitable licence to that Effect is obtained from the East India Company." The race for the trade of the Columbia River was on. The victor would be determined, however, not by who got there first, but by war.

Another threat to the NWC was the Hudson's Bay Company's intrusion into the area between Lake Nipigon and Lake Winnipeg, sometimes known as the "Little North." Lying within the HBC's chartered realm, the NWC considered this territory its Monontagué department. With supplies of beaver dwindling, the company determined to keep the district's small harvest of fur for itself. In September 1809, a NWC clerk, Aeneas Macdonell, and his men seized goods which an Indian had just received as credits from the HBC at Eagle Lake (northeast of Lake of the Woods). As HBC servants rushed to save their company's property, Macdonell slashed at one John Mowat, but Mowat grabbed a pistol and shot Macdonell dead.[6]

According to Duncan Cameron, the NWC proprietor of Lake Winnipeg, Macdonell had acted in self-defence when attacked "with premeditated design" in this "Heinous Crime." What later befell Mowat and his colleague, James Tate, is not pleasant, if Tate's journal of their experiences is correct. John Haldane, the NWC proprietor of Monontagué, arrested Mowat and sent him and Tate to Rainy Lake where the wounded Mowat spent much of the winter in chains.[7]

On May 29, 1810, the two were sent to Fort William with the injured Tate forced to paddle. The fort's proprietor, Kenneth MacKenzie, treated them well, ordering that the prisoners be given rum, bread and butter for breakfast and fish, venison and beer for dinner, welcome repasts after wild rice (often raw) and grease to eat on the way. Confined in the common gaol for two weeks, Mowat was charged with murder. Passing sentence was Angus Shaw, a magistrate for the Indian Territories under the Canada Jurisdiction Act, NWC agent since 1808 and William McGillivray's brother-in-law.

For the next few weeks, Mowat was kept in irons for fourteen hours each night. On July 16, he became ill, "a lamentable scene to see the poor man laying with his arms cut with the fetters and his body all broke out with boils."[8] His request for medicines refused, Tate received permission from the fort's James Taitt to tend to Mowat's needs.

On August 17, Mowat was sent to Montréal by canoe in handcuffs, crying as he left. Tate followed by schooner for the Lake Superior lap of the voyage. His journal sheds much light on life under the North West Company. On the Sunday before Mowat departed, "The proprietors of the Norwest Company made an auction of dressed moose skins, and the Canadians from Montréal gave from forty to forty-five livres for each skin."[9]

Tate's revelations about his journey are also illuminating. After drinking with the schooner's captain, possibly McCargo, the intoxicated partners A.N. McLeod, Alexander McKenzie, and Angus Shaw beat the captain unmercifully until some sailors rescued him. At Montréal, Tate was jailed with Mowat, who arrived in irons five weeks after leaving Fort William.

In March, 1811, Tate was freed, but Mowat was found guilty of manslaughter. Judge James Reid, another brother-in-law of McGillivray, passed sentence: six months in the common jail and branding on the left thumb. In September, two years after the Eagle Lake affair, Mowat was released and branded. Deranged from his experiences, he vanished en route to England into the wilds of northern New York.

Thanks to the Canada Jurisdiction Act and North West Company's connections to Lower Canada's justice system, the company suffered no penalties for its actions at Eagle Lake. Its loss of a promising clerk induced some caution, though, for the company tried to end violence by a futile proposal for the division of trading territories with the Hudson's Bay Company.

For the Nor'westers at Fort William, 1811 was not a good year. Hoping to influence the Hudson's Bay Company to share its trading territories, it purchased £15,000 in HBC stock. The NWC's shares supplemented those already acquired by Sir Alexander Mackenzie through another HBC shareholder, the Earl of Selkirk, who was avidly buying up stock for himself. When Mackenzie discovered Selkirk's purpose, their alliance ended. Selkirk had learned in Mackenzie's *Voyages* about fertile lands in the Red River valley. The visionary colonizer had already settled dispossessed Highlanders on Prince Edward Island in 1803 and at Baldoon, Upper Canada, in 1804. Now he decided to establish a similar settlement in Assiniboia.

Selkirk's projected colony, however, straddled the North West Company's canoe route to the Athabasca and impinged on lands inhabited by buffalo, source of the pemmican which provisioned the NWC's western canoe brigades.[10]

Thomas Douglas, Fifth Earl of Selkirk, portrait perhaps by Raeburn. *Courtesy of TBHMS, 972.2.324, copy of LAC C-1346.*

The wintering partners at Fort William in 1811 knew nothing of Selkirk's plans but the NWC's London agents did. As HBC shareholders, Sir Alexander Mackenzie, Edward Ellice and Simon McGillivray tried to stop the scheme but lacked majority control. That February, the Hudson's Bay Company granted Selkirk 116,000 acres of its chartered territory in Assiniboia. The Red River Settlement would extend eastward to the height of land between Hudson Bay and the Kaministiquia river system.

In vain, Edward Ellice warned Selkirk that the Nor'westers would stop at nothing to destroy his colony. In Ellice's words, the NWC's wintering partners were:

> ...a set of men utterly destitute of all moral principle or the feelings of honour prevalent in

71

civilized society, men who were in general of the lowest origin, selected from among the indigent relatives of the leading partners…they would not scruple to commit any crime which was necessary to effect the views of their associates in the concern.[11]

Through letters to the *Inverness Journal,* signed "Highlander," Simon McGillivray unsuccessfully tried to frighten would-be settlers with prophecies of isolation from "the rest of civilized Mankind" and almost certain danger from "warlike Savage nations." He did succeed, however, in convincing the Nor'westers that Lord Selkirk and the Hudson's Bay Company shared a common goal: to destroy the North West Company:

The committee of the Hudson's Bay Company is a mere machine in the hands of Lord Selkirk. *He must be driven to abandon it* [the settlement] for his success would strike at the very existence of our Trade.[12]

In the next few years, the North West Company fought for its very existence on many fronts. It battled Astor's American Fur Company south and west of the Upper Lakes and on the Pacific Coast. It also opposed the Hudson's Bay Company in the "Little North," on the Red River and throughout the northwest. Despite temporary victories, ultimately the Nor'westers would find no defence against two inexorable forces driving development in North America: the crusade by the United States of America to fulfill its Manifest Destiny and the advance of agriculture and settlement to the detriment of the fur trade.

72

10   FORT WILLIAM AND THE WAR OF 1812

In the midst of the 1812 *rendezvous*, William McKay arrived unexpectedly at Fort William by express canoe carrying news that the United States of America had declared war against Great Britain. A retired partner, McKay was the brother of Alexander MacKay who had joined the Pacific Fur Company's sea expedition to the Columbia River in 1811, and later met a violent death on a trading mission when Indians attacked the *Tonquin* at Clayoquot Sound on Vancouver Island. Ironically, William McKay's tidings led the North West Company to take possession of Astoria which his brother had helped found for the American John Jacob Astor.[1]

The United States had declared war in response to Britain's seizure of American ships trying to break the British naval blockade of Napoleonic France. For many U.S. Congressmen, war over control of Atlantic shipping lanes provided an excuse to fulfill their expansionist ambitions by conquering Canada. For Montréal merchants, however, the war presented an opportunity to regain territories lost in 1783 to the new United States of America, and at the same time dispose of Astor's threatened takeover of the southwest trade.

William McKay had left Québec on June 25 with orders for the British garrison at St. Joseph's Island and for the North West Com-pany at Fort William from Governor General Sir George Prevost, commander of His Majesty's forces in British North America. Both establishments were to dispatch expeditions immediately to Michilimackinac and take it by surprise. As "a small testimony of their esteem," the partners at Fort William requested that McKay accept a gift of two hundred guineas.[2]

The Fort William detachment reached Michilimackinac two days after Captain Charles Roberts and his Canadian Volunteers of Fort St. Joseph had seized the island and fort without a shot. As a result of this, the first action in the war, British forces held onto Michilimackinac until hostilities ended. By seizing this strategic fur trade distribution centre on the straits between Lakes Huron and Michigan, the military hoped to secure the loyalty of tribes on both sides of the Upper Lakes to the Crown—and to the Montréal fur trade. In American hands, Michilimackinac would threaten the St. Mary's River canal and portage some fifty miles northwest, through which passed all North West Company shipments between Fort William and Montréal.

Backed by the NWC's pledge of "Cordial and active Cooperation" with Britain, William McKay later claimed that it was he who 'procured all the arms, ammunition, provisions,

73

Colonel William MacKay, 1816, oil on canvas attributed to Levi Stevens. In the War of 1812, the Nor'wester MacKay (also spelled McKay) served as Captain in the Corps of Canadian Voyageurs, the 5th Select Embodied Militia Battalion of Lower Canada and the Michigan Fencibles. As lieutenant-colonel, he led the Fencibles in the capture of Prairie du Chien. After the war, he was superintendent of Indian Affairs at Drummond Island and then at Montréal where he died in 1832. *Courtesy of Notman Photographic Archives, McCord Museum of Canadian History, Montréal, M17684.*

74

action from the partners at Fort William:

> …it was determined to send as many men as could be spared, without detriment to the business, to *Lac la Pluie* to help getting the packs out in as much haste as possible, and Mr. McLellan volunteered to go and conduct the same–and the same time to use his influence to send out as many Indians as could be induced, to accompany us for the safeguard of the Company's Furs to the French River [linking Lakes Huron and Nipissing to the east on the canoe route to Montréal]. And that Mr. James Grant should go to Fond du Lac [at the western tip of Lake Superior] on the same business; that Mr. Shaw and the Gentlemen going to Montréal, and as many as could be spared, should set out in the *Invincible* with a supply of arms ammunitions & Provisions for St. Maries–then to act as circumstances require.[4]

Writing to Donald McIntosh, the NWC's forwarding agent at Sandwich, that July 16, "Mr." McKenzie boasted that of 1200 "young gentlemen and engagés" mustered, one hundred would depart the next day along with a hundred Indians and that five thousand inland Indians were in reserve. The fall of Michilimackinac sent the American General at Detroit, William Hull, into a state of terror. Several thousand Indians in Michigan defected to the British and McKenzie's intercepted letter revealed that the NWC had thousands more Indians at its disposal. Rather than face such a fearsome force, Hull surrendered Detroit to the British, an action for which he would be court-martialed for treason. Ironically, the British had little faith in their Indian allies, especially as supplies of provisions, tobacco, liquor and trade goods dwindled.[5]

To prove their patriotism, several Nor'westers volunteered the military services of themselves and those of NWC *engagés*. Before the war, Prevost considered recruiting two corps of voyageurs, one from the North West and the other from the South West Company. As mili-

ships, etc. of the North West Company for the use of the Government." These material contributions to the war had motives both commercial and patriotic. The NWC's defence needs coincided with those of British North America. As General Prevost ordered Captain Roberts: "…you will to the utmost of your ability afford every assistance and Protection Possible to Promote the Interest and Security of the North West Company."[3]

Getting the company's 1812 fur returns safely to Montréal from Fort William demanded quick

tary officers, any traders captured by the enemy would be treated as prisoners-of-war and not as "free-booters, or plunderers." On commissioning the Corps of Canadian Voyageurs, Prevost gave its officers, all current or retired Nor'westers, the authority to the enrol "those who are now or have been voyageurs" living in various parishes.[6]

On October 1, the Corps was embodied in Montréal. Its officers included Lieutenant-Colonel William McGillivray, Majors Angus Shaw and Archibald N. McLeod, Surgeon Henry Munro, Captains Alexander McKenzie [the Emperor], William McKay, John McDonell, Jean Pierre Rastel de Rocheblave, James Hughes and Kenneth MacKenzie. (During the latter's rotation to Montréal in 1812, Hugh McGillis replaced him as proprietor at Fort William.)[7]

The Corps had its first engagement on October 23 at St. Regis just across the St. Lawrence River from Cornwall on Montréal's line of communication to the Great Lakes. Here Ensign Pierre Rototte, Sr., his sergeant and six of his men died in action, the war's first casualties. St. Regis fell into American hands, but one month later British forces recaptured this strategic spot.

On November 20 at Lacolle on the Richelieu River, the American Colonel Zebulon Montgomery Pike commanding west Lake Champlain met the Nor'wester, Captain William McKay, in action but met with less success than when confronting another Nor'wester, Hugh McGillis, at Leech Lake in 1806. This time, Corps forces led by McKay and other military units stopped Pike's invasion thrust towards Montréal. In recognition of the North West Company's war efforts, William McGillivray was appointed to the Legislative Council of Lower Canada on January 25, 1813. He was now the Honourable Lieutenant-Colonel William McGillivray.[8]

With high praise for "their zealous and disinterested service," the Governor-General ordered the Militia Corps of Voyageurs disbanded just six months after its formation. As the theatre of war had moved to the Great Lakes, the need for these defenders of the St. Lawrence perhaps had vanished. Or could it be, that voyageurs "proved extremely inefficient & totally defective in point of discipline," as Lord Selkirk later charged? William McGillivray's mixed-blood son, Lieutenant Joseph McGillivray, apparently agreed with Selkirk's assessment of the voyageurs' character:[9]

In moments when danger ought to have produced a little steadiness, they completely set discipline at defiance, and the volatile volunteer broke out into all the unrestrained mirth and anti-military familiarity of the thoughtless voyageur.

Lieutenant McGillivray, however, did not dispute the fighting ability of these French-Canadian guerrillas:

Notwithstanding these peculiarities, the *voyageurs* were excellent partisans, and, from their superior knowledge of the country, were able to render material service during the war.

But were the North West Company's motives in raising the Corps entirely patriotic? Lord Selkirk described the creation of the Corps as "ingenious." On government pay over the winter of 1812–1813, he alleged, the disbanded voyageurs were on hand in Montréal for the 1813 summer journey to Fort William. This saved the company the trouble of finding manpower, a scarce commodity during wartime. The Nor'westers countered Selkirk's denunciations by pointing to their service as officers without pay, and "without emolument," in the Corps which they themselves had raised.[10]

In 1814, obtaining voyageurs for the journey to Fort William proved formidable and costly. The NWC's disbursements for that year's outfit included, "A. Landriaux his expenses at LaChine; Ditto for his expenses going home to advertise the men who did not appear at La Chine"; "Antoine Landriaux for warning the men from the lower & upper Parishes including his Board in town;" and

75

a month later, "Paid R. Dillon's Travelling Expenses to L'Assomption Berthier Yamaska Sorelle & warning men who did not make their appearance in the Spring & engaging others."[11]

During most summers, Landriaux served as the storekeeper at Fort William where he supervised the storage and distribution of corn and other provisions. In Lower Canada, he now used his authority as a militia officer to overcome the voyageurs' reluctance to head into a possible war zone. The company paid generous advances to those who did sign up and to their families. It also hired some hundred Iroquois as reinforcements for its canoe brigades. With government support, the North West Company managed to keep its trade goods and furs moving despite the destruction of Sault Ste. Marie and its schooners, the *Nancy, Perseverance* and *Mink*.[12]

Far from the St. Lawrence-Great Lakes war zone, the North West Company scored a victory over the Americans without combat. William McKay's arrival at Fort William with news of war coincided with David Thompson's arrival from the Pacific Ocean with news of discovery. Thompson had found the long-sought Northwest Passage by river to the Pacific Ocean, having undertaken his voyage believing that the NWC and Astor had come to a partnership about the Columbia trade. No matter that on completing his voyage from the Athabasca Pass down the Columbia River to the sea in 1811, he found, as half-expected, the Pacific Fur Company's post, Fort Astoria, already established. The declaration of war presented an opportunity to rectify the situation.

Seizing the moment, the Company dispatched two expeditions to the Columbia from Fort William. John George McTavish who accompanied Thompson to Fort William now headed an overland voyage back west to Astoria. Donald McTavish and John McDonald of Garth, William McGillivray's brother-in-law, left Fort William for England, crossing the Atlantic on the *Isaac Todd*. Reaching the Columbia first, the over-

land group convinced the Pacific Fur Company partners to sell Astoria and its contents to the North West Company rather than surrender to British naval forces on the way. This they did on October 16, 1813 for $80,500.[13]

The *Isaac Todd* sailed from England in February 1813, with the *Phoebe* as naval escort. At Rio, McDonald transferred to the *Phoebe* and off Chile to the *Raccoon,* a naval sloop of war. When the *Raccoon* reached the Columbia on November 29, Astoria was already in North West Company hands. Determined to take Astoria as a prize of war, Captain William Black raised the Union Jack, claimed Astoria and region for the King, and re-named the tiny post "Fort George." The *Isaac Todd* with Donald McTavish did not reach Astoria until April 1814, eighteen days after McDonald's departure for Fort William.

Meanwhile, the defeat of British naval forces on Lake Erie in September 1813 made it essential for British officials *and* Montréal merchants to keep the Americans out of Lake Huron.

Working in Old Fort William's shipyard, the late Albert Leon is seen constructing a replica of the North West Company's schooner *Perseverance*, which was destroyed at Sault Ste. Marie in the War of 1812. *Courtesy of Fort William Historical Park.*

Michilimackinac was strengthened by the appointment of Lieutenant-Colonel Robert McDouall of the Glengarry Light Infantry as commandant. Because of his wilderness experience, Major William McKay had escorted McDouall up the now invaluable Yonge Street route to Nottawasaga and safely up Lake Huron. Now in command of the Michigan Fencibles, a provincial corps composed of "Canadians enlisted from the service of the Traders," McKay volunteered to re-capture Prairie du Chien.

At the confluence of the Wisconsin and Mississippi rivers, this strategic post had earlier been occupied by the Americans who renamed it Fort Shelby. If United States forces were not driven out:

> ...tribe after tribe would be gained over or subdued, and thus would be destroyed the only barrier which protects the great trading establishments of the North West and Hudson's Bay Companies.[14]

On July 19, 1814, McKay accepted the American surrender of Fort Shelby, now re-named Fort McKay, a tribute to the Nor'wester and now lieutenant-colonel who ensured "British superiority in the Wisconsin area and on the Waters of the Upper Mississippi."[15]

Unfortunately for the Nor'westers, Britain lost its superiority on Lake Huron. At Fort Joseph, U.S. naval forces destroyed the fort and seized the *Mink*, a NWC schooner destined for St. Mary's River where the *Perseverance* waited to carry its lading of flour to Fort William. At the Sault, the Americans destroyed the company's locks and canal, buildings and horses, but found that Nor'westers had set the *Perseverance* ablaze to prevent its capture by the enemy. But at Michilimackinac for the expected *coup de gras,* the American ships met defeat as Robert McDouall and his Menominee allies drove the attackers off.

Suffering severe casualties, the Americans then headed to Nottawasaga where the NWC's

William McGillivray's brother-in-law John McDonald of Garth left Fort William for England in 1812, sailed to Astoria round the Horn, then travelled overland to Fort William in 1814 when he retired on his two shares to Cornwall, Ontario. There he built a Regency cottage known today as Inverarden. *Courtesy of FWHP, copy of original in private possession.*

Nancy, now in British service, lay hidden upriver. Before they could seize their prize, the *Nancy* and its valuable cargo were destroyed by fire, but whether from enemy or British shelling is unclear. Undeterred, the Americans next targeted the vulnerable link between the St. Mary's and French rivers on the canoe route to Michilimackinac and Fort William. Thanks to daring and bad weather, Lieutenant Miller Worseley, R.N., captain of the scuttled *Nancy*, had his revenge by capturing the enemy's vessels, the *Tigress* and the *Scorpion*. Lake Huron had been secured for the safe transport of NWC trade goods and British military supplies.[16]

Superior Rendezvous-Place

Back in 1812, John McDonald of Garth had left Fort William for Astoria by way of England and Cape Horn. Two years later, he was back at Fort William after a three-month journey across the continent from the Pacific coast. McDonald informed the assembled Nor'westers of the "highly advantageous" sale of Astoria to the North West Company. Then, retiring on his two shares worth £10,000, he left Fort William with the former PFC clerk Gabriel Franchère and four other passengers in a Montréal canoe manned by fourteen voyageurs.

Near Michipicoten, McDonald's party met a small canoe carrying Captain Robert McCargo and the crew of the *Perseverance*. McCargo told of narrowly escaping the American raid on the Sault and of his scuttling the cargo-laden *Perseverance*. The company undoubtedly was grateful that McCargo had safely hidden the *Recovery* at Isle Royale on western Lake Superior in an inlet today known as "McCargo Cove."[17] Eluding the Americans, McDonald reached Montréal safely as did the express canoes of William McGillivray

Opposite top: View of Mackinac Island from Round Island, 1820, by Seth Eastman. A nineteenth-century engraving after a watercolour sketch by the artist. In the first action of the War of 1812, British forces captured both this strategically placed fort and the Island of Michilimackinac to ensure the loyalty of Indians on both sides of the border, as well as the security of the NWC's transportation routes between Montréal and Fort William. *Courtesy of Mackinac State Historic Parks, Mackinac Island, Michigan.*

Opposite bottom: Michilimackinac on Lake Huron, oil on canvas, by William Dashwood circa 1820. Commissioned by Colonel Robert McDouall, British Commander of Fort Mackinac, it depicts Mackinac Island and Fort Mackinac following the battle of 1814 and is based on the 1813 print by Richard Dillon after Thomas Hall. McDouall had the artist add the captured prizes *Tigress* and *Scorpion*, as well as himself. He is wearing his shako and the distinctive green uniform of the Glengarry Light Infantry Fencibles. *Courtesy of Mackinac State Historic Parks, Mackinac Island, Michigan.*

and Archibald Norman McLeod. McGillivray awarded an extra $5.00 to each of his twelve-man crew, six from the Cournoyer family from Sorel. McLeod paid the same amount not only to his voyageurs, but he rewarded Hugh McKay, Fort William's piper and butler, the grand sum of £10, Halifax currency. The lilt of bagpipes could not but quicken Highland fervour to fight, not just the Americans, but another enemy altogether in a conflict heating up in the Red River valley far from the war zone on the Great Lakes.[18]

In December 1814, the Treaty of Ghent ending the War of 1812 decreed the return of all captured territories to their original owners. Out on the Pacific, the ownership of Astoria remained in dispute. Did it belong to the North West Company by right of purchase or had it legally been captured as a prize of war by Captain Black? In 1818, the Joint Occupancy Treaty gave Britain and the United States equal access to the Columbia district lying between Russian Alaska and Spanish California. The North West Company and its successor, the Hudson's Bay Company, however, held sway there until American settlers began moving into the Oregon Country in the 1840s.[19]

For the North West Company, the "unfortunate Cession of the Fort and Island of Michilimackinac to the United States" roused "strong apprehensions" about the security of the international boundary. The friendship of Indians now irrevocably in American territory must be preserved, William McGillivray admonished Sir George Prevost, not only for the sake of the fur trade but to preserve the safety of Upper Canada. To that end, McGillivray urged a strong military presence, not at Sault Ste. Marie and not on St. Joseph's Island, but "on the high Islands near the *Detour*" (presumably Manitoulin or Cockburn Island) as close as possible to Michilimackinac.[20]

Who won the War of 1812? Both Canada and the United States claimed victory, but the

79

North West Company knew that it had lost its last chance for dominion over what the Americans call the "Old Northwest" between Lakes Huron and Michigan, and the region south and west of Lake Superior. In vain had the British captured Michilimackinac and Prairie du Chien on behalf of King and the Montréal fur trade. The Company had suffered severe property losses in war and the final loss of its southwest trade in peace despite William McGillivray's futile attempt to salvage something from diplomatic defeat. But when the Nor'westers met at Fort William in 1815, this setback to company fortunes would not be the only disaster foretelling the downfall of the North West Company.

80

11   THE PEMMICAN WAR

The irreconcilable differences between Lord Selkirk and the North West Company over his Red River Settlement revolved around one question: "Whether extensive and fertile regions in British regions in British North America are ever to become inhabited by civilized society?" To this question posed by Selkirk's publicists, the Nor'westers retorted, "Colonization is at all times unfavourable to the fur trade." The NWC, therefore, did all it could to obstruct the Selkirk colony's threat to its very existence.[1]

In 1814, the issue was forced by pemmican, the dried pounded buffalo meat which nourished western voyageur brigades. But the Selkirk colony, too, needed pemmican; its settlers were starving. On January 8, 1814, Governor Miles Macdonell of Assiniboia issued a proclamation forbidding its export from HBC lands. With this authority, Sheriff John Spencer seized four hundred ninety-pound bags of buffalo meat from the NWC that May at La Souris. In July, the Nor'westers meeting at Fort William responded:

The Intentions of Miles McDonnell and the Heads of the Hudson Bay interests were evident. They Supposed the Communication with Canada cut off by the Events of the War last Campaine—and by depriving the Company of the Provisions collected in the Interior

the People must have starved and the Business totally stopped.[2]

Before the NWC business could be stopped, the Nor'westers determined to destroy the colony by removing its leaders and dispersing the settlers. But how to do this with any semblance of legality?

In May 1814, a general military order renewed the commissions William McGillivray and Archibald Norman McLeod had held in the now disbanded Corps of Canadian Voyageurs. These appointments applied to the Militia and Provincial Rank for the Indian and Conquered Countries, but Sir George Prevost authorized Colonel McDouall at Michilimackinac "to grant commissions to any gentlemen who should be recommended by Mr. McGillivray to serve in the Corps of Voyageurs in the Indian & Conquered Countries."

Lord Selkirk later challenged this confusing order naming the disbanded corps. In the meantime Lieutenant-Colonel McGillivray quickly recommended that most officers in the original unit be commissioned at their former or higher rank and that Duncan Cameron, who had not previously served, be named captain.[3]

In 1814, Major Archibald Norman McLeod was one of two agents representing McTavish,

81

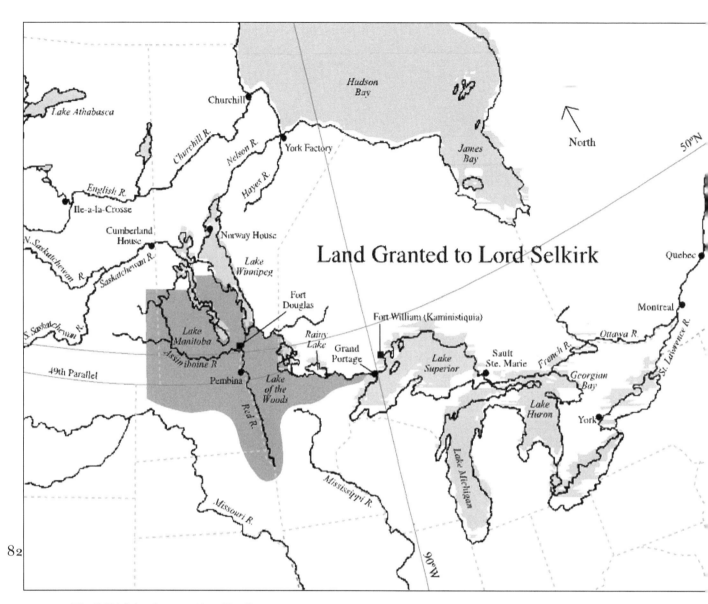

The Selkirk land grant, 1811. Totalling 116,000 square
miles, the grant extended south to the limit of the
HBC charter at the source of the Red River and east
to Savanne Portage at the height of land between the
St. Lawrence and Hudson Bay watersheds, just 120
miles by canoe from Fort William. *Courtesy of Chris-
tine Rains, cartographer, reproduced from Dorothy
Morrison,* Outpost: John McLoughlin and the Far
Northwest, *74, courtesy of Dorothy Morrison and Adair
Law, director, Oregon Historical Society Press.*

McGillivrays at Fort William. As Justice of the Peace for the Indian Territories, McLeod sent Captain Cameron to the Red River with warrants to arrest those responsible for the pemmican embargo. He also ordered Cameron to persuade the colonists, by whatever means, to leave the colony for Canada. But since Cameron had no uniform, McLeod lent him his outfit with all the accoutrements of a major.

Far from the war in the "conquered countries" (Michigan and part of Wisconsin), Cameron arrived at Fort Gibraltar, the NWC post at the Assiniboine and Red River junction, under the guise, "Captain, Voyageur Corps, Commanding Officer, Red River." The ploy worked. "In the King's name," the uniformed Cameron ordered the settlers to evacuate the settlement. One hundred and forty settlers accompanied him to Fort William on their way to a promised better life in Upper Canada while sixty colonists fled to Hudson Bay. After setting the colony afire, Cameron headed back to Fort William arriving the following spring with Macdonell and Spencer as prisoners and with the settlers bound for Canada.

Since William McGillivray had legislative duties at Québec in 1815, his brother Simon, a partner in both McTavish, Fraser and McTavish, McGillivrays, represented him at the Fort William *rendezvous* that year. During his stay, the company held a ball to which the settlers were invited. For Simon, the occasion was a great success:

A Ball is given in the evening to the Colonists, the Ladies of the Fort &ca. and all is fun & good humour. Our officers appear in uniform for the first time and dancing kept up till daylight.[4]

Under house arrest in an adjacent bedroom, Miles Macdonell had a different reaction:

Last night there was a ball to which all the Settlers from Red R. & their women were asked.

The Servants of the N.W. Co. thought that they had as good a right to be at the ball as the Settlers, went there in a body & continued to the end. There was not much drinking but they danced reels incessantly & made a dreadful noise. I could not get a wink of sleep.[5]

One might ask, as did Lord Selkirk, under what authority did the partners appear in uniform in 1815, months after hostilities with the United States had ceased? And when Simon Fraser took a "Uniform Coat with two Epaulettes to it" with him to Athabasca in 1815, did he do so "to pass himself off for a field officer," as Miles Macdonell alleged? Macdonell had grave comments about Cameron's use of uniforms in both 1814 and 1815:

Mr. McLeod had lent a suit of Uniform, a Sword & Sash &c last year to Mr. Duncan Cameron to pass himself off at Red R. as a Captain. He has now given him a new Suit to return there again.[6]

Through Lord Selkirk's intervention in 1816, Sir John Sherbrooke, the new Governor-in-Chief and Commander of the Forces, was "pleased to Cancel and Annul" the commissions of those designated as officers in the Corps of Voyageurs.[7]

A settler who had deserted to the North West Company, George Campbell had special status at the *rendezvous* of 1815. On the Red River, he had sown discontent among the colonists by persuading them of the settlement's bleak prospects. At Fort William, he received a reward of £100 for his services and a place at the dinner table next the partners and above the clerks. These honours for betrayal perhaps prepared the colonists for what came next: they would be loaded into heavy, open boats and forced to row them by themselves along Lake Superior and down Lake Huron to Upper Canada where they settled forty miles north of York.

Simon McGillivary by Richard Ramsay Reinagle. Depicted in full Masonic regalia, Simon became the first Provincial Grand Master of Upper Canada in 1822, at the same time William served as Provincial Grand Master of Lower Canada. *Courtesy of Fort William Historical Park, copy of LAC C-176.*

In 1815, the Nor'westers had won the first round of the Pemmican War, thanks in part to their uniforms. But they had lost the War of 1812. The southwest, seemingly guaranteed for Britain and the Montréal merchants by Roberts' seizure of Michilimackinac and McKay's capture of Prairie du Chien, now indisputably belonged to the United States as determined by the Treaty of Ghent. Soon, the Americans would control the North West Company's Fond du Lac Department, the area between the Pigeon and St. Louis rivers stretching from Lake Superior to the Red River.

Despite the destruction of Selkirk's colony and dispersion of its settlers, the partners came to the 1815 *rendezvous* in a foul mood. Fortunately for posterity, Simon McGillivray left a diary of his summer at Fort William. This only extant day-by-day behind-the-scenes account of a *rendezvous* paints a graphic picture of the wintering partners' discontent.[8]

Daniel McKenzie, whom Simon barely mentions, was at Fort William that summer on his way to Canada. McKenzie had retired in 1814, perhaps because the company had expressed disappointment with his failure to "bring out some Provisions for the support of the general Stock at Head Quarters." McKenzie, for his part, held a long grudge against the Montréal agents. Back in 1809, he had confided in Duncan Cameron about "our worthy Directors":

…their plan is to get Rid of their old experienced & money'd Partners to make room for Froth, Pomp & Ostentation. Had we thought and acted for ourselves we should now be both rich & respected and we should not have an addition to our titles of "McG's Geeze."[9]

The "worthy Directors" soon had reason to regret Daniel McKenzie's discontent. They also had reason to regret their earlier failure to promote a certain clerk, Colin Robertson, to a partnership. Robertson wasted no time in seeking revenge. He offered his services to the Hudson's Bay Company in 1809, along with advice based on his own experience on how to defeat the Nor'westers at their own game.[10]

Under contract to the HBC in 1815, Robertson led a canoe brigade manned by former NWC voyageurs along the Nor'westers' trade route to the Red River where he re-established Selkirk's colony. From there, his travelling companion, John Clarke, another former Nor'wester, went on to mount an opposition to the North West Company in the Athabasca country. To the Nor'westers, Robertson's expedition proved that Lord Selkirk and the Hudson's Bay Company shared one goal: the total destruction of the North West Company.

In spite of this threat from outside, the partners lashed out at one another. They gossiped about Kenneth MacKenzie's rumoured replacement of Alexander McKenzie (the "Emperor") as Sir Alexander Mackenzie & Company's agent at Fort William. They grumbled about John McGillivray's purported inability to oppose the HBC in the Athabasca, alleging that his surname alone qualified him for his long proprietorship, this of the person Colin Robertson described as "a good Trader liked by the Indians and attached to the Company."[11]

The partners also voiced dissatisfaction with Archibald Norman McLeod as "too arbitrary and hot…his language offends them &ca." After the *rendezvous*, Magistrate McLeod "went down" to Montréal because of illness, but in 1816, he was back at Fort William in fighting form.

Rather than face inevitable confrontation from the HBC, many Nor'westers demanded rotation (a year's leave) or retirement. The explorer Simon Fraser and Robert Henry refused to winter in the Athabasca, or even meet the late and possibly endangered Athabasca canoes. The clerk Simon McGillivray (William's son) did "go in" to meet the canoes and then wintered with another Athabasca proprietor, Samuel Black. The HBC Governor George Simpson would later observe that Black was "the strangest man" he ever knew. McGillivray and Black would use any means to challenge the Bay's invasion of Athabasca.

In 1815, Dr. John McLoughlin of Lac la Pluie, who had been promoted to his long awaited proprietorship the previous year, showed "in a young Partner presumptuous conduct" when he declined an Athabasca posting. He also refused to go to Lac des Isles (described in the 1808 minutes as "Interior of Nipigon"), a proposal so insulting that he accepted the Athabasca after all. But by "neglecting his medicines," McLoughlin had his way. His posting from 1815 to 1820 would be Fort William. Through strength of personality, Simon McGillivray managed to fill all places for the coming winter, although "ten partners talk of leaving the Country next year & most of them in disgust."[12]

The tobacco situation was especially troubling. The winterers had plenty of plug but no Brazilian or Northwest twist, the Indians' favourite. The NWC's enemy, John Jacob Astor, had cornered the market by making NW twist available to Colin Robertson and the HBC. After much acrimony, James Leith, the Nipigon

85

proprietor, went to York, only to return five weeks later with "plenty Carrot but that will not suit the Indian Trade particularly the provision posts." Without the preferred tobacco, the partners had reason to fear the enemy's incursion.[13]

The Nor'westers also complained about their losses in the Columbia. After realizing their dream of finding the Northwest Passage to the Pacific, they had launched a trade with China from the West Coast under license from the East India Company, which held the British monopoly over commerce in Asia. The North West Company sent three missions from Fort George (Astoria) to Canton with their new wintering partner Angus Bethune as supercargo in 1814 and in 1816.[14]

Sadly for the North West Company, its anticipated riches from the Columbia Adventure did not immediately materialize, at least for the wintering partners who bore the costs of the unfavourable exchange rate between the British and Canadian pound. The company's trade with the Far East continued, but in American bottoms. In 1815, Colin Robertson accurately described the Nor'westers' plight:

> The North is now ripe for a rebellion, their finances are at the lowest ebb, their promises to the Young Gentlemen are nearly exhausted, the American War and the rigid economy they have pursued, since the Fur Trade has become their own, has reduced their Inventories in Athabasca so low, and raised their Indian standard so high, that the Natives cannot kill a sufficient quantity of Beaver to supply their wants.[15]

"Everybody says there will be a terrible storm next year as from the scanty outfit…and the Columbia losses," Simon McGillivray lamented as the 1815 *rendezvous* drew to its close. Everybody was right about the storm though not its cause. Who could predict that in 1816 Duncan Cameron would be arrested and sent to England for trial, that the NWC's Fort Gibraltar on the Red River would be destroyed, or most incredibly of all, that Fort William itself would come under military occupation?

86

1 2   BEFORE THE STORM

In October, 1815, Jean-Baptiste Lagimodière left the Red River for Montréal some 1800 miles away. A freeman and former North West Company employee, Lagimodière carried welcome news for Lord Selkirk: Colin Robertson had re-established Selkirk's colony and now awaited its new governor Robert Semple and eighty new settlers. Travelling south of Lake Superior via Fond du Lac by snowshoe, Lagimodière met no interference from the Nor'westers. Selkirk, then wintering in Montréal, sent Lagimodière back to the Red River with instructions to Robertson that "the North West Company must be compelled to quit their intrusive possessions upon my lands…[but] under a legal warrant from the Governor."[1]

Lagimodière was not so lucky on his return. When Archibald Norman McLeod reached Fort William on June 2, he immediately sent orders to James Grant, the proprietor of Fond du Lac, to stop Selkirk's messenger at all costs. On June 16, Pierre Bonga "the Negro" and several Indians intercepted Lagimodière and his three companions, beat them up and seized Selkirk's packet addressed to Robertson. Placed under arrest, the Lagimodière party "were brought to Fort William in the North West Company's boats" where they arrived on June 18, the day before the calamity on the Red River.[2]

All winter, the Nor'westers had anticipated a clash with the HBC. To their horror, Colin Robertson had re-founded the settlement and worse, destroyed Fort Gibraltar, captured Duncan Cameron and sent him to England for trial.

The news from Montréal was just as bad. Selkirk's recently published *The Fur Trade in North American with Observations on the North West Company of Montréal* exposed that company's alleged misdeeds. Also in Montréal, rumours circulated of Selkirk's plan to lead an expedition of demobilized soldiers to the Red River. The rumours proved correct. Fresh from theatres of war in Europe, India and North America, veterans of the Swiss De Meuron and De Watteville regiments had offered their services to Selkirk in return for free land at the Red River and payment for the voyage.[3]

William McGillivray could not stop Selkirk's expedition, but he could see that it ran short of food. In the presence of Kenneth MacKenzie at Montréal, he engaged the retired Daniel McKenzie to buy up provisions at Michilimackinac and Drummond Island before Selkirk's party could. This is the reason Daniel McKenzie was at Fort William in 1816. After obtaining provisions as ordered, he stood ready to do what was required of him.[4]

Writing from Fort William the previous summer, Kenneth MacKenzie had cautioned Duncan

87

Cameron, "Do not for God sake commit yourself in either action or writing—prudence prevents misfortune," advice Cameron ignored. At the time of his arrest at Fort Gibraltar, Cameron had just written James Hughes at Fond du Lac, "I wish that some of your *Pilleurs* who are fond of mischief and plunder, would come and pay a hostile visit to the sons of Gunpowder and riot...not that I would wish them to Butcher anyone *God forbid*."[5]

In June, 1816 McLeod had the *Pilleurs* or "Pillagers" very much in mind when he ordered the department's clerks, William Morrison and Eustache Roussin, to lead them to Lac La Pluie and the Red River. (Constant warfare with the Dakota had earned the Fond du Lac Ojibwa a reputation for exceptional bravery in battle and thus the name "Pillagers.") "You will explain to the Chiefs that we have King's officers and a few soldiers along with us so that there is not the least doubt of the Justice of our cause," McLeod wrote, somewhat deceptively. The "King's officers" were demobilized De Meurons, the NWC's guests; the soldiers were a few De Meurons whom the NWC hired before Selkirk could.[6]

The Nor'westers had little success in persuading either the peaceable Saulteur Ojibwa and Cree along the Red River or the Pillager Ojibwa of Fond du Lac and Lac La Pluie to attack the settlement. It was a different story with the Bois-Brulés (or Métis), the mixed-blood offspring of Native women and NWC personnel living in the Red River valley. The Brulés' livelihood and culture revolved around the buffalo hunt and preparation of pemmican and grease for the fur trade; they had much to lose should the lands on which the buffalo roamed were given over to farming.

In March 1816, Alexander Macdonell, founder of the NWC's Fort Gibraltar at the Red and Assiniboine rivers (and Miles Macdonell's cousin), predicted the coming confrontation:

I remark with pleasure the hostile proceedings of our neighbours [the Brulés]. I say pleasure because the more they do the more Justice we will have on our side. A storm is gathering to the Northward ready to burst on the rascals who deserve it. Little do they know their situation. Last year was but a joke. The new nation under their leaders are coming forward to clear their Native soil of intruders and assassins.[7]

On June 19 1816, the new Métis nation did come forward under its mixed-blood leader Cuthbert Grant, a NWC clerk and William McGillivray's ward. Did the Brulés act on their own or had Alexander Macdonell whipped them into a frenzy? Did they ride peacefully by Fort Douglas or were they decked in war-dress and armed with guns and tomahawks? Could bloodshed have been avoided had Governor Semple not gone out to meet them? Did the North West Company have any control at all over the Brulés who, insisted William McGillivray, were the real possessors of the land on the Red River?

Expecting a confrontation, the North West Company partners left Fort William for the Red River in June, but arrived shortly after Governor Semple clashed with the Brulés at Seven Oaks on June 19. "I thank providence that the Battle was over before we got there as it was our intention to storm the fort," the NWC clerk Robert Henry later wrote from Fort William. In that battle, Semple and twenty-one settlers met gruesome deaths at the hands of the Brulés, if the testimony of survivors is correct.[8]

Daniel McKenzie had travelled separately to the Red River to see his son Roderic despite McGillivray's plea that he remain at Fort William. "For God's sake, then let there be no blood-shed," McGillivray urged but too late. The battle was over when McKenzie met his son heading a party of Brulés. Roderic asked if they had done right. They were right in defending themselves, Daniel could only reply.

Magistrate A.N. McLeod conducted six settlers back to Fort William as prisoners, some

88

bound in chains for the long canoe journey. At the fort, they languished over the hot summer in the common gaol, a place, John Bourke, the colony's storekeeper, later testified:

> …that had been used as a privy, in which light was not admitted, except through crevices between the logs, of which the building was constructed, and in which an intolerable stench prevailed.[9]

The complicity of the North West Company in the Seven Oaks Massacre (or "Incident" in *The Canadian Encyclopedia*) became subject to much debate on both sides of the Atlantic. Lord Selkirk heard the news when he reached Sault Ste. Marie *en route* to the Red River with his military reinforcements. Changing his mind to travel west from Lake Superior by the St. Louis River, Selkirk had himself sworn in as Justice of Peace for the Indian Territories. He then altered his course towards Fort William.

During their anxious wait for Selkirk's arrival, the partners had some singular business to attend, thirty packs of fur which their clerk and leader of the Métis, Cuthbert Grant, had seized from the HBC at Qu' Appelle. As Alexander McKenzie and Simon Fraser sorted the annual returns in the Pack Stores and prepared their invoices, they listed the HBC furs separately from the NWC's but replaced the HBC's mark QA by the NWC's RR.[10]

Fort William was a receptacle of the Nor'westers' plunder, Selkirk would charge, his proof not only stolen furs but also presents packaged up in the Equipment Store for the Bois-Brulés. Soon after June 19, A.N. McLeod distributed outfits to some Brulés assembled at Rainy Lake, but as he explained to them, his supplies ran out:

> My kinsmen, my comrades, who have helped us in the time of need, I have brought clothing for you…I have forty suits of clothing; those who are most in need of them, may have these, and, on the arrival of the canoes in autumn, the rest of you shall be clothed likewise.[11]

Were these suits of clothing rewards for service at Seven Oaks, or merely the usual equipments supplied to the Brulés each year? In the so-called pamphlet war which ensued after June 19, Lord Selkirk and the North West Company both published persuasive, and contradictory, arguments about the purpose of these gifts to the Brulés who had fought the settlers.

At least one NWC employee at Fort William looked forward to Selkirk's coming. Forced to work after his *engagement* expired in 1816, the angered blacksmith Alexander Fraser traded three moose skins for shoe leather to one Chatelain in Selkirk's advance party then encamped on a nearby island. McGillivray had already threatened to jail the obdurate Fraser for contacting Chatelain earlier; now he had James Taitt bring the "traitor" before Dr. McLoughlin.

"You damned rascal, how durst you sell any thing to our enemies? I would hang you for a copper," McLoughlin roared before delivering a few blows and sending Fraser to "a small square building made of hewn logs, without any light, wherein was a quantity of human excrement." After more than ten days in the common gaol's noxious conditions, Fraser relented. He signed another three-year contract; Taitt then released him and sent him back to the forge.[12]

As Selkirk's party neared the fort, a long-time NWC clerk Edward Harrison wrote his will. Harrison bequeathed his estate to two natural sons in Canada and three daughters and a son, Thomas, in the northwest. The document makes no mention of Josephte, the Cree mother of his children. By some quirk of history, Thomas Harrison later married Apolline Lagimodière, a daughter of Jean-Baptiste who had been at Fort William in 1816 under arrest. Lagimodière had sided with the Red River settlers in their struggle against the Métis; paradoxically, his grandson

Old Fort William interpreter Daniel McGoey in the Blacksmith's Shop. Blacksmithing was one of the trades essential to the functioning of Fort William. The NWC's extraordinary measures to keep blacksmith Alexander Fraser in its employ must be seen within the context of the looming crisis created by Selkirk's impending arrival at the Fort. *Courtesy of Fort William Historical Park.*

Louis Riel would lead Indian and Métis resistance to settlement in 1870 and 1885.[13]

On the eve of Selkirk's arrival, Daniel McKenzie, a reputed drunkard, quite soberly wrote his son Roderic at the Red River Settlement with advice about behaviour as a clerk under the new partner, Allan Macdonell, at Swan River:

> The Law at present is very Strick respecting offences committed in the Indian Country you must take great care how you act. You are to defend your master & the Companys property if attacked but never to be the aggressor.[14]

The gentlemen had been pleased with Roderic's conduct on the Red River, Daniel added, while noting, "Burk, Pritchard and the Blacksmith are in prison here & it is supposed that they will be <u>Hung</u>."[15]

On August 12, the fort's people watched in silence as a flotilla of canoes and *batteaux* carrying Lord Selkirk, Miles Macdonell and red-uniformed soldiers entered the Kaministiquia River to the sound of drums, pipes and trumpets. Little did the spectators or the intruders realize that Selkirk would occupy Fort William for another nine months.

13   FORT WILLIAM OCCUPIED

As his canoe had sped westward across Lake Superior, Lord Selkirk plotted his strategy, fully confident that his military brigade could overcome any resistance it might meet at Fort William. Besides the hired De Meurons and de Wattevilles, his force included Sergeant John McNabb and six regulars of the British 37th Foot assigned, at Selkirk's insistence, by order of the Colonial Office to protect his Lordship from anticipated attempts on his life.[1]

On August 12, Selkirk's flotilla of boats and canoes passed Fort William and set up camp upstream on the opposite bank of the Kaministiquia River. Selkirk first demanded and obtained the release of the imprisoned Red River colonists still at the Fort. (The NWC had already sent Burke and the blacksmith to Montréal for trial.) He then interviewed them about the events of June 19 which left twenty-two settlers dead.

The prisoners' version of the tragedy gave Selkirk reason to implicate all North West Company partners in the slaughter. As a magistrate, he ordered William McGillivray's arrest on charges of "conspiracy, treason and being accessory to murder." McGillivray "acted as a gentleman, read the warrant, and immediately prepared to accompany us," Sergeant McNabb later declared. The agent Kenneth MacKenzie

and the fort's proprietor, Dr. John McLoughlin, accompanied McGillivray as bail, but Selkirk ordered them placed under arrest.[2]

Selkirk now sent a party of De Meurons to apprehend the partners who had not yet left for the interior. John McDonald FD (FD for Fort Dauphin to distinguish him from John McDonald of Garth) tried to bar their entry to the fort, but managed to close only one door of the gate when soldiers rushed through the other and seized him. He was then brought before Selkirk along with Alexander McKenzie, Hugh McGillis, Simon Fraser, Allan Macdonell and Daniel McKenzie. Protesting to Selkirk, the wintering partners described the scene:

> "…between fifty and sixty disbanded and intoxicated soldiers" with "bayonets fixed, and shouting a most horrid huzza!…spread a general terror amongst the inhabitants of the Fort."[3]

Sgt. McNabb viewed the drama differently:

> Much praise is due to Captain D'Orsonnens, for his cool and determined conduct. Lieutenant Fauche co-operated with the most laudable zeal and correctness, and the men behaved with the most exemplary propriety.[4]

Volunteer re-enactors portray the De Meurons, Lord Selkirk's mercenary soldiers, during Lord Selkirk's siege of Fort William in August 1816. *Courtesy of Fort William Historical Park.*

But Lieutenant Friederich von Graffenried probably came closest to the truth:

> Because the soldiers were dressed half in uniform and half in civilian clothes, and we the Officers wore short jackets and were armed with swords and pistols, we resembled a band of robbers…Our men, however, were in no mood to fool around, and broke down the gate. Fortunately no shot was fired, otherwise we could not have restrained our men from plundering, and in all likelihood blood would have been spilled.[5]

To prevent blood from spilling may have been the Nor'westers' reason for not defending the fort. McDonald later alluded to another. As Justice of the Peace for the Indian Territories and the western territories of Upper Canada, Selkirk

possibly had the right to make arrests. Defying his warrant could constitute an obstruction to justice which might have no defence in Canadian courts.

Promising not to commit or allow "hostile measures," the arrested gentlemen returned to the fort where soldiers secured their papers. All co-operated except McDonald who locked his

Opposite top: Map of Fort William, circa 1816. Drawn by Lord Selkirk on onion skin paper, this map shows the outline of the Fort and the surrounding area, including farm plots. *Courtesy of Fort William Historical Park, copy of Archives of Ontario, MU3279, F481.*

Opposite bottom: Detail from Selkirk's sketch plan of Fort William, drawn on the reverse side of the map. This almost indecipherable sketch of the main square was invaluable to the Old Fort William reconstruction project. *Courtesy of Fort William Historical Park, copy of Archives of Ontario, MU3279, F481.*

92

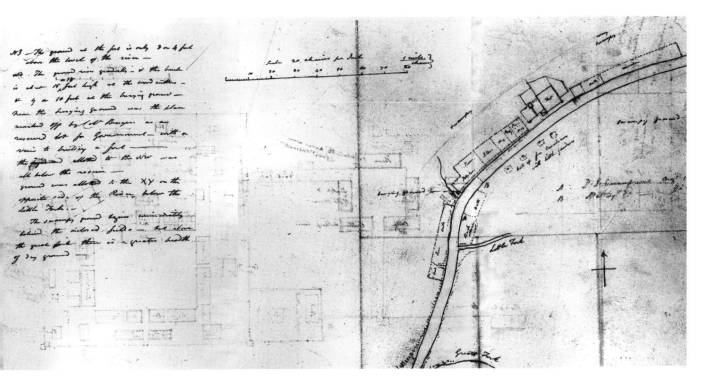

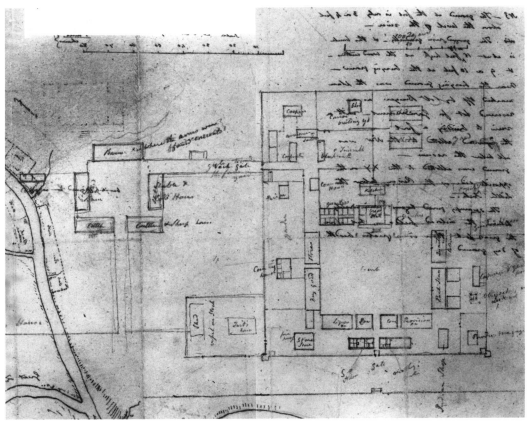

FORT WILLIAM OCCUPIED

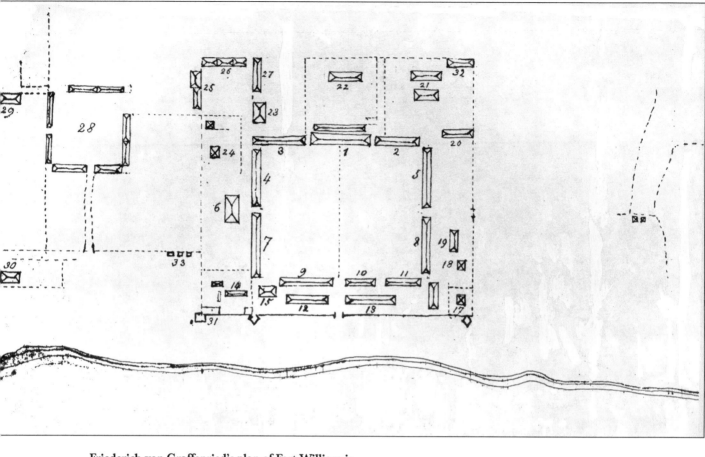

Friederich von Graffenried's plan of Fort William is less well-known and is useful for comparison. *Courtesy of Fort William Historical Park.*

94

room and gave the key to his "little girl." The soldiers broke down the door and found McDonald's desk open and his papers gone. That night, the partners furtively broke seals and frantically burnt company and private papers in the mess house kitchen.[6]

Unfortunately for the Nor'westers, but not for historians, the disgruntled blacksmith Alexander Fraser reported these activities to Lord Selkirk who ordered any undestroyed documents brought to his tent. These records became part of the evidence in later trials; some found their way into the Red River Settlement Collection and others ended up at the Selkirk estate on St. Mary's Isle, Kirkcudbright, Scotland where they were burned in a fire in 1940.[7]

A search found four cases of guns and forty fowling-pieces hidden in a hayloft and eight barrels of gunpowder stashed outside the fort. The weapons had been concealed "to effect the rescue of the partners arrested, and to destroy the party of the Earl of Selkirk," the blacksmith Fraser reported. Always fearful of a "massacre," Selkirk ordered the fort seized.[8]

Selkirk now examined all of his prisoners, except one, about the affray of June 19. The retired partner Daniel McKenzie could wait. William McGillivray acknowledged no responsibility on his or the company's part for attacks on Selkirk's colony. Since Cuthbert Grant "considers his situation as a Chief more important than his office as a Clerk," McGillivray argued, it would have been dangerous to interfere. Besides, the Brulés were "justifiable if they did arm themselves." It was an "extraordinary infatuation" on the part of Semple, to go out "into the Plains to attack the halfbreeds."[9]

Deciding to send the partners to Canada for trial, Selkirk ordered the canoes readied and crews selected for the voyage. Perhaps Kenneth MacKenzie had a premonition. The day before his departure, he wrote his will. As the Nor'westers embarked, he called out to Daniel McKenzie, "If ever I am acquitted, I'll blow out your brains." Kenneth suspected his kinsman, who had yet to be interrogated, of collaboration with the enemy.[10]

On August 17, the arrested partners embarked in three canoes manned by Iroquois instead of by crews "usually employed for the canoes of the agents." William McGillivray later complained that one canoe suited for fifteen passengers carried twenty-two. As proof of Selkirk's cold-heartedness, McGillivray's manservant had not been allowed to accompany him.[11]

On August 26 gale force winds blew hard from the west, but McGillivray insisted that conditions on Lake Superior were favourable, Lieutenant Fauche later reported. The canoes raced for safety towards Isles des Erables at the eastern end of the lake, but the overloaded vessel capsized in the surf on the rocky shoals. Kenneth MacKenzie, two De Meurons, and six

A sketch of William McGillivray's room in Fort William's Great Hall by Lord Selkirk. This view frames the view of the centre square of the fort. Note the furniture, probably made by Fort William tradesmen. *Courtesy of Fort William Historical Park, original in Archives of Ontario, MU 3279.*

Squall on Lake Superior, May 1845, by Henry James Warre. Conditions must have been like this or even worse when the canoe carrying the arrested Kenneth MacKenzie capsized and he and eight other passengers drowned on Lake Superior in August 1816. *Courtesy of LAC, C-031288.*

Iroquois drowned; Dr. John McLoughlin nearly succumbed. MacKenzie's body was taken to Sault Ste. Marie for burial; Dr. McLoughlin's health took years to recover.[12]

With Selkirk's permission, McGillivray appointed senior clerks from the Montréal counting-house "to superintend, direct, and govern" company affairs at Fort William in the absence of the partners. Late in the shipping season on August 21, the clerks implored Selkirk to allow the immediate shipment of NWC goods and furs to their destinations. The Company's property remained at the fort, however. Selkirk kept it as collateral and also as supplies for the fort's unusually large population over winter. Selkirk had another reason for his intransigence.

Stopping the North West Company's trade would hasten the day of his enemy's collapse.[13]

Selkirk now turned his attention to the dissident, Daniel McKenzie. Was he a "weak-kneed boozer" or did Selkirk use Colin Robertson's assessment of McKenzie as "very stupid obstinate and of doubtful attachment to the Company" to extract wanted answers from this bitter man? Daniel's letters convey erudition not stupidity. Although Robertson's assessment did not include "dissipated," this was the slur which his captors tried to make stick.[14]

McKenzie had nothing to say about North West Company perfidy when Selkirk interrogated him on August 20. Then the unthinkable happened; Selkirk had Daniel, a North West

Company partner *and* a gentleman, thrust into the *common* gaol, the prison for lesser ranks. There he joined four *engagés* and freemen, including his "negro servant" from Fond du Lac, Pierre Bonga, who had been arrested for seizing Lagimodière in June.

The putrid jail conditions had not improved under Selkirk. McKenzie "was kept in the dark, except as to such light as pervaded the chinks in the building, there being no window in the dungeon in which he was so confined." To console him, his guards lavishly plied him with liquor, but whether at his insistence or by Selkirk's orders remains in doubt.[15]

After two wretched days, Daniel co-operated. In an audacious proposal addressed to Miles Macdonell, he argued that, as the only North West Company partner at Fort William, he had the right to act on the company's behalf and to dispose of the company's stores and property as he wished. He also had the right to "sell the buildings and the Soil on which they are built— provided I can find a purchaser." Since the company had not paid him his due, he could keep the proceeds and any surplus until legally required to pay other creditors (the partners).[16]

McKenzie's letter opened the prison door. Immediately, he ordered the clerks to unlock the fort's stores and offices. In a letter dated September 3, McKenzie told Selkirk "all" he knew about the Red River disturbances. When he visited his son Roderic in July, he had taken a brigade of forty to fifty Iroquois with him at William McGillivray's request but, refusing to winter there, he returned to Fort William. McGillivray had also advised him not to tell Selkirk anything that "would shew that the NWC have a control over the Half Breeds."[17]

By September 18, McKenzie's "derangement of mind" had advanced. He sold the fort's movable property to Lord Selkirk (provisions, goods, furnishings, tools, animals) on condition that the £60,000 worth of furs in the Pack Stores be kept in trust along with one of Selkirk's properties worth £2,000 in annual rent, the transaction to be referred to arbitrators in London. The fact that McKenzie had no knowledge about who these arbitrators might be strongly suggests that the idea of the sale was not his.[18]

As a partner, Daniel claimed the right to act on behalf of all NWC shareholders. According to English law, single partners had such rights, Miles Macdonell wrote the wintering partners, allegedly on Daniel's behalf. Broadly hinting that they join the Hudson's Bay Company, Miles assured them that his Lordship wanted the Athabasca trade to continue, but under the HBC. Wouldn't the winterers prefer that their earnings go directly to themselves rather than to the "Nabobs of Montréal"? Most partners had pondered this very question long before Miles taunted them about their financial woes.[19]

To fulfill the sale agreement, the fort's assets were carefully recorded, first by building, as "Inventory of Goods &c. at Fort William as sold by D. McKenzie to the Earl of Selkirk 18th September 1816" and then alphabetically as "Recapitulation Inventory of Goods &c…" These lists of merchandise, provisions, tools and farm animals give valuable insights into the material culture of the fur trade.[20]

Now that McKenzie had met his Lordship's expectations, Selkirk sent him to Canada as a Crown witness against the Nor'westers. At Sault Ste. Marie, the Nor'westers helped him come to his senses. At Drummond Island on November 11, he formally protested his treatment at Selkirk's hands, and at Nottawasaga he swore before a notary that nothing he had told Selkirk was true. His letter of September 3 had been "a tissue of lies," mostly dictated by Miles Macdonell, "a *dictator*, a *monitor*, or an *amanuensis*." In or out of jail, Miles Macdonell and officers of the De Meurons had kept him "in a state of inebriety and actual derangement of the mind."

In 1818, McKenzie published his response to Selkirk's charge that his "tergiversation" had

98   **Daniel McKenzie's tombstone in the Blue Church Cemetery near Prescott, Ontario. The names of Daniel's wife Margaret Graves, son George, and daughters Margaret and Winn are inscribed on the reverse, as is the unsubstantiated claim that Daniel and Roderick McKenzie were with Sir Alexander Mackenzie at "discovery of the Mackenzie River."** *Courtesy of Marion Elizabeth Fawkes, from* In Search of My Father, *28–29.*

been engineered by the North West Company. This wordy, passionate pamphlet touches on more than his dealings with Selkirk; it also concerns his family. On August 10 he had written his son Roderic: "You must support yourself, your Sister & Mother." Daniel later changed his mind for he begged Selkirk to allow his wife and children accompany him to Montréal. Selkirk refused, promising that they would be well cared for at Fort William.

This was not the case, Daniel charged. His wife, Margaret Graves, and his children received none of the provisions left for them. (They survived on salt fish, bread, grease, flour and Indian corn.) Put in a house outside the fort, Mrs. McKenzie defended herself with pistols when soldiers tried to remove her. Eventually, she and the children, Elizabeth, Andrew and William, did follow Daniel to Upper Canada. Thanks to the £1,500 in damages for false imprisonment, McKenzie bought a farm in Augusta township north of Brockville where he lived with his family until his accidental death in 1832.[21]

As winter closed in, Lord Selkirk adjusted to months ahead "without any intercourse with the civilized world." Never one to stay idle, he sent the De Meuron units in extreme weather to occupy Michipicoten, Lac la Pluie and Fond du Lac, the latter in United States territory. From Lac la Pluie, Captain D'Orsonnens and Miles Macdonell proceeded to Fort Douglas, the HBC post on the Red River, now occupied by the North West Company. Surprising the partner Archibald McLellan, they arrested him for instigating the murder of a settlement official, Owen Keveny, while being taken to Fort William as a prisoner after the June 19 disaster.[22]

Selkirk had a passion for building roads. He hired Indians to mark out a road southwest from Fort William, to Arrow Lake on the U.S. border, and hence to Rainy Lake "by blazing as the Americans call it, or plaquer as the Canadians," the project to be completed by spring, so "they can work upon it next summer." (How long, one wonders, did Selkirk expect to occupy the fort?) He also planned a road from Grand Portage to Arrow Lake where he had a depot built for storing goods moved by horse and wagon or sleigh from Lake Superior. This scheme to circumvent the Dog Lake route to Rainy Lake came to naught with Selkirk's withdrawal from Fort William.[23]

Much to Selkirk's dismay, the Nor'westers were released on bail in Montréal, thanks to friends in Canada's government and judiciary. Since ignominiously leaving Fort William as arrested felons, they had tried everything to regain their great emporium. In September, they sent John Johnston JP, from Saint Mary's with a

polite, but futile, request to relinquish the fort. On November 12, one Constable Robinson arrived with a warrant for Selkirk's arrest on charges of forcible entry and detention. Selkirk sent him off with the message that he would never yield the fort to anyone but the King's soldiers.

In November, Pierre de la Rastel Rocheblave, the Montréal agent replacing Kenneth MacKenzie, headed towards Fort William on the *Invincible* with Deputy Sheriff William Smith of Sandwich. November is not a good month for sailing on Lake Superior. When the schooner left St. Mary's on the 14th, there was no danger, Captain McCargo said, but McCargo proved wrong:

> Toward the middle of the traverse of la Pointe aux poissons Blancs [Whitefish Point], a violent wind from the North West came up, the weather turned cold, which, in a moment, froze the sails and cables, so that they were powerless to manage the vessel. It was driven between la point aux poissons Blancs, and la rivière au Brochets [Pike River] where it was shipwrecked [without loss of life].[24]

It would be spring before anyone could reach Fort William from the east. At the request of both sides, the government at Québec appointed a commissioner to investigate crimes perpetrated by the other. Selkirk learned of the commission in March and of the revocation of all appointments, including his, as magistrates under the Canada Jurisdiction Act. When he discovered that his actions would unlikely be sanctioned in court, he removed himself from Canadian jurisdiction before William Benjamin Coltman could make his appearance at Fort William. On May 1, he departed for the Red River with most of his entourage.[25]

On May 29, William McGillivray re-possessed the fort one month before Coltman arrived with Simon McGillivray and Pierre Rocheblave in a North West Company canoe manned by North West Company voyageurs. Coltman would balance this lack of impartiality by refusing to arrest Selkirk when he caught up with him at Fort Douglas.

Over in England, the Prince Regent had issued a Proclamation requiring "the mutual restoration of all property captured during these disputes and the freedom of trade and intercourse with the Indians until the trials now pending can be brought to a judicial decision…" In Canada, the Prince Regent's wishes became official as the "Proclamation of the 3rd of May." Despite the Proclamation, the battle continued, and not only in the courts, but also throughout the northwest from the banks of the Kaministiquia River to the Athabasca country.[26]

101

Lieutenant Robert Irvine
Woman at Fort William, 1811
Watercolour
Courtesy of Fort William Historical Park.

102

Frances Anne Hopkins
Canoes in a Fog, Lake Superior, 1869
Oil on canvas
Collection of Glenbow Museum, Calgary, Canada.

SUPERIOR RENDEZVOUS-PLACE

Artist unknown
William McGillivray
Oil on canvas
*Courtesy Fort William Historical Park, copied by kind
permission of Gianni Lombardi, Rome.*

104

Eastman Johnson
Ojibwe Women at Grand Portage, 1857
Courtesy of Fort William Historical Park.

105

Attributed to Levi Stevens
Colonel William MacKay, 1816
Oil on canvas
Courtesy of Notman Photographic Archives,
McCord Museum of Canadian History, Montréal.

106

William Dashwood
Michilimackinac on Lake Huron, circa 1820
Oil on canvas
Courtesy of Mackinac State Historic Parks,
Mackinac Island, Michigan.

Artist unknown
Portrait of John McDonald of Garth, circa 1803
Oil on canvas
Courtesy of Fort William Historical Park.

Richard Ramsay Reinagle
Simon McGillivray, circa 1824
Courtesy of Fort William Historical Park.

14   "A Strange Medley"

With Fort William firmly in North West Company hands, a "strange medley" of people from lands far and near gathered at Fort William for the *rendezvous* of 1817. In mid-August, the Astorian Ross Cox found a broad diversity of ethnic origins:

> England, Ireland, Scotland, France, Germany, Italy, Denmark, Sweden, Holland, Switzerland, United States of America, the Gold Coast of Africa, the Sandwich Islands [Hawaii], Bengal, Canada, with various tribes of Indians, and a mixed progeny of Creoles, or half-breeds. We *had one East Indian from Bengal, two negroes, and the DeMeurons were a mixture of nearly every nation in Europe.* What a strange medley![1]

As already seen, Anglo-Scots, French Canadians, Ojibwa and their mixed progeny formed the basis of year-round Fort William society, but what of individuals from other backgrounds who had assembled there that summer? Selkirk had left a small contingent of De Meurons to protect the new Hudson's Bay Company post located nine miles up the Kaministiquia River at Pointe de Meuron. Veterans of far-off battles, this mixture of Swiss, German, Lithuanian and other European nationalities had undoubtedly picked up hangers-on all the way from Bengal to the Gold Coast.[2]

The "two negroes" seen by Cox could have been Pierre Bonga and one of his sons. Descended from West Indian slaves owned by a British commandant at Michilimackinac, Pierre served Alexander Henry the Younger at Pembina in 1800. The 1812 apprenticeship *engagement* of his son John Baptiste, at age fourteen, to Archibald Norman McLeod identifies Pierre as an interpreter at Fort William. But when Selkirk had him jailed in 1816, he belonged to the Fond du Lac Department where earlier he had served under Daniel McKenzie. On Pierre's release from Fort William's "common gaol" in 1817, he apparently remained at the fort that summer. The second "negro" may have been John Baptiste or Pierre's second son, Etienne (Stephen in English) who had been baptised in 1808 at St. Gabriel's Church in Montréal; he perhaps was the 19-year-old Stephen Bonga of Montréal who signed as middleman for three years at Norway House in 1821.[3]

The Montréal clerk, Jasper Vandersluys, accounts for Holland. A bookkeeper in the NWC's Montréal counting house, Vandersluys accompanied the agents to Fort William each summer. In August 1816, he was one of two clerks given charge of the fort on the arrested

109

partners' departure for Montréal. After the Napoleonic Wars, the North West Company hired more Europeans as clerks. Some had German or Polish names, but they lacked one qualification for promotion, "family connexions."[4] The Norwegian, Willard Ferdinand Wentzel, a NWC clerk since 1799, had already made this discovery as Ross Cox noted in an oblique commentary about credentials needed for promotion:

> Having no family connexions to place his claims in the prominent point of view which they ought to occupy, and being moreover of an honest unbending disposition, his name was struck out of the house-list of favourite clerks intended for proprietors.[5]

Cox's American may have been Daniel Williams Harmon of Vermont who joined the NWC as an apprentice clerk in 1800. Harmon had no "family connexions" but did become a partner in 1818. By then not enough suitable clerks were available to replace older partners anxious to quit the company. Most new clerks with expectations had Scots names, some still fresh out from the Highlands but others natives of Glengarry in Upper Canada.

The Hawaiians were adept boatmen. It is not surprising that in 1817 many found their way to Fort William from the Pacific coast. They were preceded at Fort William by Naukana whose astonishing story reflects the global linkages forged by major trading companies. In 1811, Naukana and twenty-four boatmen boarded John Jacob Astor's ship, the *Tonquin*, at Hawaii on its way to the Columbia River. He was at Astoria when David Thompson reached the Columbia's mouth later that year. Exchanging a voyageur too "weak for the hard labour of ascending the river" with the Astorians for Naukana, Thompson took him on his journey back to Fort William. In his narrative, he described the Hawaiian as:

> …a powerful well-made Sandwich Islander, (whom we named Coxe, from his resemblance to a seaman of that name); he spoke some English, and was anxious to acquire our language, and would act as Interpreter on our ship from England to this river.[6]

Thompson and Naukana reached the fort in July, 1812 just as the Nor'westers had learned of the American declaration of war against Britain. Donald McTavish and John McDonald of Garth took Naukana with them to England where they embarked on their expedition to claim the Pacific Northwest coast for Britain. On November 30, 1813, Naukana was back at Astoria, by then in North West Company hands. In August 1814, all Hawaiians on the Columbia, including Naukana, were returned to the Islands but, in 1823, he accompanied the Hawaiian king and queen to England where he had an audience with King George IV. In 1827, Naukana returned to the Columbia. There, the Hudson's Bay Company employed him until 1843 when Dr. John McLoughlin hired him as a swineherd on a meadow still called Coxe's Plain. Naukana's son William later founded a colony of Hawaiians near today's Vancouver, British Columbia, where descendants of Naukana still reside.[7]

According to Ross Cox, the peoples at Fort William also represented a rich diversity of religious backgrounds:

> Here were assembled on the shores of this inland sea, Episcopalians, Presbyterians, Methodists, sun-worshippers, men from all parts of the world, and whose creeds were "wide as the poles asunder," united in one common object, and bowing down before the same idol.[8]

Strangely, Cox made no mention of Roman Catholics such as the French-Canadian voyageurs and a few Nor'westers like Simon

Fraser, John McLoughlin and Pierre Rocheblave. By "sun-worshippers" perhaps he meant the local Ojibwa, the Iroquois from around Montréal and perhaps a scattering of Cree and other tribal origins. But the idol this strange medley worshipped in common had no temple at Fort William, unless the counting-house be considered as such. Under the British, the fur trade managed quite happily without moralistic meddling from the clergy. All that changed when the Red River Settlement became more or less permanent with all the trappings of European society including organized religion.

Before 1816, Selkirk had urged the Roman Catholic Bishop, Joseph-Octave Plessis, at Québec to appoint a mission which would put his Red River colony "on a more solid footing." The Seven Oaks disaster halted the first attempt but, in 1818, Plessis dispatched three missionaries to the settlement. En route, they received a warm welcome at Fort William from NWC agent Pierre Rastel de Rocheblave and at Pointe de Meuron from HBC officer, Jean Baptiste Lemoine. The NWC, like the HBC, had never before championed Christianity in the hinterland, but now that a Catholic mission would be established in Assiniboia, with or without their sanction, the two firms found it expedient to cooperate with the church.[9]

Journeying into regions beyond Christian influence, the missionaries were shocked to discover marriages *à la façon du pays* with progenies of unbaptized children. Also disturbing were "poor infidels who live in ignorance, and who think that all they have to do in the world is to hunt in order to be able to barter for rum and other things."[10]

With its superior resources, Fort William outdid the struggling HBC post in welcoming the missionaries. On June 21, mass was said at Fort William, perhaps for the first time under British rule. The NWC sent fresh food to the impoverished HBC post and requested the NWC interior posts to feed the missionaries en route to the Red River. "All is free," thanks to the North West Company, Joseph-Norbert Provencher gratefully wrote his bishop from Rainy Lake.[11]

When the missionary Pierre-Antoine Tabeau arrived at Fort William in 1820, he, too, was "received with all the decorum customary on the part of these gentlemen":

> A large chamber and two smaller rooms have been given us for lodgings, and a very large room for our chapel…we have had our altar mounted beneath the dais…and have hung the intervening space with a beautiful embroidered cloth upon which are hung images and little crosses in abundance, placed in Indian symmetry to conform to local taste. We began to say Mass and have continued to do so once only on week days and twice on Sundays and feast days.

Tabeau, a missionary, had doubts about any lasting success, though. Few Natives were willing to be confessed, "and even fewer still are doing so with benefit."[12]

That same year, however, the missionary Joseph Crevier could report "much progress in the catechism of certain children, especially at Fort William." As well, "wives of several Protestant men [were] already instructed in the same way and asking me to marry them." The best news of all was Dr. McLoughlin's announcement that wood for a chapel "was all cut ready for construction at the expense of the North West Company."[13]

The missionaries had been fortunate to find Rocheblave and McLoughlin at Fort William. As Catholics, they supported the church's aim to save souls in the wilderness. But Rocheblave and McLoughlin were not typical traders, as Bishop Plessis well knew. The NWC refused to give the missionaries transportation into the Athabasca country (where the NWC and HBC were engaged in mortal combat, it must be added). By 1820, the church could no longer count on even the HBC:

Worship of Manitou, Lake of the Woods, 1873, a lithograph from a drawing by F. A. Verner. The local Ojibwa clung onto their old religion despite the efforts of missionaries from Québec from 1817–1821. After the Jesuits established their mission at Fort William in 1849, the conversion of Natives to Christianity continued slowly. *Courtesy of TBHMS, 972.2.466.*

The death of Lord Selkirk has resulted in much confusion for the Hudson's Bay Company, which is not very favorable to the Catholic religion, and, between ourselves, the North West Company is still less so.[14]

In 1821, the attitude of the fur companies to Catholicism proved irrelevant. After the rival companies amalgamated, the Hudson's Bay Company allowed Joseph-Norbert Provencher, the future Bishop of St. Boniface, to continue his mission at the Red River, but it cancelled plans for a chapel at Fort William. No permanent structure devoted to Christianity would be erected on the Kaministiquia until 1849.

On regaining Fort William in 1817, the Nor'westers strengthened its defences against future attack by adding a portcullis to the main gate, building bastions at the rear corners and buying an extensive armoury of war-surplus weapons. As the Hudson's Bay Company escalated its drive into the interior, violence between the rival companies escalated. Prepared to meet any invasion of Fort William, the North West Company also tried to ruin the HBC's trade at Fort de Meuron.

Dr. McLoughlin, who had been arrested by Lord Selkirk in 1816 and sent to Canada for trial, returned to Fort William on bail the next year. In 1818, he had to travel to York to appear in court as an accessory to murder where he was acquitted. Once more he returned to Fort William, though reluctantly. He "had an offer to enter into Business in the civilized world – if I do not accept the proposal – it will be from want of capital." But McLoughlin had legal costs besides responsibility for his children's schooling. He never would retire to the "civilized world."[15]

McLoughlin's absences and his duties as proprietor led the NWC to hire Dr. William Scott in 1818 as Fort William's surgeon. Scott's three-year contract stipulated that when "not occupied by his professional duties, to give assistance in the stores or in conducting the trade…in the same manner as other clerks." McLoughlin could now devote himself to combating the HBC at Pointe de Meuron.

One example of McLoughlin's aggressive tactics is the case of Visinat, a freeman working for the HBC. McLoughlin had the freeman arrested "for stealing a chicken and killing or helped to kill a cow and her calf." Visinat escaped, "having been abused more and more every day and even kicked….Dr. McLoughlin struck him and he bore the mark for several days. …They are terrible those N-W when it comes to carry out justice themselves…," lamented Lemoine, the master at Pointe de Meuron.[16]

112

By spring, food shortages forced Lemoine to beg Dr. McLoughlin for provisions. McLoughlin's terms were harsh: HBC men were not to make or mend canoes or build stores or houses until the HBC repaid the NWC with provisions of similar quality. He was "not to send to the Interior or to the Sault;" and "should any Indians go to your House you are not to Trade with thems [sic] but send them to Fort William."[17]

Fort William had the food, the goods and the men to outdo Pointe de Meuron. If tempted to visit the HBC, usually by liquor, the Indians lived in terror of discovery. At Fort William, they were "corrected and beat according to the will and pleasure of the Master," Lemoine wrote. To the rival firms, however, the skirmishes on the Kaministiquia were trivial affairs compared to the larger war being waged out in the Athabasca country.

As violence begot violence and arrest followed arrest, both sides behaved as if they had never heard of the Prince Regent's Proclamation requiring "all parties in the northwest to keep the peace." Most sobering was the death by starvation of Nor'wester Benjamin Frobisher who had escaped a HBC ambush of an NWC brigade at Grand Rapids on the Saskatchewan River's entry into Lake Winnipeg.

Some winterers seemed willing to declare a truce. Dr. McLoughlin protested "that no good had been derived from those violent measures, that even the Indians themselves laughed at them." In 1820, the Hudson's Bay Company sent a promising young officer from Britain to bolster its forces in the Athabasca. En route, George Simpson visited Fort William, ostensibly to deliver a copy of the Prince Regent's Proclamation. Dr. McLoughlin warmly welcomed the future governor of the Hudson's Bay Company on this, his first of many visits to Fort William.[18]

As the NWC agreement of 1802 neared its conclusion in 1822, most wintering partners wished to replace their Montréal agents with another supply house altogether, an idea carefully nurtured by Colin Robertson. Strife in the interior simply aggravated their discontent.

In 1820, Robertson arrived at Fort William in close confinement. Acquitted in 1818 on charges of destroying Fort Gibraltar, this nemesis of the North West Company had led a HBC expedition to the Athabasca. At the HBC's Fort Wedderburn, Samuel Black arrested him and at Fort Chippewyan kept him in a log privy for eight months before sending him to Montréal for trial. En route, Robertson escaped. As he headed yet another HBC campaign towards the Athabasca, the Nor'westers seized him at Grand Rapids and brought him to Fort William under arrest.

At Fort William, Archibald Norman McLeod offered Robertson freedom on condition that he stay out of the Athabasca for one year. "I eyed the fellow with such perfect contempt," Robertson wrote, "that he rose from his chair, and with his highland accent observed, 'You shall not see Montréal untill (sic) the ice takes this year.' " William McGillivray begged Robertson to seek reconciliation or a "junction" between the two companies, something Lord Selkirk had refused but which the agents considered their only "salvation." On the Ottawa River while under escort to trial in Montréal, Robertson again escaped, this time via the United States to England.[19]

In 1820, the North West Company held its last annual meeting at Fort William. Eighteen Nor'westers refused to consider joining a renewed NWC in 1822. Instead, they sent John McLoughlin and Angus Bethune to London to negotiate with the Hudson's Bay Company. A fellow passenger on the Atlantic crossing happened to be the Nor'westers' escaped prisoner, Colin Robertson, who later described what happened when a gratuity was solicited for the crew:

Our friend the Doctor had put down his name, and I took up the pen for the same purpose, but perceiving Bethune waiting I turned round to Abby Carriera, "Come Abby put down your

In this re-enactment, North West Company wintering partners debate policy with Montréal agents in the Fort's Council House. *Courtesy of Fort William Historical Park.*

name, I don't like to sign between two North Westers." "Never mind, Mr. R.," replied Monsr. Carriera," remember our Saviour was crucified between two thieves."[20]

In the long run, the fate of the NWC was decided, not on the Kaministiquia nor in the Athabasca, but in London where Edward Ellice, now Member of Parliament for Coventry, and his fellow merchant, Simon McGillivray, had the final say. Turning McLoughlin and Bethune aside, the HBC accepted the overtures of the two agents who signed the HBC-NWC union agreement on behalf of themselves and of William McGillivray in Montréal.

For Ellice, the North West Company was just one of many far-ranging interests in Britain and America. For Simon McGillivray, the North West Company had been his *entré* into London financial and social circles. Neither had any sentimentality about the name of the united company as long as it paid healthy dividends.

In 1821, a much stranger medley gathered at Fort William than Ross Cox had observed in 1817. The unthinkable happened in 1821 when Nor'westers and their former foes met together to learn their fate in the new Hudson's Bay Company. But, as William McGillivray himself would lament, what really doomed the North West Company, and with it Fort William's function in the Montréal fur trade's east-west transportation system, was geography.

In his assessment, the NWC lost to a "Chartered Company, who brought their goods to the Indian Country at less than half the Expence that ours cost us."[21]

The vast distance from Thunder Bay to saltwater continues to bedevil the Canadian Head of the Lakes as the transshipment centre for manufactured goods from the east and staple products from the west.

15   FORT WILLIAM, 1821

In 1821, the North West Company convened once more at Fort William but this time in joint assembly with the Hudson's Bay Company This meeting had few decisions to make. Its purpose was to inform the gathering of decisions already made about the selection, duties and classification of traders in the amalgamated firm.

In a sense, the imperial design promoted by Sir Alexander Mackenzie in his *Voyages* of 1801 had come to pass. This coalescence of the NWC and the HBC would combine his proposed "Fishery in the Pacific with the Fur Trade of the Interior from the East to the West Coasts." The union, enabled by the deaths of Mackenzie and Lord Selkirk in 1820, also helped fulfill Selkirk's colonial ambitions by securing the Red River Settlement's right to survive. The British Government officially sanctioned these enterprises on the Columbia and Red rivers as deterrents to American expansion northward.[1]

In the new 100-share Hudson's Bay Company, the London committee assumed overall management of the trade but, on the ground, the NWC's wintering partners fared rather well. A Deed Poll dated March 26, 1821, divided the forty shares allotted to traders into eighty-five: two each to twenty-five chief factors, one each to twenty-eight chief traders and the balance for retirees. (In British merchant companies, agents in charge of trading stations, or factories, were known as factors.) Fifteen chief factors and seventeen chief traders were Nor'westers, but that was to be expected; the HBC could hardly match the experience, energy and enterprise of its former enemies.[2]

To implement the "Agreement for carrying on the Fur Trade," the HBC sent its director Nicholas Garry to North America. Garry sailed from London to New York with John McLoughlin and Angus Bethune, but at Montréal McLoughlin turned back to Europe. Still suffering from his near-drowning in 1816, and no doubt depressed by being outmanoeuvred in London, he sought medical treatment from his brother, Dr. David McLoughlin, in Paris. Garry accompanied William and Simon McGillivray in their express canoe on the journey from Montréal to Fort William.[3]

The tension at Fort William must have been unbearable as traders of both camps had to reconcile themselves to working with former enemies. But "Simon carried everything off without even the semblance of opposition," Colin Robertson observed. "The wintering partners are the most conforming and accomodating [sic] set of gentlemen I ever met with…. All is peace and harmony, except for poor Bethune who is sent to Coventry."[4]

115

116

Map of the North-West Territory of the Province of Canada, by David Thompson. Completed in 1814, the original of this map hangs in the foyer of the Ontario Archives. Seen here is the hand-copied version com- missioned by Old Fort William for display in the reconstructed Great Hall. *Courtesy of FWHP, hand-drawn copy of original at the Archives of Ontario.*

FORT WILLIAM, 1821

Yes, the Nor'westers' Enemy No. l, Colin Robertson, was back at Fort William, trying "to laugh not to be angry at my enemies" and "pacing the *Fort* at full length" just to remind the principals of his presence. Despite his efforts to bring this moment about, he had no assurance of a posting. The McGillivray and Selkirk interests had agreed to exclude their most contentious combatants from the new HBC. The Nor'westers Peter Skene Ogden and Samuel Black, scourges of the HBC in the northwest, and Alex Macdonell, the reputed instigator of the Seven Oaks slaughter; and the HBC's men were Colin Robertson and John Clarke, organizers of the HBC's offensive in the Athabasca, and Governor William Williams, ambusher of the NWC brigade at Grand Rapids in 1819.

The proscribed gentlemen eventually did get placements except for Macdonell who would make his home in Glengarry County. (In 1821, that haven of retired Nor'westers elected him to the Upper Canada Legislative Assembly.) Williams was still an HBC governor, but of the Southern Department only. The larger and more productive Northern Department came under the jurisdiction of the company's rising star, George Simpson. Robertson would be chief factor at Norway House.

John McLoughlin and Angus Bethune were rewarded for their rebellion against the Montréal agents with chief factorships at Rainy Lake and Moose Factory respectively. They still owed the Montréal agents more for the cost of each outfit since becoming partners in 1814 than credited to them for the returns. The War of 1812 and skirmishes at Red River and the Athabasca had taken their toll of NWC profits. In fact, McLoughlin's "total partnership income was zero."[5]

The prestigious chief factorship at York Factory went to John George McTavish whom Williams had arrested in 1819 and sent to England for a trial which never took place. Made a partner in 1813, McTavish took charge of Astoria on its purchase by the NWC in 1813 and, in 1820, he replaced McLoughlin as proprietor at Fort William. "Liberal in opinions, gentlemanly in his manners and moderate during the late contest," in Robertson's view, McTavish restored York Factory, headquarters of the HBC's Northern Department and its major sea port, on the model of Fort William.[6]

As if to symbolize Fort William's lost status, McTavish had the paintings of Lord Nelson and the Battle of Trafalgar removed from the Great Hall and shipped to York Factory. These gifts of William McGillivray to the North West Company stayed in their packing case until around 1835. They then hung in the York Factory mess house where they remained until 1928.[7]

The same packing case carried three maps from Fort William which were sent from York Factory to Michipicoten in 1833. Perhaps one was David Thompson's preliminary map of the west which the geographer forwarded to Fort William in 1813. This evidence of NWC accomplishments featured the explorations of Sir Alexander Mackenzie, Simon Fraser, and Thompson himself, all under company auspices, as well as the location of over fifty NWC posts in the west. Thompson's draft map from Fort William had several errors, including a non-existent Caledonia River between the Fraser and the Columbia and others which Selkirk's hydrographer, A. B. Becker, noted in 1816 that "even a school boy could hardly be expected to fall into." Thompson's perfected map, which never did hang at Fort William, is on view at the Ontario Archives in Toronto.[8]

Since goods, provisions and stores formed part of the capital stock each company brought into the united firm, careful inventories had to be taken at all forts, posts, stations and depots. The NWC's agent Pierre Rocheblave assumed this task at Fort William, wasting too much time, in Robertson's view, deciding whether *capots* were three or three and a half ells in size. Back in Montréal, Rocheblave undertook the inventories at the NWC's eastern divisions and tried to help Thomas Thain straighten out the NWC accounts. In 1822, McGillivrays, Thain and Company, with Thain in charge, was established for this purpose. A director of the Bank of Montréal, founded by his cousin John Richardson of Sir Alexander Mackenzie & Company in 1817, the overworked and over wrought Thain never did manage to end the chaos.[9]

In 1821, many Nor'westers quit Fort William and the fur trade forever. The old warrior, Archibald Norman McLeod, retired to Scotland, and the recent NWC partner Daniel Harmon brought his "country" wife and family with him back to Vermont. "Having children by her," Harmon explained, "I consider that I am under moral obligation not to dissolve the connexion, if she is willing to continue it."[10] Some traders left their wives and children behind when they retired from the trade, but others, like David Thompson in 1812 and Harmon in 1821, brought their families with them when settled in the east.

Now redundant, three clerks also left Fort William forever: physician Dr. William Scott, storekeeper Captain Antoine Landriaux, and superintendent, Mr. James Taitt. As seen earlier, Taitt retired with his family to Chatham in Lower Canada along with Captain Robert McCargo and his wife Nancy McKay, the daughter of Alexander MacKay and Marguerite Waddens MacKay McLoughlin. As also noted, two sons of the McKay-McCargo marriage would marry two daughters born to James Taitt and Susan McKenzie from the Assiniboine.[11]

The diversion of traffic from Fort William to York Factory saw the York boat replacing the birchbark canoe as the fur trade's major carrier on larger waterways. Longer than the fragile Montréal canoe, the sturdy forty-two foot York boat carried twice its cargo and needed fewer men. A whole way of life now changed for many *engagés* who faced unemployment whether in Canada or the interior. To lower manpower costs, the HBC encouraged a labour surplus. The Governor and Committee in London did not "wish any Canadian men to be reengaged for more than One year, as there must be more men in the Country than can be usefully employed hereafter."[12]

In 1821, the NWC used its surplus inventory as payment for employees as seen in the "Account of Goods Given to Winterers out of the Equipment Shop at Fort William for Services

Left, restored headstone to the memory of Susan, William McGillivary's mixed-blood wife. Upon the HBC's surrender of its land to the CPR in 1883, the graves at Fort William's burying ground were removed to Mountainview Cemetery; *right*, marker placed on Susan's grave by Fort staff in 1990. *Photos by Glenn Craig.*

rendered the North West Company including Sundries for the Pack Store." But the new HBC assumed the debts accumulated by many NWC employees, again to lessen labour costs. As the thrift-driven HBC Governor in London explained, the Bay would "retain those men who may be in debt to the Company that they may be made to work out their debts."[13]

On July 21, Nicholas Garry "left F.W. & never in my life have I left a Place with less Regret." At posts along their way to York Factory, he and Simon McGillivray read out the terms of the Deed Poll to disbelieving Nor'westers and inspected "the Depots and Inventories of Property" belonging to both companies. The man who gave his name to Fort William on Lake Superior also had no personal regrets. But as a true businessman, William McGillivray did lament "the loss of this trade to Montréal & the immediate district in its vicinity," valued at £40,000 a year.

"I part with my *old troops* to meet them no more in discussion on the Indian trade," he wrote his friend, the Hon. Rev. Dr. John Strachan of York. Recognition of the fact that the North West Company had lost out to the Hudson's Bay Company weighed heavily on his mind. Poignantly linking the NWC's lifespan with his own career, McGillivray reminisced: "I was the first English Clerk engaged in the Service of the N.W. Co. on its first Establishment in 1784, and I have put my Hand and Seal to the Instrument which closes its *career*–and *name* in 1821."[14]

McGillivray's letter makes no mention of his Native wife, Susan, nor of his three mixed-blood sons. Little is known of Susan, except her name and date of death, August 26, 1819, apparently at Fort William. These are inscribed on her tombstone erected by her three sons by William as are their names, Simon, Joseph and Peter. Former NWC clerks and now wintering partners, Simon Jr. and Joseph McGillivray, became chief traders in the new HBC.

North West Company Achievement of Arms, 1823. On the initiative of William and Simon McGillivray, the Company acquired a coat of arms in 1823, and in 1825 their family crest carried much of the same symbolism. Today, the City of Thunder Bay commemorates the NWC in their city coat of arms. *Courtesy of Fort William Historical Park, copy of LAC C-8711.*

William McGillivray and his brother Simon, (Senior), however, did have a sense of history. In their view, the North West Company had preserved much of North America for Britain. Their petition for a family coat of arms in 1825 flaunted the company's exploits:

> By its exertions, North America had been discovered and explored from the lakes of Canada to the Pacific Ocean and the frozen or Polar Sea, by which discoveries and establishments founded by the said company extensive territories have been added to His Majesty's Dominions.[15]

The Fort William which William McGillivray left in 1821, only eighteen years after presiding at the North West Company's first *rendezvous* on the Kaministiquia River, now had the status of a minor Hudson's Bay Company post. No longer a destination, the fort became a waystation to somewhere else. For the next sixty years, the post's year-round population would typically include a factor, a few clerks and *engagés*, some free Canadians and mixed-blood families. And in the vicinity, hunting, fishing, gathering, and providing services upon which Fort William depended, were still the peoples who were there when the traders came.

During that 1821 gathering, two Ojibwa chiefs marched into Fort William's great hall preceded by an English flag and accompanied by "all the Tribe." As the chief's address to William McGillivray makes clear, they were no better off than in 1798 when they signed away, by an invalid agreement, their lands along the Kaministiquia River.

Some of his people could not be present, the chief apologized. Many had been afflicted by measles, others by hunger. Hunger had led one of his clan to murder his father "that he might feed on his Body" and to kill his whole family of ten

"that it might not be known." But there was another reason for the small attendance: "A black Bird had decoyed away some of his Followers." Despite the black Bird's whisperings of changes to the trade, though, the chief promised to still rely on "his great Father," William McGillivray.[16]

Without mentioning the merged firm's name, McGillivray assured the chief that, although the North West Company had joined the Hudson's Bay Company, the united firm would treat with the Indians as before. They, therefore, had no reason to listen to the black bird beckoning from across the border with the United States.

With the merger of 1821, the old competition to the Kaministiquia River from Hudson Bay to the north vanished, but competition from the south had already resurfaced when the American Fur Company took over NWC operations at Fond du Lac in 1817. Now, as a Hudson's Bay Company post, Fort William faced an immediate challenge—to prevent Indians on both sides of the Pigeon River from trading with the Americans.

121

In 1821, York Factory replaced Fort William as depot and port for the northwest and Michipicoten replaced the fort as depot and port for Lake Superior. Goods for Lake Superior came from James Bay by the Michipicoten River route and Superior's fur returns reached seawater the same way. The Lake Superior Department belonged to the HBC's Southern Department covering the St. Lawrence watershed. Its governor was William Williams until 1826 when the Northern Department's governor, George Simpson, assumed control over the company's entire North American operations.[1]

Fort William's first manager under the HBC, Alexander Stewart, held the rank of chief factor, but he would be its only manager to do so. Stewart had been among the Nor'westers who purchased Astoria from the Pacific Fur Company in 1813; now he presided over Fort William's transfer to the HBC. According to Simpson, Stewart won "influence over Indians by his kind treatment and patient attention," qualities perhaps deemed useful during the HBC's first years of operation along the American border.[2]

In 1824, Chief Trader Roderick McKenzie Sr. succeeded Stewart as post manager. Although "honest" and "well-meaning," in Simpson's view, McKenzie "never was possessed of abilities which

could qualify him to fill such a situation to advantage." Fort William possibly did not need more able men. They were required in the Northern Department, the HBC's chartered territories in the Arctic watershed where the fur trade flourished.[3]

McKenzie left Fort William with his Native wife, Angélique in 1829, and later married her in a Protestant ceremony. Stewart, however, abandoned his ailing wife and six of their children when he left Fort William. The feelings of Stewart's wife "when expressed with the freedom and violence that these half-breeds are apt to shew" were "as cruel to understand as to witness" Such starkly different treatment by traders of their Native wives contrasts the tragedy of many marriages *à la façon du pays* with the felicity of others.[4]

Under the Hudson's Bay Company, little changed for the fort's year-round residents, their seasonal trading, farming, fishing and upkeep duties continuing as before. What differed from the past was Fort William's altered status from *rendezvous-place* to mere waystation on the old voyageur canoe route. Among its renowned passersby were Captain John Franklin and his 1825 expedition via the Mackenzie River to seek an Arctic route to the Pacific Ocean and, in the late 1840s, parties searching for Sir John's party which had disappeared in the Arctic in 1845.

122

After 1821, many visitors were surveyors whose work helped "open up" the west.

Lieutenant Henry Wolsey Bayfield, a hydrographic surveyor under British Admiralty orders to chart the Great Lakes, made Fort William his Lake Superior base in 1821. He first leased the NWC's ten-year old *Recovery* from the HBC, but later commissioned the vessel whose ribs are seen in Selkirk's 1816 sketch of the fort. The second *Recovery* was set afloat on October 18, 1823:

> About 1 p.m. the new Schooner was launched in the presence of the Officers & men of the Naval Surveying party; and of the Whole of the Company Servants at the Fort. She was named the "Recovery" and went off the Stocks in good Style, under a discharge of nine Guns from the Fort, and nine rounds of Small arms from the men in the Government employ who were drawn out on the occasion.[5]

Ready for service in May, 1824 the *Recovery II* served as Bayfield's supply ship. On the survey's completion in 1825, the HBC had the schooner laid up and sold, not for its unseaworthiness, but because its sailors were "a great pest to us at Fort William, their idle dissolute habits interfering with the regular ones of our establishments, owing to the liquor served out to the former."[6]

The "government employees" at the *Recovery II*'s launching in 1823 belonged to the international joint commission created by the Treaty of Ghent in 1814 to determine the exact boundary from Lake Superior to Lake of the Woods. Based on the faulty Mitchell map of 1755, the disputed boundary shows a supposed Long Lake waterway instead of the Pigeon River. One commissioner, David Thompson, had explored the boundary waters twenty years before. In 1823, he left no written description of Fort William, but Dr. J. J. Bigsby of Great Britain and the American Major Joseph Delafield did. Aware of the fort's reputed grandeur, they could

Sir George Simpson by William Notman, Montréal. Governor Simpson made several flying visits to Fort William on his regular inspections of HBC posts. *Courtesy of TBHMS, 972.5.13.*

not help but note its decline. The fort was "a large picketted square of dwellings, offices, and stores, all now in comparative neglect," Bigsby wrote, while Delafield observed:

> Fort William is a very large establishment in decay....We were 6 or 8 at table in a hall that was large enough to dine 300, and the whole establishment look'd as if it had been run in correspondence with the hall. There is a handsome square of ground neatly levelled, &c. within the pickets, the hall on one side facing the entrance, and empty warehouses and useless offices on the other three sides.[7]

The commissioners may have agreed about Fort William's decline, but they disagreed about the boundary's location; the British proposed

123

the St. Louis River flowing into Fond du Lac and the Americans arguing for the Kaministiquia. They finally compromised on the Pigeon River. In 1842, the Webster-Ashburton Treaty confirmed this choice but kept the Grand Portage trail in U.S. territory open to American and British subjects alike.[8]

As already seen, the North West Company operated on U.S. soil until Congress barred British traders in 1816. The next year, John Jacob Astor's American Fur Company acquired the NWC's Fond du Lac Department and with it many former NWC employees. By 1822, the AFC confronted HBC traders in the United States at Grand Marais, Grand Portage and along the border. "In order to keep our opponents on their own side of the boundary," wrote Ramsay Crooks, the AFC general manager, "our clerks or traders are to be made customhouse officers."[9]

One Indian chief to exploit the competition was "Espagnol" or "the Spaniard" whose band hunted on U.S. territory. To lure him to Fort William, the HBC plied him with lavish presents, but its traders never trusted him. "A troublesome and expensive customer," the Spaniard demanded that the HBC supply him at Grand Marais not Fort William.[10]

The fort's Ojibwa undoubtedly hoped that competition might end their misery. As John Haldane, Chief Factor of the Lake Superior District, reported in 1824:

> In winter few fish are taken anywhere—this the poor Indians feel severely—almost everything then becomes an article of food,—that is capable of being eaten—and they are at the same time pinched with cold from their scanty covering. Indeed were it not for the supply of European Woollens, which they received from us in the fall, they would literally require to lie dormant the whole winter...in these parts they must depend on the Company even for Leather & Parchment to make themselves Mockassins & Snow Shoes.[11]

In 1829, the Native population of the Fort William District was still small, forty-nine men and boys, fifty-one women and ninety-five children. One-quarter of these lived on American soil and traded with the AFC. Yet these few were "far too many for the district and the furs about it." Beaver now made up one-sixth of the fort's annual returns compared to one-third in former years.[12]

The HBC also faced inroads from independent traders on Lake Superior. In 1833, the HBC and the AFC joined in opposing the intruders by agreeing to separate spheres of operation. The AFC gave up its Pigeon River posts and the HBC stopped trading at Grand Portage. The firms still competed, though, as Indians from Nipigon were drawn past Fort William to the AFC post at Grand Portage. After the AFC's failure in 1842, competition from independents intensified. In 1863, the HBC's new governor, Alexander G. Dallas, deemed Fort William the most important post on Lake Superior as the place for watching American traders who "make excursions toward Lac La Pluie, to Nipigon, the Pays Plat and other points on the north shore of Lake Superior."[13]

In the 1830s, a new natural resource industry began at Fort William. Lake Superior's fisheries, which traditionally sustained the region's posts over winter, now became a flourishing commercial enterprise with markets in the Canadas and the United States. By 1839, Fort William alone had seventeen fishing stations whose salt trout and whitefish found lucrative markets in Cleveland and Detroit.[14]

In 1838, the fort exported 280 barrels of fish and kept 120 for provisions. At around 200 pounds per barrel, this amounts to 80,000 pounds altogether. Although the fisheries remained productive, the American market became less profitable, partly through competition. The HBC stopped exporting fish in the mid-1860s although the industry continued on Lake Superior under various auspices.[15]

Superior's economic diversification continued apace. Pre-contact Indians had traded local copper

124

The Mission of the Immaculate Conception at Fort William, circa 1880. Construction of the Jesuit mission on the Kaministiquia River began in 1848 but in 1905 it and the Fort William Band were forced to move upriver to make way for the Grand Trunk Pacific Railway Company's terminals. *Courtesy of TBHMS, 981.39.154.*

throughout North America and, in the early 1770s, Alexander Henry the Elder operated a short-lived copper and silver mine at Michipicoten. In 1845, mineral discoveries on the lake's southern shore brought exploration parties to the Canadian side. The Fort William post now entered its phase as a retail outlet for customers outside the fur trade by acting as a supply and mail distribution centre for the prospectors.

Some of Canada's leading fur magnates also fared well from mineral exploration. In 1846, fifteen thousand acres of mining lands south of Thunder Cape were transferred to Sir George Simpson, Peter McGill, nephew of fur baron James McGill, and Montréal financier, the Honourable George Moffatt, a former XYC and NWC clerk. Each held stock in the Montréal Mining Company which held the largest block of mining locations on Lake Superior while the HBC itself acquired patents to 400 acres at Lake Nipigon.[16]

The rush to stake claims between Sault Ste. Marie and the Pigeon River took place with no regard to Superior's Native peoples whose num-

bers came to 1240 in 1849. The Indians protested to the Crown but, at Mica Bay north of the Sault, armed conflict erupted. Deeming "it desirable, to extinguish the Indian title" to territories on Lake Superior and Huron, the Canadian Government began negotiations for the surrender of Indian lands.

Native interests would best be served by ceding their territories in return for reserves safe from mining ventures or settlement, the government promised. In 1849, Thomas Gummersall Anderson, Superintendent of Indian Affairs for Canada West, began talks at Fort William with chief Peau de Chat and the Illinois. Peau de Chat demanded:

> Besides a reserve on both banks of the river where we are living, we ask for thirty dollars a head (including the women and children) every year to the end of the world, and this should be in gold, not in merchandise. Besides, we ask the Government to pay the expenses of a school master, a doctor, a blacksmith, a

125

carpenter, an instructor in agriculture, and a magistrate.

According to the Father Nicolas Frémiot who witnessed the meeting, Anderson rebuked the assembled Indians, pointing to the fate of American Indians who gave up "their money, even their blankets, for a glass of water mixed with a little whiskey" and soon would be pushed beyond the Mississippi. In 1848, Frémiot and Father Pierre Choné had founded the Jesuit Mission of the Immaculate Conception up the Kaministiquia River from the HBC post. Already active across the U.S. border, the Jesuit Order became the first non-fur trade institution on the Canadian side of Lake Superior.[17]

In 1850, the Robinson-Superior Treaty between the Crown and "the principal men of the Ojibwa Indians inhabiting the Northern Shore of Lake Superior" was signed at Sault Ste. Marie. Giving the Indians the right to hunt and fish on Crown lands, it granted Peau de Chat and "his tribe" a reserve commencing "about two miles from Fort William (inland)…so as not to interfere with any acquired rights of the Honorable Hudson's Bay Company."[18]

The HBC zealously aided the negotiations. The annual payments of £1 (or $6.00) for each Indian within the Superior District at Fort William or Michipicoten would be spent at the posts as soon as collected. But the treaty did have one drawback. Indians on reserves could be tempted into farming, an activity engaged in by those congregated around the mission. This is one reason for Governor Simpson's unsuccessful attempt to stop the Catholic mission which would "become exceedingly injurious to the Company's interests." Like the North West

Rescue Steamer Off Fort William, 1859, by William Armstrong. With the promontory now known as the "Sleeping Giant" in the background, the *Rescue* heralds the new age of steam transport at Thunder Bay, soon to replace the old age of canoe travel. Welcoming the *Rescue* are a large canoe from the HBC post and canoes manned by Indians. *Courtesy of TBHMS 972.220.32.*

126

John McIntyre, family and friends. McIntyre was the HBC chief trader at Fort William from 1858 to 1878. His wife, Jane, is seen holding the baby. *Courtesy of TBHMS, 977.113.381.*

Company before, the HBC adamantly opposed any independent agricultural activity by Indians within its sphere of operations.[19]

The Jesuits themselves may not have been entirely altruistic for they well knew the difficulty of making Christians out of nomads. Even their converts were "obstinate" in their paganism. As well, not all Indians living near the fort adopted the new faith. Some thirty-two families of "heathens" lived in encampments across from the fort while many Indians preferred living within their hunting territories. Fort personnel had to go inland to obtain their furs to keep the Indians from taking them to the United States or even James Bay.

In 1855, the new Sault Ste. Marie canal on the American side of St. Mary's River admitted steamships to Lake Superior. In 1858, the first steamer to dock at Thunder Bay, the *Rescue*, carried mail from Collingwood for Winnipeg. As a sandbar barred steamship access to the Kaministiquia, a new port at The Landing on Thunder Bay (the future Port Arthur) became the start of a wagon-water route to the west named for its surveyor, Simon Dawson.

The *Rescue* was greeted by canoes filled with Indians and by Fort William's manager "in a huge gondola rowed by twenty Indians singing their boating songs." Yet the HBC had the mail contract cancelled. It did not welcome this threat to its monopoly over postal service.[20]

Neither did the HBC welcome employment opportunities for Indians provided by surveyors and mining venturers. In January 1847, Thomas C. Childs, agent of the British American Mining Company, assured Chief Trader John McKenzie that, while he occasionally fed the Indians out of pity, they were not "loitering about me, making frequent visits, and being fed for days at a time." He also promised not to allow any private trading for moccasins or boots. In March, however, he explained that a shortage of men had forced him to hire Indians for the shafts.[21]

For the Ojibwa, however, this onward march of progress did not prove entirely beneficial. In 1859, Canada West's Indian and Crown Lands Departments negotiated the surrender of one-third of the Fort William Reserve, some 6300 acres of arable lands then laid out in Neebing township for sale at bargain prices.[22]

Probably few at the time recognized that John McIntyre's posting as manager of Fort William in 1855 signalled a dramatic change to fur trade society at Thunder Bay. A Highland Scot, the HBC clerk brought his English wife, Jane, and their four children with him from New

127

Top, Here the Stone Store built by the NWC and other HBC structures are seen amidst the CPR's encroaching transshipping operations as the steamer *Australasia* takes on coal while grain elevator "A" in the background augurs the Wheat Boom era of the early 1900s. *Courtesy of TBMHS, 978.61.81.*

Bottom, Built by the North West Company to store perishables over winter, the Stone Store was the last fur trade structure to survive. Seen amidst the CPR's rail yards in this photo, the Stone Store was razed in 1902 to make way for expansion of CPR operations at Fort William. *Courtesy of TBHMS, 977.113.386.*

Brunswick House near James Bay where he had been stationed for six years. The fort's first trader with a non-Native wife and family, McIntyre was also its first senior officer to stay and settle in the area. Made a factor in 1873, McIntyre retired from the HBC in 1877 and died at Fort William in 1899.[23]

The Fort William of 1899 was not the fur trade post but the town of that name. The transition from post to municipality was one in which McIntyre himself participated. The HBC always tried to confine Indians to the fur trade, but McIntyre availed himself of other opportunities. In 1864, he was "in the 'clouds' about mining" after "an offer of $10,000 for 200 acres of land at Fort William," and in 1865, he obtained a mining patent of 400 acres at Black Bay.[24]

The McIntyres introduced a new kind of gentility to Fort William as Mrs. McIntyre did her best to emulate the lifestyle of English upper middle class society.[25] The commanding officer's wife no longer was unseen when dignitaries called; Jane herself acted as hostess to George Simpson and other luminaries. On Christmas Day, 1855, she gave birth to Duncan, the first non-Native child born at the fort. Only nine "whites," including two women, lived along Superior's entire north shore outside HBC posts in 1860, but before long British-dominated communities arose on Thunder Bay and upriver from the fort at West Fort William.

In 1864, seldom did non-Native wives of HBC senior officers accompany their husbands on their tours of duty. Yet when Edward Hopkins, chief factor of the Montréal District in which Fort William now belonged, visited the fort on company and private mining business, his English wife came along. Frances Anne Hopkins' paintings of canoe travel are hugely popular still for their evocative portrayal of a vanishing culture dominated by Natives and French Canadians. In her enthralling *Canoes in a Fog, Lake Superior*, she painted her husband and self into the last of three craft heading towards

the unknown on that misty inland sea, while her less romantic *Voyageurs at Dawn* realistically depicts fur trade social relationships within the material culture of canoe travel.[26]

The Toronto engineer William Armstrong was another artist. He first came to Thunder Bay on the *Rescue* in 1858 and acquired 120 acres of land with mineral rights on the Kaministiquia River in 1863. His living, however, came primarily from depictions of peoples and places on the route to and beyond Thunder Bay.[27]

During the military expedition's stop-over at Thunder Bay, John McIntyre gained some prominence by persuading Colonel Garnet Wolseley of the Kaministiquia River's merits for moving troops and supplies. Wolseley also used the Dawson route, but obstacles along both courses added weight to the growing demand for a railroad link to the Red River. Acrimonious debate between promoters of the Kam and the Bay as ideal sites for the Canadian Pacific Railway's Lake Superior terminus did not end when the Canadian Government chose West Fort in 1875. The CPR would follow the old voyageur route along the Kaministiquia stretch of its run to the west, but it would use Prince Arthur's Landing as a rail and shipping depot.

Since the lower Kaministiquia best suited the CPR's transshipment needs, the re-organized railway company chose the HBC post as the site for its grain elevators and freight sheds in 1882. The CPR's half-interest in HBC property expedited the agreement of March 9, 1883, to transfer all HBC's lands at Fort William to the railway, the transaction no doubt facilitated by the principal shareholder of both firms, Donald Smith.

Smith had entered the HBC in 1838 as an apprentice clerk on the Gulf of St. Lawrence. By 1883 he was a director in both the Hudson's Bay Company and the Canadian Pacific Railway and in 1897, he would be 1st Baron Strathcona and Mount Royal. As a principal shareholder of the Bank of Montréal and its President in 1887, Smith brings to mind the Montréal merchants in the XY and then the North West Company,

129

Indians on the bank of Kaministiquia River at West Fort waiting for treaty money. *Courtesy of TBHMS, 972.50.14.*

especially John Richardson, a founder of the Bank of Montréal in 1817. Certainly, Fort William's role as the funnel for fur under the NWC and then for wheat under the CPR contributed to the wealth of Montréal's commercial classes in both eras.

In 1878, the HBC had already moved its retail shop for the area's growing population from the old post on the Kaministiquia River to Simpson Street in the future town of Fort William's emerging business sector. By this time local Indians no longer relied on the Hudson's Bay Company to sustain them. As Thomas Richards, the HBC's clerk, explained in 1883:

> The fur trade is a failure, as the Fort William Indians are not hunting fur this year they are for the most part employed in the shanties and Railroads.[28]

On July 18 that year, a small notice appeared in Fort William's *Weekly Herald*:

> The Hudson Bay Post at Fort William, which has been in existence upwards of one hundred years, has been closed, on account of the business being so small that it does not pay.[29]

In 1882, the first CPR train arrived at Thunder Bay from Winnipeg, its cars laden with prairie grain for transshipment into east-bound lake freighters. In 1886, the first transcontinental train stopped on its way from Montréal, its cars carrying passengers and freight to British Columbia and points in between. In the twentieth century, the site of the Fort William post resumed the same role it had under the North West Company as the "gateway of commerce" to the west.

130

17   FORT WILLIAM HISTORICAL PARK

In 1902, the Canadian Pacific Railway demolished the last surviving building from Fort William's fur trade era to make way for its expanding transshipping business on the Kaministiquia River. With the razing of the North West Company's century-old Stone Store, all visible evidence of the great rendezvous-place vanished.[1]

In the early 1900s, the municipality of Fort William's thriving business and professional classes aspired to preserve the area's historical heritage. Soon after its founding in 1908, the Thunder Bay Historical Society commissioned the monument which still stands "in the gateway of the early fur traders as well as in the 'golden gateway' through which now pass the vast Canadian traffic and commerce between the East and the West."[2]

Sporadically over the next decades, local history enthusiasts—and tourist promoters—floated the idea of rebuilding Fort William to the era of the North West Company. After the Second World War, talk of reconstructing the fort coincided with North America's burgeoning heritage movement. In 1960, Fort William's City Council formed an Old Fort William Reconstruction Committee, but its proposal to finance the project through taxation met decisive defeat in a municipal plebiscite.

During Canada's Centennial in 1967, restorations or reconstructions of historic buildings and sites proliferated across the country. At the Lakehead, centennial celebrations featured a Fur Traders Rendezvous Dinner at Lakehead University's Great Hall. The hall simulated the North West Company's Great Hall at Fort William, its windows painted to portray an approaching canoe brigade paddling across Superior's Thunder Bay towards the Fort. Costumed voyageurs, traders and ladies in nineteenth century attire with a menu of roast moose, beaver tail, Lake Superior trout and blueberry crumble imparted the "atmosphere and flavour" of festivities at Fort William a century and half earlier.[3]

Somewhat astounded at discovering Fort William's prominent role in Canada's fur trade, newcomers to the Lakehead joined long-time residents in advocating the old fort's reconstruction. (At the time, Ontario school texts mentioned Grand Portage, but not Fort William, as the Nor'westers' inland headquarters.) Their zeal coincided with the popularization of Canada's fur trade history through books, films, conferences and voyageur canoe expeditions along historic fur trade routes.

In 1968, Kenneth Dawson, an archaeology professor at Lakehead University, received

Ontario Government backing for preliminary excavations of the site. With Selkirk's drawings of Fort as a guide, his purpose was to locate evidence of North West Company structures and verify their dimensions and construction materials. The site's sixty-year occupation by the Hudson's Bay Company and by the Canadian Pacific Railway for another eighty years had obliterated most NWC remains. Student archaeologists met this challenge by digging each day between the tracks and ties of a working railway yard and then backfilling the excavations. Their findings included the foundations of the Great Hall, palisade posts and other remnants of NWC activities.[4]

Dawson's public lectures on his archaeological discoveries drew widespread enthusiasm for the reconstruction. Fort William's Progressive Conservative MPP, Jim Jessiman, lobbied for provincial financing as did George Macgillivray, publisher of the Fort William *Daily Times-Journal*. Macgillivray also used his paper to publish articles on the North West Company and the McGillivray clan history.[5] Reconstruction of Fort William to its NWC period became virtually inevitable, and politically expedient.

But was an accurate reconstruction feasible? One historical consultant advised against the project for lack of evidence. Experts in heritage restoration, however, convinced the government otherwise. In 1970, the Ontario Government established the Fort William Archaeological Project (FWAP), under the Lakehead University administration, to continue excavations and compile comprehensive historical documentation. It also hired National Heritage Limited (NHL), through its parent company, Pigott Construction of Hamilton, to produce a master plan.

Entitled "Fort William, Hinge of a Nation," and dedicated to The Honourable William McGillivray, the plan ranged from solid documentation to such practicalities as anticipated costs and projected attendance figures. Yet its

Members of the Fort William Archaeological Project Team are seen excavating between the CPR rail lines at the original site of Fort William during the early 1970s. *Courtesy of Fort William Historical Park.*

tone was lofty and its message nationalistic. From their command post at Fort William, the plan exhorted, the Nor'westers had forged the cartographical entity known as Canada. For that reason, Fort William under the North West Company became "the hinge of a nation."

On January 20, 1971, Ontario's Prime Minister, the Honourable John Robarts, announced to the Thunder Bay Chamber of Commerce that "Reconstruction of Fort William will begin this spring." The undertaking, however, would not be on the original site. It would be at Pointe de Meuron, once occupied by Lord Selkirk's De Meurons and the Hudson's Bay Company. The reconstruction, though, would be on the low-lying Pointe along which flows the meandering Kaministiquia River. The 125 acres of wooded and fallow land would also accommodate a visitor information centre and parking lot, staff and maintenance facilities, a working historical farm with pasturage, a marina and walking trails.

The project came under Ontario rather than Canadian auspices for two reasons. The federal National Sites and Monuments Board supports historical projects on original locations only. Besides, Ontario already operated major heritage sites elsewhere: Old Fort Henry at Kingston, Sainte-Marie-among-the-Hurons at Midland and Upper Canada Village near Morrisburg. Northwestern Ontario could also benefit from the economic spin-off effect of a similar undertaking at Thunder Bay.

Robart's announcement did not meet universal acclaim. Those favouring the original site protested this violation to historical authenticity. Among them were Historical Society members (including this writer), Lakehead University professors, and residents living at the original site. Clairvoyants warned that the chosen site was located on a flood-plain. At the Ontario Legislature, Jim Foulds, the NDP MPP for Port Arthur, predicted that the reconstruction would become the "Disneyland of the North."[6]

Fort William's original site admittedly had certain drawbacks. Much of it lies under several lines of railway tracks as well as houses, churches and businesses of the "East End." The

This aerial shot of Old Fort William is shown in its setting on Pointe de Meuron. *Courtesy of Fort William Historical Park.*

133

As part of Old Fort William's Educational Programs, school children have opportunities to participate in specialized activities. Here, school children re-enact the cannon salutes with which Fort William greeted incoming canoe brigades and schooners. *Courtesy of Fort William Historical Park.*

cost of buying out the CPR and other property owners was deemed prohibitive. Across the Kaministiquia River, huge oil tanks mar the view; commercial and pleasure vessels ply its waters; train and truck traffic assails the ears. Far removed from the sights and sounds of modern commerce, Pointe de Meuron would best convey the ambience of the fur trade era.

What to call the reconstruction? Old Fort William seemed a logical first choice, but that was the local name for the original site. Fort William Historical Park thus came into use, though briefly. The final choice was Old Fort William after all, its name until 2003 when it once more became Fort William Historical Park.

In 1971, National Heritage Limited began construction. On July 3, 1973, Her Majesty Queen Elizabeth II officially opened the Fort with only three historic buildings complete: the Naval Shed, Taitt's House and Boucher's House. Still, visitors found the site impressive. To their surprise, Fort William had not been some wilderness outpost but a vast complex of some forty structures. Among the other revelations were the North West Company's use of schooners, as well as the familiar birchbark canoes, and the Fort William naval yard for building and repairing ships and batteaux.

It took ten years to construct and furnish the entire historic area. National Heritage hired experts to research architecture and construction methods and such materials as window glass, nails, hardware, paint, shingles, brick, stone and timbers. A government-appointed authenticity committee scrutinized designs; skilled tradesmen then gave fastidious attention to each structure's outward appearance. They used broad axes to finish machine cut timbers, for example. No visible circular saw marks allowed!

Research for the fort's furnishings was just as exacting as seen in reports for National Heritage on trade goods, tools, farm implements, medicines and medical instruments, cooking and baking equipment, household and office furniture, naval stores and canoe building materials. Old Fort William took charge of the interpretive, furnishings and research programs in 1975.

In museum lingo, "interpretation" refers to the art of giving meaning to what viewers see and experience. The Fort's mission was, and is, to interpret to its visitors the roles of the North West Company and Fort William in Canadian history within the context of early nineteenth century fur trade society and its material culture. Built to represent Fort William in 1815–16, years well-documented by records from Lord Selkirk's occupation, the reconstruction focuses its interpretation on that time.

The Fort's primary interpretive method is "living history." Animators in period costume portray individuals from the NWC era. In historic roles, qualified staff uses authentic tools to produce iron and tinware, barrels and even canoes for use at the fort or for sale. On the farm, they tend animals and sow and reap; in the bake house oven and kitchen fireplace, they make bread and prepare food for consumption.

134

A schooner built at the fort is now at Ontario's Naval Establishments in Penetanguishene.

In dramatizations, wintering partners and Montréal agents debate policy in the Council House; canoes arrive at the wharf from the west to the skirl of bagpipe and the salute of cannon; occasionally, the blacksmith Alexander Fraser may be arrested and thrown into jail for not renewing his contract. Lord Selkirk and his De Meurons seize Fort William, interrogate the Nor'westers, and send them off under arrest to Montréal by canoe.

At Ojibwa Keeshigun, First Nations groups demonstrate their traditions in song, dance, food and crafts. FWHP also celebrates Native culture at the Indian Encampment outside the palisade. Birchbark wigwams and such activities as stretching and tanning pelts help Native interpreters re-create the ambience in which their forbears once lived. Ironwares and clothing of Native design and British fabric reveal the blending of imported manufactures and Native material culture. The encampment's realism has led some visitors to ask, "Do the Indians live here all year round?" "No," is the reply. "They live in apartments or houses in town, just like our other staff."

After its opening in 1973, Old Fort William was subject to criticism. The Fort William Archaeological Project contended that the contractor had often ignored its findings. One of its researchers pointed to inaccurate building details, such as railings added for visitor safety to the Corn Stores stairs, but not present on the original buildings.[7]

In 1990, Lakehead University Professor Patricia Jasen probed the debate between authenticity purists and the demands of tourism. According to Jasen, "The anxiety to entertain tourists turns the interpreters' attention away from the acquisition of historical knowledge and towards a preoccupation with making sure that visitors enter into the spirit of the thing and have a good time."[8]

Some criticism of OFW concerned its interpretation of Native life. In September 1996, a respected native elder told *Anishinabek News* that the Fort did not "do justice to the contributions of the Native people in the fur trade." *Anishinabek News* had its own criticisms. "The terrible abuse our people went through is never recalled for visitors to see what really happened two hundred years ago."

To such comments, the response might be that the Indian Encampment is the only area at the Fort where the interpreters' ethnic origins actually match those of the persons being portrayed. Obviously, the Fort cannot hire as many Ojibwa as were present in 1815 just as it cannot hire one thousand French-speaking voyageurs or even twenty or thirty gentlemen with thick Highland accents. And while staff may discuss some of the more unsavoury aspects of the fur trade, discretion and safety forbid their re-enactment.

A full-fledged living history project is expensive as is the maintenance needed to prevent reconstructed buildings from decaying as rapidly as the originals. Fort William Historical Park operates under the jurisdiction of the Ontario Government. Like most arts and cultural organizations today, it is subject to severe cutbacks. This means fewer seasonal staff for the summer tourist season each year. Nonetheless, FWHP provides many heritage-related programs throughout the year: summer day camps for children, winter overnight visits for school classes and adult courses in period crafts are just some examples.

In 1996, a proposal to close the Fort's splendid research library as a cost-saving move provoked an outcry from the public and the City of Thunder Bay's Arts and Heritage Committee. The library survived. Now located in the Fort's Administration Building, this well-appointed facility officially re-opened in 2005 as the "Jean Morrison Canadian Fur Trade Library."[9]

In response to government demands that the Fort generate more revenue, planning since 1990

135

Peter Collins, chief of the Fort William First Nation and descendant of Antoine Collin, canoe builder at Fort William under the NWC and HBC, then Minister of Tourism, Cam Jackson, and Bearskin Airlines vice-president, Cliff Friesen, unveil the "Learning Wigwam" at Old Fort William. *Courtesy of Thunder Bay* Chronicle-Journal, *October 2, 1999.*

has evolved "from a program-driven to a market-driven approach."[10] FWHP is a popular venue for banquets, weddings and conferences. The best example of its market-driven policy, though, is Rock the Fort, a hugely popular, and contro-

versial, concert held in 2005 and 2006, attracting some 80,000 people altogether and generating over $5 million in combined *economic spin-off.*

Some argue that the market-driven emphasis is counter-productive.[11] Yet despite debate, FWHP has more than met its primary goal: to represent the significance of Canada's fur trade to the public, including visitors from far and wide and researchers at all levels of education. Beyond its gates, the fort runs outreach programs for schools and community groups. At the annual Great Rendezvous, it welcomes re-enactment groups from across North America and even Europe.

Among the organizations and individuals making the fort their focus is Lakehead University's Outdoor Recreation Department, which launched a canoe brigade from Lachine in 1984 to celebrate Ontario's, and the North West Company's, Bicentennial. Later, canoe expeditions led by Professor Jim Smithers traced Sir Alexander Mackenzie's voyages to the Arctic and Pacific oceans. Canoeists travelling alone or in groups still make Old Fort William a stopover point on their journeys along fur trade canoe routes.

Genealogy was not one of Old Fort William's original mandates, yet the Fort's existence has led descendants of Native women and North West Company personnel to share their family trees or discover their links to fur trade society. Previously ignored, the shared ancestries of Natives and non-Natives are now acclaimed as an integral part of Canada's heritage.

As a means of generating revenue and *off-setting expenditures,* Fort William Historical Park seeks partnerships with business. While some have little or no bearing on Fort William's heritage, others offer innovative opportunities for interpreting the past. In 1999, Bearskin Airlines joined with the Fort to further promote Aboriginal culture. A Learning Wigwam *on the heritage site* teaches Ojibwa traditions and culture to visitors, students, and First Nations groups. Among those turning the sod for this venture was the then Chief of Fort William First Nation, Peter Collins,

Jr., a descendant of Antoine Collins, Fort William's canoemaker and fisher in the 1800s.[12]

Since its opening, the Fort's historical site has provided a unique setting for making films in partnership with cinema and television producers. Using the latest in computer technology, the award-winning CD-ROM *Northwest to the Pacific: A Fur Trade Odyssey* is *an educational (and entertaining) multi-media tool* on Fort William's pivotal role in North America's fur trade, providing cross-disciplinary study units in science and technology, cultural dynamics and a Teacher's Guide.

Academics and purists often criticize "Playing fort." "You can't bring it all back," Professor J.M.S. Careless quite correctly observed about OFW at an Ontario Historical Society meeting in Thunder Bay in 1975. "Why, it doesn't even smell." (*He might not have visited the working farm or savoured aromas in the Historic Kitchen.*) Yet public history, despite its flaws, has many values. Just by imparting, no matter how imperfectly, an awareness of the distinct roles of the First Nations, the French and the British in the fur trade, including that of Native women and their mixed-blood

progeny, FWHP provokes a deeper understanding about the nature of Canadian society, past and present, for thousands of people, young and old, from Canada and many other countries.

Quite shamelessly, the Fort promotes what is known as "nation-building" history by conveying the North West Company's part in exploring and developing Canada's transportation routes from the St. Lawrence River west to the Pacific Ocean and north to the Arctic. By demonstrating the skills and workmanship of men and women at Fort William some two centuries ago, it also fosters appreciation of our forebears' ingenuity.

Fort William Historical Park has now existed longer than the original North West Company's fabled inland headquarters. Only the future will tell whether market forces will allow its survival as a living history museum in years to come. But whatever happens, this reconstruction of the North West Company's Superior Rendezvous-Place will continue to make Canadians aware of their fur trade heritage and of the peoples who made it happen.

137

APPENDIX
MANAGERS IN CHARGE AT FORT WILLIAM

NORTH WEST COMPANY

Dr. Henry Munro (clerk)	1803–1805
Kenneth MacKenzie (clerk)	1805–1808
Kenneth MacKenzie (proprietor)	1808–1812
Hugh McGillis (proprietor during MacKenzie's "rotation" to Montréal)	1812–1813
Kenneth MacKenzie (proprietor)	1813–1815
Dr. John McLoughlin (proprietor)	1815–1816
Thomas Douglas, the Earl of Selkirk (commandant)	1816–1817
Dr. John McLoughlin (proprietor)	1817–1820
John George McTavish (proprietor)	1820–1821

HUDSON'S BAY COMPANY*

Alexander Stewart (Chief Factor)	1821–1824
Roderick McKenzie Sr. (Chief Trader)	1824–1829
Donald McIntosh (Chief Trader)	1830–1833
Donald McKenzie (Chief Factor in charge of district)	1833–1834
William Nourse (Clerk)	1834–1835
Donald McIntosh (Chief Trader)	1835–1838
John Swanston (Clerk)	1839–1842
Hector McKenzie (Clerk)	1843–1844
John McKenzie (Chief Trader)	1845–1850
Peter McKenzie (Chief Trader)	1851–1852
Francis Ermatinger (Chief Trader)	1852–1853
F. Boucher (Chief Trader)	1854–1855
John McIntyre (Clerk)	1855–1873
John McIntyre (Factor)	1873–1877
Richard Hardisty (Factor)	1877–1878
Thomas A. Richards (Clerk)	1879–1883

* Information about HBC post managers at Fort William, courtesy of Anne Morton, Head, Research & Reference, HBCA.

NOTES

INTRODUCTION

1 See Jean Morrison, "Ethnicity and Violence: The Lakehead Freight Handlers Before World War I," in Gregory S. Kealey and Peter Warrian, eds., *Essays in Canadian Working Class History* (Toronto: McClelland & Stewart, 1976) 143–160.

2 *The 1996 Canadian Encyclopedia Plus* (Toronto: McClelland & Stewart, 1995; CD-ROM) describes this event as the "Seven Oaks Incident."

3 Information courtesy Alexander Ross, City of Thunder Bay Archivist.

4 An incorrect spelling of Dr. John McLoughlin's name.

5 Fort William *Morning Herald*, July 3, 1913.

1 HOW IT ALL BEGAN

1 Anishinabe is spelled variously as is Ojibwa.

2 See Victor G. Hopwood, *David Thompson: Travels in Western North America, 1784–1812* (Toronto: Macmillan, 1971) 92, for Thompson's view on the value of manufactured goods to the Indians; and Carolyn Gilman, *Where Two Worlds Meet: The Great Lakes Fur Trade* (St. Paul, Minnesota Historical Society, 1982) for an illustrated examination of goods exchanged for furs.

3 Adam Smith, *The Wealth of Nations* (New York: Random House, 1937) 590.

4 James J. Talman, *Basic Documents in Canadian History* (Toronto: Van Nostrand, 1959) 19–23. For an excellent overview of HBC history, see Glyndwr Williams, "The Hudson's Bay Company and The Fur Trade: 1670–1870," *The Beaver* (Autumn 1983 Reprint).

5 Yves F. Zoltany, "Daniel Greysolon Dulhut" in *Dictionary of Canadian Biography* (University of Toronto Press), Vol. 2, 261–64 gives the date as 1683, while J.P. Bertrand, *Highway of Destiny* (New York: Vantage Press, 1959) 5–8 argues convincingly for 1679.

6 James A. Mountain, "An Historical Outline of Kakabeka Falls Provincial Park," Research Report for Ontario Ministry of Natural Resources, 1973, 48. *The Kaministikwia River Fur Trade Canoe Route,* (Ontario MNR, n.d.) 14.

7 D.G.G. Kerr, ed., *A Historical Atlas of Canada,* (Toronto: Thomas Nelson & Sons, 1960) 21.

8 For more about the early Ojibwa, see Carolyn Gilman, *The Grand Portage Story* (St. Paul, Minnesota Historical Society Press, 1992), Chapter 2, 24–42; also Laura Peers, *The Ojibwa of Western Canada, 1780–1870* (St. Paul, Minnesota Historical Society Press, 1994), Chapter 1, 3–26. See also "Glossary of Indian Tribal Names," in *Dictionary of Canadian Biography*, III (Toronto: University of Toronto Press, 1974) xxxi–xlii.

9 William W. Warren, *History of the Ojibwa People* (St. Paul: Minnesota Historical Society, 1984 [lst pub., 1885]) 76–94.

10 Cited in Stanley Ryerson, *The Founding of Canada* (Toronto: Progress Books, 1963) 179–80.

2 BRITISH TRADERS AT GRAND PORTAGE

1 See Gilman, *The Grand Portage Story,* Chapter 3, "Across the Divide."

2 Alexander Henry, the Elder, *Travels and Adventures in Canada and the Indian Territories between the Years 1760 and 1776*, ed. James Bain (Edmonton: Hurtig, 1969 [lst pub. 1901]) 43–45. The entire speech is given.

3   Henry, *Travels and Adventures,* 43–45; Warren, *History of the Ojibway People,* 210–214.

4   Bertrand, *Highway of Destiny,* 91; Gilman, *The Grand Portage Story,* 51.

5   Glyndwr Williams, "The Hudson's Bay Company and The Fur Trade: 1670–1870," 35–41.

6   This information is largely drawn from Heather Devine, "Roots in the Mohawk Valley: Sir William Johnson's Legacy in the North West Company" in Jennifer S. H. Brown, W.J. Eccles and Donald P. Heldman, eds., *The Fur Trade Revisited: Selected Papers of the Sixth North American Fur Trade Conference, Mackinac Island, Michigan, 1991* (East Lansing: Michigan State University Press, 1994) 217–242.

7   For more information on McTavish, see Fernand Ouellet, "Simon McTavish," *Dictionary of Canadian Biography,* Vol. 5, 560–7.

8   For Pond's fur trade career, see Barry M. Gough, "Peter Pond," *Dictionary of Canadian Biography,* Vol. 5, 681–6.

9   Gilman, *The Grand Portage Story,* 63–64.

10 Elizabeth Arthur, ed., *Thunder Bay District, 1821–1892* (Toronto: Champlain Society, 1983) xxiv. Mitchell's map is reproduced in D.G.G. Kerr, ed. *A Historical Atlas of Canada* (Toronto: Thomas Nelson, 1960) 35.

11 See Gordon Charles Davidson, *The North West Company* (New York: Russell & Russell, 1967 [1st pub. 1918]) 190–91, for Simon McGillivray's early career.

12 Harry W. Duckworth, ed., *The English River Book: A North West Company Journal and Account Book of 1786* (McGill-Queen's University Press, 1990); and Barry Gough, *First Across the Continent: Sir Alexander Mackenzie* (Toronto: McClelland & Stewart, 1997) 57–77. Both books give the background to this period.

13 Scots, even in the same family, used various and inconsistent spellings for names beginning "Mac" or "Mc."

14 For Mackenzie's expeditions, see W. Kaye Lamb, ed., *The Journals and Letters of Sir Alexander Mackenzie* (Cambridge: Cambridge University Press, 1970) and Gough, *First Across the Continent.* Lamb argues that Mackenzie acted under NWC orders; Gough argues that Mackenzie acted independently.

15 The distance is given in W. Kaye Lamb, "Sir Alexander Mackenzie," *Dictionary of Canadian Biography* Vol. V, 541.

16 Gilman, *The Grand Portage Story,* 90.

17 David Thompson, cited in James A. Mountain, "An Historical Outline of Kakabeka Falls Provincial Park," 47.

3   NEW FORT KAMINISTIQUIA

1   HBCA, A.12/7, fo. 228i–228j. "Conveyance of Land at Fort William from the Indians to the North West Company. Printed in Victor P. Lytwyn, "The Anishinabeg and the Fur Trade" in Thorold J. Tronrud and A. Ernest Epp, *Thunder Bay: From Rivalry to Unity.* (Thunder Bay Historical Museum Society, 1995), 36.

2   Warren, *History of the Ojibway People,* 293.

3   Lamb, *Mackenzie,* p.490: LAC, RG 10, Vol. 3, Indian Affairs, Upper Canada 1809–1814, Gore, Francis, Lieutenant-Governor, "Reply to William McGillivray that He May Not Lease the Land, 13 Feb. 1809"; McGill University Library. Rare Book Collection, John McDonald of Garth Papers, McDonald to _____, Gart, 15 April 1858. (McDonald is commonly described as "of Garth" although he referred to his retirement home at Cornwall as "Gart." Known as Inverarden today, the home is owned by Parks Canada; see Robert J. Burns, "Inverarden: Retirement Home of Fur Trade John McDonald of Garth," Parks Canada, *History and Archaeology,* 25, 1979.)

4   Barry Gough, ed. *The Journal of Alexander Henry the Younger, 1799–1814,* Vol. 1 (Toronto: Champlain Society, 1988) 140.

5   Notarized copies of *engagements* entered into at Montréal are in the Archives Nationales du Québec à Montréal. Fort William Historical Park's library has a collection of photocopies, with index cards, of *engagements* pertaining to NWC employees. For the cost of the move see "Some Account of the Trade Carried on by the North West Company," *Report of the Public Archives of Canada, 1928,* 70.

6   LAC, RG8, British Military Records, "C" Series, Vol. 263, 8019. McTavish, Frobisher & Company to Lieutenant-Governor Peter Hunter, Montréal, April 1802.

7   Mary Shivers Culpin and Richard Borjes, "The Architecture of Fort Union: A Symbol of Dominance," in Thomas C. Buckley, ed., *Rendezvous: Selected Papers of the Fourth North American Fur Trade Conference, 1981* (St. Paul: 1984) 135–140.

8   Gabriel Franchère, *Journal of a Voyage to the North West Coast of North America in the Years 1811, 1812, 1813, and 1814,* ed. W. Kaye Lamb (Toronto: Champlain Society, 1969) 180. See Chapter 10 following for more on Astoria.

9   Ross Cox, *The Columbia River,* eds. Edgar I. Stewart and Jane R. Stewart (Norman: University of Oklahoma Press, 1957) 332. Italics in quote added by author.

10 Culpin and Borjes, "The Architecture of Fort Union," 140.

11 In Northwestern Ontario, this enmity is recalled at Sioux Lookout on Lac Seul and at Sioux Narrows on Lake of the Woods where, according to tradition, the Ojibwa repelled a Dakota attack. The name Dog or *chien* comes from an effigy of a dog dug by the Dakota, it is said, into the steep portage between the Dog River and the upper Kaministiquia, to taunt the Ojibwa of an humiliating defeat. Today, dense forest almost obliterates the depression. See "Place-Names," an undated article from the Toronto *Globe* published in the Thunder Bay Historical Society, *Papers of 1926–27 and of 1927–28*, 80–83.

12 LAC, RG 8. "C" Series, Vol. 382, 406–8.

13 Gough, *Alexander Henry's Journals*, Vol. I, p.144. Spelling is shown as in the text.

14 See Jayson Childs, "Stone Construction at Old Fort William," (TBHMS, *Papers & Records*, 1999), 17–32.

15 "Some Account of the Trade Carried on by the North West Company," *Report of the Public Archives of Canada, 1928*, 62.

16 W. Kaye Lamb, ed., *Sixteen Years in the Indian Country: The Journal of Daniel Williams Harmon* (Toronto: Macmillan, 1957) 70.

17 "Courts of Justice in the Indian Territory," *Report of the Canadian Archives for 1892*; A.S. Morton, "The Canada Jurisdiction Act (1803) and the North-West," *Transactions of the Royal Society of Canada*, May, 1938.

18 Marjorie Wilkins Campbell, *The North West Company* (Toronto: Macmillan, 1957) 141.

19 Lamb, ed., *The Journals and Letters of Sir Alexander Mackenzie*, 415–8; James P. Ronda, *Astoria & Empire* (Lincoln and London: Nebraska University Press, 1990) 29–30.

20 Ronda, *Astoria & Empire* 30–31.

4 WILLIAM'S FORT

1 LAC, MG 19 E 1, Selkirk Papers. List of North West Company partners and magistrats in the Indian Territory (prepared by Colin Robertson for Lord Selkirk) 187–88.

2 W. Stewart Wallace, ed., *Documents Relating to the North West Company*, (Toronto: Champlain Society, 1934) 470.

3 Gustavus Myers, *History of Canadian Wealth* (Chicago: Charles H. Kerr, 1914) 66.

4 Wallace, *Documents*, 249–50.

5 Lamb, *Sixteen Years in the Indian Country*, 105.

6 Selkirk Papers, 13655–6.

7 Washington Irving, *Astoria; or Anecdotes of an Enterprise beyond the Rocky Mountains* (Portland, Oregon: Binfords & Mort, 1967 [1st pub. 1836]) 17. This work was commissioned by John Jacob Astor.

8 Alexander Ross, *The Fur Hunters of the Far West*, ed. Kenneth A. Spaulding (Norman, Oklahoma: University of Oklahoma Press, 1958 [1st pub. 1856]) 7, 18–20. For more about Astoria, see chapter 10.

9 Max Weber, *The Protestant Ethic and the Spirit of Capitalism*. trans., Talcott Parsons (New York: Charles Scribner's Sons, 1958 [1st pub. 1904–5]) 2.

10 For a fascinating history of the paintings' perambulations, see Margaret Arnett MacLeod, "The Riddle of the Paintings" in *The Beaver* (December 1948) 7–11. Long thought to be the work of Dulongpré of Montréal, they were executed by the artist and colonizer William Berczy. See also John André, *William Berczy: Co-Founder of Toronto* (Toronto: Borough of York, 1967) 61.

11 See Clifford P. Wilson, "The Beaver Club" in *The Beaver* (March 1936) 19–24. Diligent researchers may be able to uncover not-so-innocent meanings for some of these toasts.

12 Lamb, ed., *The Journals and Letters of Sir Alexander Mackenzie*, 98.

13 Cox, *The Columbia River*, 8–9.

14 The Earl of Selkirk, *A Sketch of the British Fur Trade in North America with Observations Relative to the North-West Company of Montréal* (London: 1816) 120.

15 Ibid, 14.

16 See Lamb, ed., *Mackenzie's Journals and Letters*, 81, for an estimate of time between ordering of goods and sales of returns.

17 Wallace, *Documents*, 113.

18 Veblen, 18. An analysis of North West Company accounting practices is given in R.A. Pendergast, S.C.B., "The Economics of the Montréal Traders," in Western *Canadian Journal of Anthropology*, Vol. 3, No. 1, 1972, 34–42.

19 £1 Hx = 24 livres Québec. = 12 livres NW = $4. See NWC account in Gough, *Henry's Journal*, I, 131–32.

20 See Wallace, *Documents*, 170–292.

5 THE TRANSFER OF GOODS

1 Gabriel Franchère, *Journal of a Voyage*, 181.

2 Arthur S. Morton, ed., *The Journal of Duncan McGillivray of the North West Company at Fort George on the Saskatchewan, 1794–5* (Toronto: Macmillan, 1929), 6–7. Cox, *The Columbia River*, 220. For McGillivray's testimony, see LAC MG 19 E1 (1), Selkirk Papers, 8297.

See also Carolyn Podruchny, "Unfair Masters and Rascally Servant? Labour Relations Among Bourgeois, Clerks and Voyageurs in the Montréal Fur Trade, 1780–1821," *Labour/Le Travail*, Spring 1999, 43–70.

3   See Allan Greer, *Peasant, Lord, and Merchant: Rural Society in Three Quebec Parishes, 1740–1840* (Toronto: University of Toronto Press, 1985) 175–193 (Chapter 7 "Habitant-voyageurs") for the fur trade's impact on Sorel.

4   For more on fur trade marriages, see Chapter 8 of this book; also Jennifer S.H. Brown, *Strangers in Blood: Fur Trade Company Families in Indian Country* (Vancouver: University of British Columbia Press, 1980) and Sylvia Van Kirk, *"Many Tender Ties": Women in Fur-Trade Society in Western Canada, 1670–1870* (Winnipeg: Watson & Dyer, 1981).

5   Information about Boucher's House comes from National Heritage Limited, "The Independent Trader," Research Report prepared for Old Fort William, 1975.

6   OFW Library. ANQ-M Records. H. Griffen Notarial Papers. Jean Marie Boucher and Messrs. McTavish, McGillivray & Co., 29 March, 1814; HBCA, Part F4/4, p. 55.

7   Old Fort William. Copied notarized engagements. Originals at Archives Nationales du Québec à Montréal.

8   Cox, *The Columbia River*, 364.

9   Wallace, *Documents*, 268, 271.

10 See National Heritage Limited, "Merchant Shipping on the Great Lakes," Volume I, Part I (1971) Research report prepared for Old Fort William. Although *bateaux* is today's usual spelling, *batteaux*, was common in fur trade documents. Prominent merchants in early Canadian shipping did considerable business for the North West Company, John Grant at Lachine, Richard Cartwright at Kingston, Robert Hamilton at Niagara, Angus McIntosh at Sandwich and John Askin at Michilimackinac.

11 F.R. Berchem, *The Yonge Street Story, 1793–1860* (Toronto: Natural Heritage/Natural History, 1996 [1st pub. 1977]), 62–74; 86–90. Percy J. Robinson, "Yonge Street and the North West Company," *Canadian Historical Review* XXIV, March 1943, No. 1, 253–265

6   "EMPORIUM FOR THE INTERIOR"

1   Cox, *The Columbia River*, 330.

2   Selkirk Papers, 9448–9456. Most of the inventories taken at Fort William are in the Selkirk Papers, 9393–9750 and 13678–13747; also in HBCA F 4.

3   Franchère, *Journal of a Voyage*, 180.

4   See *Dictionary of Canadianisms according to Historical Principles* (Toronto: Gage, 1967) for Hudson's Bay blanket, point blanket, four-point blanket, pointed blanket, three-point blanket, two-and-a-half point blanket, and two-point blanket.

5   LAC, MG 19 (A 41), James Keith Papers.

6   Charles McKenzie, "The Missouri Indians" in L.R. Masson, *Les Bourgeois de la Compagnie du Nord-Ouest* (Quebec City, 1889–90; rpt., New York: Antiquarian Press, 1960) Vol. 1, 383–86.

7   Ibid, 385.

8   Marius Barbeau, *Assomption Sash*, National Museum of Man, Facsimile Edition, 1972, and Barbeau, "Country-Made Trade Goods," in *The Beaver* (September 1944), 16–19.

9   HBCA, F. 4/10, pp. 78–79. North West Company Account Book, Cash Disbursements for 1817–18.

10 See Selkirk Papers, 9393–9487 for Inventory of Goods &c. at Fort William…. 18th September 1816 and 9488–9526 for Recapitulation Inventory of Goods &C…. See also A.M. Taylor, "Fort William: Structures and Space" (Research Report for Fort William Archeological Project, 1976), 241ff for an analysis of the Stone Store's function.

11 See Selkirk Papers, 2155–6 for citation re pork.

12 Wallace, *Documents*, 276.

13 Ibid, 268. The "Saints in Parliament" probably refers to William Wilberforce, MP, whose Society for the Suppression of Vice campaigned against slavery and the use of alcohol in the North American fur trade.

14 A. S. Morton, ed., *The Journal of Duncan McGillivray*, 47; George Nelson, "A Winter in the St. Croix Valley, 1802–3," eds. Richard Bardon and Grace Lee Nute, *Minnesota History,* March 1947, 7.

15 Cox, *The Columbia River*, 330.

16 See H.D. Smiley, "Tobacco in Indian Trade" in *Harvesting Shadows: Untold Tales from the Fur Trade,* (Manhattan, Kansas: Sunflower University Press, 1990) 25–30; also Marius Barbeau and Clifford Wilson, "Tobacco for the Fur Trade," *The Beaver*, March 1944, 38.

17 Gough, *Henry's Journal*, Vol. 1, 189–90.

18 Public Archives of Manitoba, Fur Trade: Fort William Collection, Item 11, "State of Packs made up at Fort William, Summer 1819."

19 Charles Hanson, Jr., "The Swanskin," in *The Museum of the Fur Trade Quarterly*, Winter 1976, 3–4; and Charles Hanson, Jr., "Castoreum" in Ibid, Spring (1979) 1–3.

20 Hopwood, ed., *David Thompson: Travels,* 160–61.

21 Mary Black Rogers, "Varieties of 'Starving': Semantics and Survival in the Sub-Arctic Fur Trade, 1750–1850," *Ethnohistory* 33/4 I (1986); Bruce White, "Give us a Little Milk: The Social and Cultural Meanings of Gift-Giving in the Lake Superior Fur Trade," *Minnesota History* 50/6 (1987).

7 THE FORT WILLIAM DEPARTMENT

1 See Jean Morrison, "Kenneth MacKenzie" in *Dictionary of Canadian Biography*, Vol., 5: 543–44.

2 McLoughlin's most recent biography is Dorothy Nafus Morrison, *Outpost: John McLoughlin & the Far Northwest* (Portland: Oregon Historical Society Press, 1999).

3 Burt Barker, *The McLoughlin Empire and its Rulers*, (Glendale, CA: Arthur H. Clark, 1959), 145.

4 It is possible that Lieutenant Robert Irvine served as the schooner captain on Lake Superior in 1811, the year he painted the illustrations of Fort William and of the Indian woman we have named Ikwé.

5 Barker, *The McLoughlin Empire*, 147.

6 Ibid, 165.

7 Ibid, p. 147. See also Dorothy Morrison and Jean Morrison, "John McLoughlin: Reluctant Fur Trader" in *Oregon Historical Quarterly*, Winter, 1980, 377–389; "Simpson's Character Book," in *Hudson's Bay Miscellany*, 176.

8 National Heritage Limited, *Fort William: Hinge of a Nation. Merchant Shipping on the Great Lakes*, Vol. I, Part I, Chapter II, James Taitt Superintendent of the Fort (Toronto: c. 1971), n.p.

9 LAC MG 19 C1, col. 16 #24 has Taitt's meteorological report.

10 LAC, MG 19, B1, Vol. l, North West Company Letterbook, August 16, 1800.

11 Information for this section is drawn largely on Old Fort William's Building Kits compiled on Transportation, Voyageur Life, the Farm, the Trades and Year-round Residences.

12 HBCA, F.4/53, pp. l85–186. Inventory of goods, Liquors, Provisions, etc., the Property of the Northwest Company, remaining at Fort William; June 20, 1821. OFW transcript.

13 "Simpson's Character Book" in *Hudson's Bay Miscellany,* (Winnipeg: Hudson's Bay Record Society, 1975), 234. In 1838, LeBlanc and his three children drowned in the Columbia River.

14 See Chapter 8 of this book for more information about the Collin family.

15 Mackenzie, *Voyages*, xxviii–xxix.

16 HBCA, B. 231/a/7. Fort William Journal, 1827–8. OFW transcript.

17 Selkirk Papers, 12834–8 gives an exposé of alleged NWC anti-agricultural actions.

8 FUR TRADE FAMILIES

1 In 1996, the North American Indians living in the City of Thunder Bay numbered 6,070 and the figure for the Métis population was 1,335 (Statistics Canada. Population by Aboriginal group, 1996 census metropolitan areas). These figures do not account for Aboriginals in the surrounding district. The 1805 census is in Gough, ed., *Henry's Journal*, Vol. 1, 188; "Some Account of the Trade Carried on by the North West Company," in *Report of the Public Archives of Canada for 1928*, (Ottawa, 1929), 65–6.

2 Selkirk Papers, No. 2 R.R.S. Day Book Kept at Fort William, 1816–1817, 9751–9638. Photocopy at OFW.

3 Peter Grant, "The Sauteaux Indians" in Masson, *Les Bourgeois de la Compagnie du Nord-Ouest*, Vol. 2, 318–9.

4 *The Diary of Nicholas Garry*, ed. W.J. Noxon (Toronto: Canadiana House, 1973), 51–2.

5 Gough, *Henry's Journals*, Vol. 1, 188.

6 Wallace, *Documents*, 211.

7 *Statement Respecting The Earl of Selkirk's Settlement upon the Red River….* [London], 1817. (Coles Canadian Collection, 1970), xcvi–ii.

8 Eloisa McLoughlin Harvey, "Life of John McLoughlin" (Banc M55 P-B12). The Bancroft Library, University of California, Berkeley; copy of typescript at Oregon Historical Society. Thanks to Dorothy Morrison from bringing this document to my attention.

9 Ibid (not paginated).

10 Descendants of fort personnel have provided much information to Old Fort William about their families but more research on this topic is warranted.

11 Ruth Swan and Edward A. Jerome, "The Collin Family at Thunder Bay: A Case Study of Metissage," in David H. Pentland, ed., *Papers of the Twenty-Ninth Algonquin Conference* (Winnipeg: University of Manitoba, 1998) 311–327; Susan Campbell, *Fort William: Living and Working at the Post* (n.p.: Ontario Ministry of Culture and Recreation,1976). Spelling of the name has undergone a transformation from Colin to Collin and now Collins.

12 TBHMS, B 4/2/1–3. Journal of Transactions and Occurrences at Fort William for 1823–4, December l, 1823.

13 Information supplied to Old Fort William by Mr. Anthony Mastaw, Sault Ste. Marie, Michigan.

14 Jean Morrison, "Kenneth MacKenzie, *Dictionary of Canadian Biography*, Vol. 5, 534–5.

15 Selkirk Papers, 8682–84.

16 OFW Library. Taitt-McCargo genealogical information from Mrs. Shirley Metz (née Taitt) of Ashland, Wisconsin. See also Jean Morrison, "Fur Trade Families Then and Now: The North West Company Connection," in *Families* (Ontario Genealogical Society, February 1997) 23–30. This Chatham is in the Province of Québec.

17 See Note 4, Chapter 5 for titles of recent works on fur trade marriages.

9 THREATS FROM ALL DIRECTIONS

1 Wallace, *Documents*. p. 221; Jean Morrison, "Alexander MacKay," *Dictionary of Canadian Biography,* Vol. 5, 532–5.

2 Elliott Coues, ed.*, The Expeditions of Zebulon Montgomery Pike*, Vol. I (New York: Dover Publications 1987; [1st pub. 1895]), 154–6; Pike-McGillis correspondence, 247–254; and Pike's "Observations on the trade, views, and policy of the North West Company…," 274–286.

3 Coues, ed., *Expeditions of Zebulon Montgomery Pike*, Vol. 1, 137–149.

4 Selkirk Papers, 9110.

5 Wallace, *Documents*, 266.

6 See "James Tate's Journal," in Glyndwr Williams, ed., *Hudson's Bay Miscellany, 1670–1870* (Winnipeg: Hudson's Bay Record Society, 1975), 95–150. For background to the NWC-HBC contest over this area, see Victor P. Lytwyn, *The Fur Trade of the Little North: Indians, Pedlars, and Englishmen East of Lake Winnipeg, 1760–1821* (Winnipeg: Rupert's Land Research Centre, 1986), 112–128.

7 For Duncan Cameron's view see "James Tate's Journal," 100.

8 Ibid, 126.

9 Ibid, 127.

10 See John Morgan Gray, *Lord Selkirk of Red River* (Toronto: Macmillan of Canada, 1963) for a sympathetic examination of Lord Selkirk and his colony. For an opposing view, see Marjorie Wilkins Campbell, *The North West Company* (Toronto: Macmillan, 1957).

11 Cited in E.E. Rich, ed., *Colin Robertson's Correspondence Book, September 1817 to September, 1922* (Toronto: Champlain Society, 1939), xlvi.

12 Selkirk Papers, 1909. Italics in text.

10 FORT WILLIAM AND THE WAR OF 1812

1 Although McKay is the most common spelling for both brothers, Alexander signed "MacKay." After serving with Fraser's 78th Highland Regiment at Québec in 1759, their father, Sergeant Donald McKay, settled on the Johnson estates in the Mohawk Valley before bringing his family to Canada as Loyalists.

2 McCord Museum, Lt. Col. Wm. McKay Papers. M7082; M7083.

3 Ibid, M7082; William Wood, ed., *Select British Documents of the War of 1812* (Toronto: Champlain Society, 1920) Vol. 1, 428.

4 Wallace, *Documents*, 261.

5 Cited in *Report of the Trial of Brig. General William Hull*. (New York 1814). (App. I, 46–48) Mr. McKenzie could have been Alexander (the Emperor) or Kenneth.

6 Much of the information on the Corps has been drawn from Walter Pretty, "The Corps of Canadian Voyageurs, the North West Company, and the War of 1812." Old Fort William Staff Report, 1987. For Gray citation, see Wood, ed., *Canadian War of 1812*, Vol. 1, 283–86; for Prevost quote, see Grace Lee Nute, *The Voyageur* (St. Paul: Minnesota Historical Society, 1955), 162.

7 I.L. Homfray, *Officers of the British Forces in Canada during the War of 1812–15* (Welland Tribune Press, 1908), 114–5; Selkirk Papers, 2096–7.

8 Homfray, 114–4; William McKay Papers; *Expeditions of Zebulon Montgomery Pike*, lxxii; Campbell, *McGillivray*, 194. Pike advanced rapidly in the U.S. Infantry. But before his appointment as brigadier-general could be confirmed, he was killed in action while leading the American assault on York, April 27, 1813.

9 Selkirk Papers, 12715; Ross Cox, *The Columbia River*, 357–8.

10 Earl of Selkirk, *A Sketch of the British Fur Trade in North America….* (London, 1816), 33–4; [Wilcocke], *A Narrative of Occurrences In The Indian Countries Of North America* (London: 1817), 134.

11 HBCA, F4/5, pp. 26–7, Cash Disbursements on Account of the Outfit of 1814.

12 See HBCA F.4/4, p. 67 for NWC decision not to charge the loss of the three schooners entirely to the Outfit of 1814.

13 Alexander Ross, *Adventures of the First Settlers on the Oregon or Columbia River, 1810–1813* (Lincoln and London: University of Nebraska Press 1986, [1st pub. 1904] 244–6,

14 Wm. McKay's Memorial. Public Archives of Canada, *Annual Report 1887* (Ottawa: 1888) p. civ. Robert S. Allan, "William McKay" in *Dictionary of Canadian Biography*, Vol. 5, 464–66.

15 F.G. Stanley, *The War of 1812 Land Operations* (Canadian War Museum Historical Publication No. 8, 1983), 64–5.

16 See Alec R. Gilpin, *The War of 1812 in the Old Northwest* (East Lansing: Michigan University Press, 1958), 242. In 1928, the *Nancy*'s hull was recovered. It is now on view at the Nancy Island Historic Site, Wasaga Beach, Ontario. See also Wood, *The Canadian War of 1812*, 112–13 and Ernest A. Cruikshank, "An Episode of the War of 1812: The Story of the Schooner *Nancy*" in Morris Zaslow, ed., *The Defended Border: Upper Canada and the War of l812* (Toronto: Macmillan, 1964), 143–153.

17 Masson, Vol. 2, 53–4. See also Gabriel Franchère, *Journal*, 317–8; Grace Lee Nute, *Lake Superior*, 119. (New York: Bobbs-Merrill, 1942) 119.

18 HBCA, F.4/5; pp. 51–60.

19 See James P. Ronda, *Astoria & Empire*, (Lincoln and London: Nebraska University Press, 1990) 302–315 for effect of the Treaty of Ghent on Astoria/Fort George.

20 See McGillivray's Memoire delivered to Prevost, March 28, 1815 in *The Canadian War of 1812*, Vol. 3, Pt. I, 529–30

11 THE PEMMICAN WAR

1 *Statement Respecting The Earl of Selkirk's Settlement upon the Red River*; (London: 1817; rpt. Coles) vii; 9.

2 Wallace, *Documents*, 290–91.

3 Selkirk Papers, 12715–8; see also p. 2540 for Lt. Col. J. Harvey's annulment of these commissions in 1816 with the list of those so commissioned in 1814, and 2495–8 for irregular circumstances under which the commissions were issued.

4 Jean Morrison, ed., *The North West Company in Rebellion: Simon McGillivray's Fort William Notebook, 1815* (Thunder Bay Historical Museum Society, 1988), 30.

5 Selkirk Papers, 17061.

6 Selkirk Papers, 17061–2.

7 Selkirk Papers, 2096–7, 2540.

8 The diary is in the Simon McGillivray Papers at the National Archives of Canada. MG 19, A 35, Volume 7 (Notebook IV-Memoranda 1815). It has been published as Morrison, ed., *The North West Company in Rebellion*.

9 Selkirk Papers, 8536–8542.

10 For biographical notes on Robertson, see Introduction in E.E. Rich and R. Harvey Fleming, eds., *Colin Robertson's Correspondence Book, September 1817 to September 1922* (Toronto: Champlain Society, 1939) xiii ff.

11 Selkirk Papers, 188.

12 Lac des Isles may be the lake of that name between Dog Lake and Lake Nipigon. Island Lake, northeast of Lake Winnipeg, has also been suggested as its location. In Wallace, *Documents*, 261, the Arrangement of Departments for 1809 lists "Lac des Isles (Interior of Nipigon)."

13 Selkirk Papers, 8588. Kenneth MacKenzie to Duncan Cameron, 27 August 1815.

14 Hilary Russell, "The Chinese Voyages of Angus Bethune," *The Beaver* (Spring 1977), 22–31; Barry Gough, "Canada's 'adventure to China,' 1784–1821," *Canadian Geographic Journal* (December 1976/January 1977), 28–37. Dr. Norman Bethune died in China in 1939 serving the People's Liberation Army against Japan. He may have never known of his great-grandfather's voyages to China, according to his cousin, Mary Larratt Smith in her *Prologue to Norman: The Canadian Bethunes*. Oakville, Ontario: Mosaic Press, 1976.

15 Colin Robertson to Lord Selkirk, cited in Rich and Fleming, eds., *Colin Robertson's Correspondence Book*, lx–lxi.

12 BEFORE THE STORM

1 Eugenie Dubec, "From Red River to Montréal by Snowshoe and Sleigh…," *Winnipeg Free Press*, March l2, 1966; Clifford Wilson, "Pritchard and Lagimodière," *The Beaver* (June 1948), 20–21.

2 *Colin Robertson's Correspondence Book*, 23, n. 2.

3 *Statement Respecting the Earl of Selkirk's Settlement*, 59–61.

4 Selkirk Papers, 13659.

5 Selkirk Papers, 8569–9;1466.

6 Selkirk Papers, 8612–4.

7 Selkirk Papers, 1467–8.

8 Selkirk Papers, 2373.

9 *Statement Respecting the Earl of Selkirk's Settlement*, Appendix, liii–liv.

10 Selkirk Papers, 4608 ff.

11 *Statement*, Appendix, xxxviii.

12 See Deposition of Alexander Fraser, in *Statement*, xcv–xcvii.

13 See Jean Morrison, "Old Fort William's Fiddler Joe Harrison…" in *Papers and Records* VII (Thunder Bay Historical Museum Society, 1979), 2–5.

14 Selkirk Papers, 8555–6.

15 *Robertson's Correspondence Book*, 8. In November, Selkirk attributed McKenzie's reputation as a "drunken dottard" to the NWC itself. In his view, McKenzie was "actuated by a principle far more honorable than a majority of his partners." (Selkirk Papers, 2918f.)

13 FORT WILLIAM OCCUPIED

1 John Morgan Gray, "Thomas Douglas, Baron Daer and Shortcleuch, 5th Earl of Selkirk" DCB, Vol. 5, 267.

2 *Statement Respecting The Earl of Selkirk's Settlement*, xcii.

3 *A Narrative of Occurrences in the Indian Countries* (London, 1817), 72–3.

4 *Statement Respecting The Earl of Selkirk's Settlement*, xciii.

5 Frederich von Graffenried, *Sechs Yahre in Canada, 1813–1819.* (Bern, 1891), (translation for FWAP in OFW library), 18–13.

6 *Statement Respecting The Earl of Selkirk's Settlement*, lxxxvii.

7 Archives Nationales du Québec a Montréal, Doucet Notarial Documents. Inventaire des papiers Pris par le Lord Selkirk au Fort William appartenants à la societé du Nord Quest. Also the Selkirk Papers. These are transcripts of originals which were destroyed when the Selkirk home burned. LAC 19 E2. Red River Settlement Records.

8 *Statement*, "McNabb" xciv; Ibid, xcvii.

9 Selkirk Papers, 8926–29.

10 Selkirk Papers, 2694.

11 *Postscript to the Statement respecting the Earl of Selkirk's Settlement…*. (Montréal, 1818) 205; [W.B. Coltman], *Papers Relating to the Red River Settlement* (London, 1819), 218.

12 *Narrative of Occurrences*, 102–3; *Earl of Selkirk's Settlement*, lxxxvii–iii.

13 Ibid, 89.

14 See Peter C. Newman, *Caesars of the Wilderness.* (Toronto: Viking, 1987) 179 for "weak-kneed boozer"; Selkirk Papers, 187–8.

15 *A Narrative of Occurrences*, 71.

16 Selkirk Papers, 13669.

17 Selkirk Papers, 13655–13664.

18 Selkirk Papers, 2811–18.

19 Selkirk Papers, 2779–85.

20 Selkirk Papers, 9393–9487; 9488–9526. See also 13678–13747 for "Remains of the Property sold by Daniel McKenzie Esq. to the Earl of Selkirk, May 1817, " taken on Selkirk's departure for the Red River.

21 Selkirk Papers, 9533. For more information about Daniel McKenzie's family, see Marion Elizabeth Fawkes, *In Search of my Father* (Toronto: Natural Heritage/Natural History, 1994). McKenzie's son, Dr. Andrew McKenzie, was the grandfather of the father she never knew.

22 Selkirk Papers, 13667.

23 Selkirk Papers, 3189–91; 3225–6.

24 Jean Baptiste Perrault, *Narrative of the Travels and Adventures of a Merchant Voyageur in the Savage Countries of Northern America* (1909–10), 165. Captain Henry Bayfield's map of Lake Superior shows "Wreck of the Schooner *Invincible*" off Whitefish Point, (Nute, 262) Near this spot, the lake carrier *Edmund Fitzgerald* sank in a storm on November 10, 1975.

25 John Morgan Gray, *Lord Selkirk of Red River*, 200–1; 209. The commissioner was the Honourable William Benjamin Coltman.

26 For more on the Proclamation see Ibid, 213. The Nor'wester Angus Shaw delivered a copy to Selkirk as his canoe neared the Red River.

14 "A STRANGE MEDLEY"

1 From Ross Cox, *Adventures on the Columbia River* (1831) as cited in George I. Quimby, "Hawaiians and De Meurons in the Upper Great Lakes," *Michigan Archaeologist, X*IV, Nos. 3–4, 167–9. Italics added. In Ross Cox, *The Columbia River*, Edgar I Stewart and Jane R. Stewart eds. (Norman: University of Okalahoma Press, 1957 [rpt.]) 333, the sentence in italics appears as a footnote.

2 Ironically, Old Fort William, the reconstruction of the NWC's fort is located at Pointe de Meuron but not on the same site as the HBC post.

3 Barry Gough, ed. *Alexander Henry the Younger's Journals*, Vol. 1, 23. In 1802, "Pierre's wife was delivered of a daughter–the first fruit at this fort, and very black one." (Ibid, 126) Perhaps she was Blanche, baptised at age nine in 1811 at St. Gabriel's Church, Montréal with her seven-year old brother George. A copy of John Baptiste's engagement is in OFW's ANQ-M files. Stephen Bonga's engagement is in HBCA F4/40.

4 ANQ-M files at OFW. Frederick Schultz, Peter Wulbrenner, Frederick Goedike, and Frederick Damien Huerter were assigned to the Montréal office. Frederic Schoffalesky, son of Baron Schoffalesky of Boucherville, and Stanislas Nicholas of Québec were engaged in 1817 as apprentice clerks.

5 Cox, *The Columbia River*, 325. Wentzel joined the NWC in 1799 and retired as a HBC clerk in 1825. He might have been comforted to know that the island at the very top of the map of Canada bears his name.

6 Hopwood, ed., *David Thompson: Travels in Western North America,* 302.

7 For more on Naukana, see George I. Quimby," Hawaiians and De Meurons in the Upper Great Lakes" *Michigan Archaeologist,* Vol. 14 (1968), 167–9 and David Kittelson, "The Role of Hawaiians in the Fur Trade," Unpublished paper presented to the Fourth North American Fur Trade Conference, 1981.

8 Cox, *The Columbia River,* 333.

9 See Grace Lee Nute, ed. and trans., *Documents relating to Northwest Missions* (St. Paul: 1942) for reports of missionaries to Bishop Plessis.

10 Nute, *Documents,* 123.

11 Ibid, 124.

12 Ibid, 128.

13 Ibid, 280–81.

14 Ibid, 295.

15 Burt Brown Barker, *The McLoughlin Empire and its Rulers,* McLoughlin to Dr. Simon Fraser, Fort William, October 10, 1817, 168–71.

16 OFW. FWAP Research Cards. "Translation of Journal of J. Bte. Lemoine, Fort William, 1817–18" in HBCA, B231/a/1, See also Susan J. Campbell, "Competitive Fur Trade Tactics: Pointe de Meuron 1817–1821" in Thunder Bay Historical Museum Society, *Papers and Records,* Vol. I (1973), 33–40.

17 Ibid, 36.

18 *Colin Robertson's Correspondence Book,* 124; Re Simpson: Marjorie Wilkins Campbell, *McGillivray: Lord of the Northwest* (Toronto: Clarke, Irwin, 1962), 282.

19 *Robertson's Correspondence Book,* 130–31. Robertson effected his escape at Philemon Wright's farm.

20 *Robertson's Correspondence Book,* 139. This letter is also reproduced in Wallace, *Documents,* 319, with slight variations in punctuation and transliteration. In Wallace, "waiting" is "writing" and "Carriera" is "Carriere."

21 *Robertson's Correspondence Book,* 126–131.

15 FORT WILLIAM, 1821

1 M.S. Wade, *Mackenzie of Canada: The Life and Adventures of Alexander Mackenzie, Discoverer* (Edinburgh and London: William Blackwood, 1927), 314–17.

2 Metropolitan Toronto Public Library. *Copy of the Deed Poll under the seal of the Governor and Company of Adventurers of England trading into Hudson's Bay,* (London, 1821). Also in *Robertson's Letters,* 327–343.

3 *Robertson's Correspondence Book,* 302–326, gives the Agreement of March 26, 1821. Upper Fort Garry at the Red and Assiniboine Rivers and its successor further north, Lower Fort Garry on the Red River were named in Garry's honour.

4 *Robertson's Correspondence Book,* 162–172, gives Robertson's correspondence from Fort William in July, 1821 to George Moffatt, a prominent Montréal merchant and former NWC clerk who became a staunch partisan of Selkirk's cause.

5 Dorothy Morrison, *Outpost,* 96.

6 Bruce F. Donaldson, "York Factory: A Land-Use History," Winnipeg: Parks Canada Manuscript Report Series, No. 44, 1981.

7 See Margaret Arnett MacLeod, "The Riddle of the Paintings," *The Beaver* (December 1948), 7–11. Since 1928, they have travelled to Winnipeg, London (England), back to Winnipeg, and then to Toronto where they are located at the Hudson Bay Company's head office.

8 MacLeod, The Riddle," 10; Selkirk Papers, 2895; Victor G. Hopwood, ed., *David Thompson: Travels,* 326–27.

9 See Pierre Dufour and Marc Ouellet, "Pierre de Rastel de Rocheblave" in DCB Vol. 7, 735–39 for information on Rocheblave's many activities after retiring from the fur trade. See also Gratien Allaire, "Thomas Thain" in DCB Vol. 7, 764–65. See also Selkirk Papers, 8448–50. George Simpson to Andrew Colvile, August l5, 1816: "The failure of McGillivrays Thain & Co. has alarmed the winterers very much. Some of them are creditors…There is no question that they [the agents] have robbed and plundered the winterers unmercifully…" Unfortunately, Dr. Kenneth Dodd, professor of history at Lakehead University, died before he could complete his study of the wintering partners' accounts.

10 Lamb, *Sixteen Years,* 194–95.

11 See Jean Morrison, " Fur Trade Families Then and Now: The North West Company Connection," in *Families,* Vol. 36, No. 1 (Feb. 1997), 23–30. Much of this information was provided by a Taitt-McCargo descendant, Mrs. Shirley Metz of Ashland, WI. This Chatham is not to be confused with Chatham, Ontario.

12 E.E. Rich and Harvey Fleming, *Minutes of Council, Northern Department of Rupert Land, 1821–31* (London: Hudson's Bay Record Society, 1940) 295.

13 See HBCA, Part B231/d/14, fo. 7d.-8., Fort William (Lake Superior) Account Book (1818–1821) for Account of Goods; also *Minutes of Council,* 295 for HBC policy.

14 Elizabeth Arthur, *Thunder Bay District,* 33 for Garry and Wm. McGillivray citations.

15 George B. McGillivray, *Our Heritage* (Thunder Bay: privately published, 1970) 22. When the Canadian Pacific Railway purchased the HBC's property on the Kaministiquia River in 1891, the stone was moved to Thunder Bay's Mountainview Cemetery, along with others from the fort's cemetery. On William McGillivray's death in 1825, Simon and Joseph (Peter had not survived) inherited £2,000 and lands in Lower Canada (DCB, Vol. 6, 456–57). See Campbell, *McGillivray: Lord of the North West*, back cover for excerpt from Grant of Arms.

16 For entire text of Grant of Arms, see "Facsimile of Grant of Arms to William and Simon McGillivray, June 6, 1823" in HBCA, F.6/5.

16 HUDSON'S BAY POST

1 Elizabeth Arthur, ed. *Thunder Bay District, 1821–1892: A Collection of Documents* (Toronto: Champlain Society, 1973) is an essential source of information about Fort William in its Hudson's Bay Company era.

2 See "The 'Character Book' of Governor George Simpson 1832," in Glyndwr Williams, ed. *Hudson's Bay Miscellany, 1670–1870* (Winnipeg: Hudson's Bay Record Society, 1975, 170.

3 "Simpson's Character Book," 185; Arthur, *Thunder Bay District* (p. 36) states that this Roderick McKenzie never belonged to the NWC; but according to Williams, *Hudson's Bay Miscellany* (p. 186), he joined the NWC in his twenties. See also Elizabeth Arthur, "Angélique and her Children," Thunder Bay Historical Museum Society, *Papers and Records*, VI (1978), 30–40.

4 Arthur, *Thunder Bay District,* 59. The same thing can be said of marriages in any culture.

5 TBHMS, B 4/2/1–3. "Journal of Transactions and Occurrences at Fort William, Lake Superior, 1823–4,"18.

6 Ruth McKenzie, ed., *The St. Lawrence Survey Journals of Captain Henry Wolsey Bayfield, 1829–1853*, Volume I (Toronto: The Champlain Society, 1984), xxiii–iv.

7 Citations from Bigsby and Delafield are in Arthur, *Thunder Bay District*, 55–9.

8 In David Thompson's view, this was "twice the area of the territory the States could justly claim. …History will place all these transactions in their proper light, and the blockhead treat of Lord Ashburton will be a subject of ridicule." See Hopwood, *David Thompson's Travels*, 152–3.

9 Carolyn Gilman, *The Grand Portage Story*, 104.

10 Susan Campbell, *Fort William: Living and Working at the Post*, 44–5; Arthur, *Thunder Bay District*, 36–7.

11 Cited in Campbell, *Fort William: Living and Working*, 93–94.

12 Printed in Arthur, *Thunder Bay District*, 62.

13 Ibid, 103.

14 Grace Lee Nute, *Lake Superior*, 120. W. Robert Wightman and Nancy M. Wightman, *The Land Between: Northwestern Ontario Resource Development, 1800 to the 1990s* (Toronto: University of Toronto Press, 1997, 15–7.

15 Campbell, *Fort William: Living and Working,* 68–7. Wightman and Wightman, *The Land Between*, 32, 43.

16 Bertrand, *Highway of Destiny*, 162–63. This was near the famed Silver Islet which produced one million dollars in 1870–71. Arthur, *Thunder Bay District*, 105–7, lists patents to mineral lands issued between 1856 and 1865 within the present district of Thunder Bay.

17 Arthur, *Thunder Bay District*, 13–16.

18 See Arthur, *Thunder Bay District*, 17–19, for text of the Robinson Superior Treaty, so named for Canada's chief negotiator, William B. Robinson, a prominent trader, Tory politician and office-holder. See also Julia Jarvis, "William Benjamin Robinson" in DCB Vol. 10, 622–24.

19 George Simpson, *London Correspondence Inward from George Simpson, 1841–42*. Ed. Glyndwr Williams with intro. by John S. Galbraith. Hudson's Bay Record Society, XXIX, xxi, 24–26. N.M.W.J. McKenzie, "Hudson Bay Reminiscences," TBHS, *Papers of 1920*, 19–24. McKenzie was ex-manager of the HBC's Eastern Districts.

20 "An Interview with Captain Dick of the S.S. Rescue (TBHS, *Papers of 1923*, 13–4) Interview first published in the Kingston *Whig*, 1886.

21 TBHS *Papers to 1967*. "Letters to the Hudson's Bay Post, Fort William Ontario," 5–8. See also Thomas Dunk, "Indian Participation in the Industrial Economy on the North Shore of Lake Superior, 1869–1940" in TBHMS, *Papers and Records*, XV (1987), 3–13.

22 A.A. Vickers, "Treaty Making with Indians," TBHS, *Papers of 1911–12*, 9–12. Vicker's account is based on the diary of his father, J. J. Vickers, a mining promoter present at the 1849 meetings in which the Fort William Indians relinquished part of their reserve in return for "protection against the inroads of the whites." See also Fort William First Nation, *Forward-Looking Solutions to Past Problems* (Thunder Bay, 1999), 3, 5.

23 See Pearl McIntyre Packard, *The Reluctant Pioneer* (Montréal: Palm Publishers, 1968) for Jane McIntyre's (her grandmother) life in the fur trade.

24 Arthur, *Thunder Bay District*, 103–4; 107.

25 Jane had been a guest at Queen Victoria's coronation ball in 1837.

26 Arthur, *Thunder Bay District*, 104n. Janet E. Clark and Robert Stacy, *Frances Anne Hopkins, 1838–1919: Canadian Scenery* (Thunder Bay Art Gallery, 1990), 19–23.

27 Janet E. Clark, Thorold J. Tronrud and Michael Ball, *William Armstrong (1822–1914)*, Thunder Bay Art Gallery, 1996.

28 Cited in Victor Lytwyn, "The Anishinabeg and the Fur Trade," in Thorold J. Tronrud and A. Ernest Epp, *Thunder Bay: From Rivalry to Unity*, 34.

29 Courtesy Thunder Bay Historical Museum Society.

17 FORT WILLIAM HISTORICAL PARK

1 See Patricia Jasen, "Imagining Fort William: Romanticism, Tourism and the Old Fort, 1821 to 1971," TBHMS, *Papers and Records*, XVVIII (1990) 1-19. Sault St. Marie, on the other hand, can still boast the fur trader Charles Oakes Ermatinger's Stone House built in 1815 and now open to the public.

2 Peter McKellar, "President's Address," TBHS, *Papers of 1912-13*, 3.

3 Lakehead University Library, AU58B. Friends of Lakehead University Collection.

4 K.C.A. Dawson, "Old Fort Played Important Role," Thunder Bay *News-Chronicle*, April 17, 1971.

5 In 1970, Macgillivray issued his articles together in a private publication entitled *Our Heritage: A Brief History of Early Fort William and the Great North West Company*.

6 This paragraph is based largely on the memory of the writer, then in graduate studies at Lakehead University. Extensive files on the controversy may be found at FWHP, TBHMS, and TBPL.

7 See Foreword to Susan Campbell, *Fort William: Living and Working at the Post* (Ontario Ministry of Tourism and Recreation, 1976) viii; Marie Taylor, "What are they doing to our history?, *News-Chronicle*, 1976.

8 Patricia Jasen, "Imagining Fort William: Romanticism, Tourism and the Old Fort, 1821 to 1971," THHMS *Papers and Records* (1990) 2-29.

9 *Chronicle-Journal*, December 23, 1996; November 5, 2005.

10 "Old Fort William: Its History and Its Programs." OFW typescript prepared by Ann Martin, 1987; updated by Marty Mascarin, 1993.

11 Livio Di Matteo, "Using private sector criteria to judge the Old Fort is foolish," *Chronicle-Journal*, November 16, 1996.

12 *Chronicle-Journal*, October 2, 1999; "Preserving Native Culture," *Bear Country In-Flight Magazine* (Fall 1999) 16-18.

ACKNOWLEDGEMENTS

Fort William Historical Park has a remarkable library of sources related to the fur trade and its era. This collection of primary and secondary materials is the result of investigations undertaken by National Heritage Limited and the Fort William Archaeological Project in connection with the OFW construction project and OFW's ongoing research programs. As OFW's historical researcher from 1975 to 1990, I not only had access to this library, but I also had the privilege of learning from OFW's staff whose expertise ranged from trades to technology to Native life to fine arts. Contact with educational and heritage institutions in Canada and the United States, and with professionals and "history buffs" from both sides of the border, deepened my awareness of the multi-faceted fur trade heritage shared by Canadians and Americans alike. To all those individuals who made this experience possible, I will always be grateful.

Superior Rendezvous-Place grew out of this background, but it could not have come to fruition without the endorsement of Old Fort William's management and the assistance of its busy staff, especially Peter Boyle, Chris Ficek, Shawn Patterson and Joe Winterburn. They not only made constructive suggestions for improving the manuscript, but they also facilitated the use of many illustrations held by OFW. As well, the Fort's seasonal researcher/librarian, Mindy Bell, cheerfully helped in many ways. Thorold Tronrud, the Thunder Bay Historical Museum Society's curator/archivist, did yeoman service in selecting and copying images from the museum's rich storehouse of historical paintings and photographs.

Ian Wilson, National Archivist, kindly allowed the use of Old Fort William's copies of materials held by the National Archives of Canada, while Miriam McTiernan, Archivist of Ontario, gave similar permission to reproduce OFW's copies of the Thomas Douglas Selkirk fonds (F481). Also at the Archives of Ontario, Greg Brown, Senior Archivist, Education Portfolio, clarified the correct description of the Selkirk documents. Others who sent information or provided illustrations include Sally Gibson, superintendent of Fort St. Joseph, and staff members at the Glenbow Museum and Archives (Calgary), the Hudson's Bay Company Archives (Toronto), the McCord Museum (Montréal), the National Archives of Canada (Ottawa), the National Gallery of Canada (Ottawa), the Royal Ontario Museum (Toronto), and the Toronto Reference Library.

The generosity in which images for this book have been made available by the following individuals and heritage organizations in the United States of America is deeply appreciated. Thanks to Dorothy Morrison of Oregon, my long-time

150

collaborator and authority on Dr. John McLoughlin, and to her fellow residents of Oregon, cartographer Christine Rains and Adair Law, director of the Oregon Historical Society Press. My thanks to the staff at the Grand Portage National Monument in Minnesota, particularly Tim Cochrane, superintendent, Pam Neil, chief of interpretation, and Dave Cooper, chief of resource management. Thanks also to Steven Brisson, Curator of Collections, Mackinac State Historic Parks, Michigan.

I am especially grateful to the City of Thunder Bay for permission to use the city's coat of arms, and to Sian Madsen, Hudson's Bay Company Corporate Archives, for confirming that the original William Berczy paintings of Lord Nelson and the Battle of Trafalgar are, indeed, at the HBC head office in Toronto.

Besides the OFW staff mentioned above, others who read all or part of the manuscript include Dr. Barry Gough, Professor of History, Sir Wilfrid Laurier University; Dr. Carolyn Podruchny, fur trade historian currently at Newberry Library, Chicago; Dr. Donald Wilson, Professor Emeritus, University of British Columbia; Trish McGowan, Thorold Tronrud, Rob Van Wyck and my best critic, Ken Morrison, all of Thunder Bay. As well, Anne Morton, Head, Research and Reference, Hudson's Bay Company Archives, corrected many of my references to HBCA material with good grace. All devoted much time and thought to their comments on errors and omissions, unclear wording and interpretation. While not always accepted, their wise council is hereby gratefully acknowledged. All errors and omissions remaining are, of course, my own responsibility.

Cathy Chapin, cartographer at Lakehead University, painstakingly prepared the maps in Chapter 1. Others who answered questions or gave encouragement include Elinor Barr, local historian; Judith Beattie, Keeper, Hudson's Bay Company Archives; Professor Jennifer Brown, University of Winnipeg; Janet Clark, former curator, Thunder Bay Art Gallery; Professor Scott Hamilton, Lakehead University; Andrew Hinchelwood, archaeologist; Murray McCance, former director, National Heritage Limited; Peter Newman, author; Ann Roddy, pharmacist; Alex Ross, City of Thunder Bay Archivist; Vivian Sharpe, Lakehead University Library; John Sims, Ontario Ministry of Tourism, Culture and Recreation; Charlie Wilkins, Thunder Bay freelance writer; and the reference staff at Lakehead University Library and the Thunder Bay Public Library. Much appreciation to my friend Shawn Allaire, former librarian at Old Fort William, for her warm support.

A big thank you to Barry Penhale, Publisher of Natural Heritage Books, for suggesting this project in the first place and for his continuing encouragement despite missed deadlines. Also thanks to Jane Gibson for her careful copy editing and indexing. And what would I have done without the close collaboration of the very competent Shannon MacMillan, Assistant to the Publisher, and her help with the illustrations? To those inadvertently omitted from these acknowledgements, my thanks and apologies.

This project owes a big debt to the electronic age. Thanks to my Mac, I discovered the world of word processing and e-mailing, both of which facilitated the project (or perhaps delayed it because of the ease of editing again and again and again).

None of this could have happened without the support and forbearance of my husband, Ken Morrison, who not only performed extra domestic duties, but who also obtained new bridge partners! His loyalty in spite of everything will be treasured always.

I am grateful to Sergio Buonocore, Manager of Fort William Historical Park, and to Kevin Anderson, Proprietor of FWHP's Gift Shop, for supporting the second edition of this book. I also wish to thank FWHP staff Peter Boyle, Marty Mascarin and Shawn Patterson for their invaluable help.

151

SUGGESTED READING

Abbot, John, Grame S. Mount and Michael J. Mulloy, *The History of Fort St. Joseph*. Toronto: The Dundurn Group, 2000.

Arthur, Elizabeth., ed., *Thunder Bay District, 1821-1892*. Toronto: Champlain Society, 1983.

Bertrand, J.P., *Highway of Destiny*. New York: Vantage Press, 1959.

Black, Arthur, *Old Fort William: Not the definitive, authorized, shrinkproof, cling-free story* .... Thunder Bay: Old Fort William Volunteer Association, 1985.

Brown, Jennifer S. H., *Strangers in Blood: Fur Trade Company Families in Indian Country*. Vancouver: University of British Columbia Press, 1980.

Buckley, Thomas C., ed., *Rendezvous: Selected Papers of the Fourth North American Fur Trade Conference, 1981*. St. Paul: 1984. The conference took place at Grand Portage, MN and Thunder Bay, ON; hence this volume contains a number of papers relating to the Great Lakes fur trade.

Campbell, Marjorie Wilkins, *McGillivray: Lord of the Northwest*. Toronto: Clarke, Irwin, 1962.

_____, *The North West Company*. Toronto: Macmillan, 1957.

Campbell, Susan, *Fort William: Living and Working at the Post*. n.p.:Ontario Ministry of Culture and Recreation, 1976.

Clark, Janet E., Thorold J. Tronrud, and Michael Bell, *William Armstrong (1822-1914)*. Thunder Bay Art Gallery, 1996.

_____ and Robert Stacy, *Frances Anne Hopkins, 1838-1919: Canadian Scenery*. Thunder Bay Art Gallery, 1990.

Coues, Elliot, ed., *The Expeditions of Zebulon Montgomery Pike*, Vol. I. New York: Dover Publications, 1987; 1st pub. 1895.

Cox, Ross, *The Columbia River*. Eds. Edgar I Stewart and Jane R. Stewart. Norman: University of Oklahoma Press, 1957.

Fawkes, Marion Elizabeth, *In Search of My Father*. Toronto: Natural Heritage/Natural History, 1994. Fawkes' father was the great-grandson of Nor'wester Daniel McKenzie.

Franchère, Gabriel, *Journal of a Voyage to the North West Coast of North America in the Years 18ll, 1812, 1813, and 1814*. Ed. W. Kaye Lamb. Toronto: Champlain Society, 1969.

Gilman, Carolyn, *The Grand Portage Story*. St. Paul: Minnesota Historical Society Press, 1992.

_____, *Where Two Worlds Meet: The Great Lakes Fur Trade*. St. Paul: Minnesota Historical Society, 1982.

Gough, Barry, *First Across the Continent: Sir Alexander Mackenzie*. Toronto: McClelland & Stewart, 1997. Also recommended for its section on "Sources," 217-224.

_____ ed., *The Journal of Alexander Henry the Younger, 1799-1814*. 2 vols. Toronto: Champlain Society, 1988, 1992.

Gray, John Morgan, *Lord Selkirk of Red River*. Toronto: Macmillan, 1963.

Henry, Alexander (the Elder), *Travels and Adventures in Canada and the Indian Territories between the Years 1760 and 1776*. Ed. James Bain. Edmonton: Hurtig, 1969; lst pub. 1901.

Innis, Harold A., *The Fur Trade in Canada: An Introduction to Canadian Economic History*. Toronto: University of Toronto Press, rev. ed. 1956; 1st pub. 1930.

Irving, Washington, *Astoria; or, Anecdotes of an Enterprise beyond the Rocky Mountains*. Portland, Oregon: Binfords & Mort, 1967; 1st pub. 1836

Lamb, W. Kaye, ed., *Sixteen Years in the Indian Country: The Journal of Daniel Williams Harmon*. Toronto: Macmillan, 1957.

_____ , *The Journals and Letters of Sir Alexander Mackenzie*. Cambridge: Cambridge University Press, 1970.

Lytwyn, Victor P., "The Anishinabeg and the Fur Trade," in Thorold J. Tronrud and A. Ernest Epp, *Thunder Bay: From Rivalry to Unity*. Thunder Bay Historical Museum Society, 1995.

_____, *The Fur Trade of the Little North: Indians, Pedlars and Englishmen East of Lake Winnipeg, 1760-1820*. Winnipeg: Rupert's Land Research Centre, 1989.

Masson, L.F.R., *Les Bourgeois de la Compagnie du Nord-Ouest; Recits de voyages, lettres et rapports inédits relatifs au Nord-Ouest canadien*. New York: Antiquarian Press, 1960; 1st pub. 1889-90, 2 vols. Many of these memoirs by Nor'westers are in English.

Morrison, Dorothy Nafus, *Outpost: John McLoughlin & the Far Northwest*. Portland: Oregon Historical Society Press, 1999.

Morrison, Jean, ed., *The North West Company in Rebellion: Simon McGillivray's Fort William Notebook, 1815*. Thunder Bay Historical Museum Society, 1988.

Newman, Peter C., *Caesars of the Wilderness*. Toronto: Viking, 1987. Newman's Chapter Notes, Bibliography and Illustration Credits are excellent reference sources.

Nute, Grace Lee, ed. and trans., *Documents relating to Northwest Missions, 1815-1827*. St. Paul, Minnesota Historical Society, 1942.

_____, *Lake Superior*. New York: Bobbs-Merrill, 1942.

_____, *The Voyageur*. St. Paul: Minnesota Historical Society, 1955.

Packard, Pearl McIntyre, *The Reluctant Pioneer*. Montreal: Palm Publishers, 1968. The life of Jane McIntyre, wife of HBC factor, John McIntyre; written as fiction.

Pendergast, R.A., S.C.B., "The Economics of the Montreal Traders," in *Western Canadian Journal of Anthropology*, III, 1, 1972.

Peers, Laura, *The Ojibwa of Western Canada, 1780-1870*. St. Paul: Minnesota Historical Society Press, 1994.

Podruchny, Carolyn, "Unfair Masters and Rascally Servants? Labour Relations Among Bourgeois Clerks and Voyageurs in the Montréal Fur Trade, 1780-1821" in *Labour/Le Travail* (Spring 1999) 43-70.

Rich, E.E. and R. Harvey Fleming, eds., *Colin Robertson's Correspondence Book, September 1817 to September 1922*. Toronto: Champlain Society, 1939.

Ronda, James P., *Astoria & Empire*. Lincoln and London: Nebraska University Press, 1990.

Ross, Alexander, *Adventures of the First Settlers on the Oregon or Columbia River, 1810-1813*. Lincoln and London: University of Nebraska Press, 1986; 1st pub.1904.

_____, *The Fur Hunters of the Far West*. Ed. Kenneth A. Spaulding. Norman: University of Oklahoma Press, 1956; 1st pub. 1856.

Thompson, David, *Travels in Western North America, 1784-1812*. Ed. Victor G. Hopwood. Toronto: Macmillan, 1971.

Town, Florida, *The North West Company: Frontier Merchants*. Toronto: Umbrella Press, 1999. Sponsored by the North West Company created in 1987 to buy out the Hudson's Bay Company's Northern Stores.

Statement Respecting The Earl of Selkirk's Settlement upon the Red River....[London], 1817. Coles Canadian Collection, 1970.

Van Kirk, Sylvia, *"Many Tender Ties": Women in Fur-Trade Society in Western Canada, 1670-1870*. Winnipeg: Watson & Dyer, 1981.

Wallace, W. Stewart, *Documents relating to the North West Company*. Toronto: Champlain Society, 1934.

Warren, William W., *History of the Ojibwa People*. St. Paul: Minnesota Historical Society, 1984; lst pub. 1885.

Wightman, W. Robert and Nancy M. Wightman, *The Land Between: Northwestern Ontario Resource Development, 1800 to the 1990s*. Toronto: University of Toronto Press, 1997.

Williams, Glyndwr, "The Hudson's Bay Company And The Fur Trade: 1670-1870" in *The Beaver* Autumn 1983, rpt. 1991.

_____, ed., *Hudson's Bay Miscellany, 1670-1870*. Winnipeg: Hudson's Bay Record Society, 1975. Contains "James Tat's Journal, 1809-12" and "The 'Character Book' of George Simpson, 1832."

Wood, William, ed., *Select British Documents of the War of 1812*. Toronto: Champlain Society, 1920. 3 vols.

Zaslow, Morris, ed., *The Defended Border: Upper Canada and the War of l812*. Toronto: Macmillan, 1964.

OTHER RELEVANT PUBLICATIONS:

Dictionary of Canadian Biography. Toronto: University of Toronto Press, 1973. Vols I-XII covering the years 1000 to 1900.

The Canadian Encyclopedia. Edmonton: Hurtig Publishers, 1988. 4 vols.

The Canadian Encyclopedia 2001. Toronto: McClelland & Stewart, 2000. CD-ROM. 6 vols.

Northwest to the Pacific: A Fur Trade Odyssey. Thunder Bay: Old Fort William, 2000. CD-ROM.

Most issues of *The Beaver* magazine and the Thunder Bay Historical Society's *Papers and Records*.

INDEX

156

158

159

INDEX

163

INDEX

ABOUT THE AUTHOR

Jean Morrison, historian at Old Fort William in Thunder Bay for 15 years, has written widely on Fort William and the North West Company. Her credits include *North West Company in Rebellion: Simon McGillivray's Fort William Notebook, 1815* (Thunder Bay Historical Museum Society, 1988, reprint 1997) and numerous articles and reviews on the fur trade and local labour history in *The Canadian Encyclopedia*, the *Dictionary of Canadian Biography*, the Thunder Bay Historical Society's annual *Papers and Records*, *The Beaver* and *Families* (Ontario Genealogical Society). Since retirement in 1990, she has served on the Ontario Geographic Names Board and the Old Fort William Advisory Committee.

In 2003, Morrison edited and contributed to *Lake Superior to Rainy Lake: Three Centuries of Fur Trade History* and, in 2004, she won the *Chronicle-Journal* Prize for her contributions to Thunder Bay's heritage. In 2005, she won the Thunder Bay Museum Society's M. Elizabeth Arthur Award for the best scholarly production on the history of Northwestern Ontario. She enjoys living in Thunder Bay where she is married to Ken Morrison. She is proud of her three daughters and four grandchildren.